# The Creation of
# an Ensemble

## The First Years of the
## American Conservatory Theatre

John R. Wilk

Southern Illinois University Press
Carbondale and Edwardsville

*Library of Congress Cataloging in Publication Data*

Wilk, John R.
    The Creation of an ensemble.

    Bibliography: p.
    Includes index.
    1. American Conservatory Theatre. 2. Repertory
theater—California—San Francisco. 3. Theater—Study
and teaching—California—San Francisco. I. Title.
PN2277.S42A468 1986    792'.09794'61    85–1698
ISBN 0-8093-1212-3
ISBN 0-8093-1213-1 (pbk.)

89  88  87  86    4  3  2  1

*Dedicated to*
*the hopes and dreams of all theatre artists;*
*to my loving parents, John and Victoria; and*
*to my wife, Betsy*

# Contents

# Illustrations

# Illustrations

# Preface

The regional theatre movement of America, backed by the matching grants of the Ford Foundation during the late 1950s and through the 1960s, opened the way for professional theatre artists to work in residence away from the New York City theatre world. The movement created a variety of organizations, many of which tried to construct their theatres in accordance with their strict ideas of what a theatre ought to be. Often these theatres grew at a slow rate and then accelerated as various funding agencies, the Ford Foundation in particular, contributed funds to sustain them. The regional theatres were nonprofit ventures, run by local boards of directors that were organized by the theatres to raise funds for the practice of the art (the prototypes of this structure had been museums and symphonies). However, as the regional movement developed during the 1960s, rifts occurred between the supporting boards—composed of business people—and the theatrical management.

The civic leaders on the boards found it necessary in some cases to dictate to the artistic personnel on the theatre's internal management. Several outstanding artistic directors lost their positions at that time, including Elia Kazan and Robert Whitehead of the Lincoln Center. Immediately following the dismissal of these two directors in 1965, William Ball, general director of the American Conservatory Theatre (ACT), wrote his theatre manifesto, which was designed to create a theatre that would be free of the nonprofit board structure of the day.

Ball's theatrical structure was an idyllic one. He wanted to create an ensemble acting company that would simultaneously train and perform in a repertory schedule. He also wanted to create a board of trustees made up of professional artists, thus distinguishing ACT from its contemporaries. Ball's first attempt with the structure, in the company he had assembled in Pittsburgh, failed because of infighting over artistic control. But the failure only served to strengthen Ball's conviction that ACT's support structure should be separate from its artistic management. After the Pittsburgh failure, ACT went shopping, so to speak, for a setting that would support its work with as few demands as possible. In 1966 Ball found that environment in San Francisco, with its strong civic leader, Mortimer Fleishhacker.

The ensemble is an ill-defined form of theatrical management by its very nature. However, through a historical survey of theatrical ensembles of Europe, including the *Comédie Française*, the Moscow Art Theatre, and the Meiningers, we can construct a definition of the theatre ensemble.

ACT's structure and function during its first years were similar to these historical examples. Nevertheless, the ideal of ensemble theatre was untested in the regional movement. Factions appeared within the ACT management in an attempt to shape the organization. Since no model of a nonprofit ensemble structure existed, these rifts were natural. The absolute artistic control of Ball, ACT's *regisseur*, was questioned during the 1968–1969 season. ACT and Ball weathered this period, and ACT continued to operate in accordance with its founding principles.

The two aspects of the ACT ensemble as Ball created it were training and professional repertory theatre. Regarding training, the conservatory of ACT began with a series of seminars called *exploratories* and evolved into a two-year school by 1972. ACT's repertory began with a large and eclectic schedule, producing twenty-seven plays during its first full season, 1967–1968. However, subscriptions dropped and costs escalated, and in 1969, faced with possible closure, ACT adapted and simplified its format.

The history of any organization shows change and development, but often the core of the organization remains the same. This was the case with ACT. By 1972, with Ball's principles intact and the continuity of his artistic control ensured, ACT had become America's prototype of an ensemble acting company in the regional setting.

I would like to express gratitude to the staff at ACT for their cooperation, and to William Ball for openly discussing ACT's survival and his own views on theatre and theatre education. Also, to those on the staff who agreed to be interviewed I am very grateful.

I am also grateful for the encouragement of Robert Goldsby, Edward Hastings, James B. McKenzie, Dennis Powers, Lawrence Hecht, Mary Garrett, Suzanne Lipsett, Robert Smith, and Robert Hazzard. I am indebted to my wife, Elizabeth Eddy, for her encouragement and guiding love during the long hours I spent on this work.

This book is not meant to be encyclopedic; not all the individuals who were involved with ACT during its first years are represented. Rather, the intention is to help clarify ACT's ideal of ensemble and eliminate any misconceptions about a company that has succeeded in its philosophies.

# The Creation of
# an Ensemble

# 1

## Ensemble Theatre Companies

The idea of an *ensemble* acting company is an organizational philosophy. However, theatrical ensemble is an ill-defined concept and an often abused term. The nearest analogy is a musical one: the simultaneous performance of all the instruments of an orchestra, or of all the voices in a chorus. In other words, the creation of a whole performance work coordinated from its several pieces. The vagueness of this definition for the theatre is obvious. Thus, the term *ensemble* has been applied to diverse theatrical organizations.

### The King's Men

The earliest example of a successful ensemble acting company might have been Shakespeare's King's Men. Gerald Eades Bently describes the group:

In 1616 the organization appears to have consisted of twelve members and various hired men, musicians, and apprentices. The twelve members were those later listed in the patent of 1619. . . .

For several years the King's Men had been playing during the summer months at the Globe on the Bankside, a large new theatre less than two years old at the time of Shakespeare's death, according to John Chamberlain, reported to be "the fairest that ever was in England." During the rest of the year the company performed at their private house in Blackfriars. Both these theatres were held in joint tenancy by the actors themselves.

This financial interest of the players themselves in their theatres must be considered a prominent factor in their success; its effect on the solidarity and permanence of the company is obvious. We have no evidence that any other groups were so organized. When other companies broke or changed houses or were reorganized, the King's Men played on at the Blackfriars and the Globe.[1]

Besides financial ties, other contingencies contributed to the cohesiveness of the company. First, all the actors performed in the same rhetorical acting mold with no acting style to model except possibly that of the medieval theatre. Thus, they enjoyed the freedom of creating a style all their own. Second, they had royal patronage, which no doubt made them feel secure of having continuous work. Third, until 1616 they also had a creative genius among their ranks who supplied them with a great deal of their staged material. His name was William Shakespeare. The financial and artistic successes that followed welded a strong ensemble company.

Shakespeare, himself an actor, had a deep understanding of the art through his own stage experience. Hamlet, the *raisonneur* of Shakespeare, is proof of his understanding of acting:

Suit the action to the word, the word to the action; with this special observance, that you o'erstep not the modesty of nature: for anything whose end, both at the first and now, was and is, to hold as t'were, the mirror up to nature; to show virtue her own feature, scorn her own image, and the very age and body of the time his form and pressure. Now this can be overdone, or come tardy off, though it make the unskillful laugh, cannot but make the judicious grieve; the censure of the which one must in your allowance o'erweigh a whole theatre of others. O, there be players I have seen play, and heard others praise, and that highly (not to speak profanely), that, neither having the accent of Christians, nor the gait of Christians, pagan, nor man, have so strutted and bellowed that I have thought some of Nature's journeymen had made men, and not made them well, they imitated humanity so abominably.

*Hamlet*, act 3, scene 2, lines 17–34

These written words are now a bit of memory, an idea placed in the mouth of Shakespeare's most famous character. The actor who spoke those words first upon the boards was

Richard Burbage (d. 1619), one of the cornerstones of the King's Men. He was also the son of James Burbage, the theatre-builder, and owned rights to the Globe and Blackfriars with his brother, Cuthbert.

The King's Men survived the deaths of both its playwright and leading actor (Shakespeare and Burbage, respectively). The company also survived political turmoil, the deaths of Queen Elizabeth I and King James, as well as many bouts with the plague (a scourge that intermittently closed all theatres and public meeting places owing to the health hazard). What finally dissolved the troupe on 2 September 1642 was a raging civil war that brought the Puritans, with their disdain for "mirthmaking," into power. On this day the House of Lords and the House of Commons resolved that,

fasting and Prayer having bin often tryed to be very effectual, have bin lately, and are still enjoyed; and whereas publike sports doe not well agree with publike Calamities; not publike Stage-Players with the Season of Humiliation, this being an Excercise of sad and pious solemnity, and the other being Spectacles of pleasure, too commonly expressing lacivious Mirth and Levities: It is therefore thought fit, and Ordeined by the Lords and Commons in this Parliament Assembled, that while these sad causes and set times of Humiliation doe continue, publike Stage-Players shall cease, and bee forbone.[2]

Thus ended one of the most prolific expressions of the stage, from 1584 until 1624, a mere fifty-eight years. The organizational qualities of the King's Men were forgotten by the time the theatres were restored in 1660, when the age of the great actor and actor-manager emerged. The unusual demands made on the actors by the benefit-performance system of the Restoration did little to encourage them to work together. Indeed, the expectations of the English audiences for "star" actors grew out of the Restoration's benefit system. The names of the great English actors from the eighteenth and nineteenth centuries are still famous today: Garrick, Siddons, Macklin, Kean, Macready, Kemble, Bancroft, Irving, and Terry. The emergence of these actors reflected a shift in English philosophy and its imperialistic expansion; here the individual took precedence.

Theatrical management was now motivated by a desire for huge and quick profits.

While names and styles changed, the prevailing emphasis on the great actor destroyed any stimuli for the creation of a true company of tightly woven performance capabilities in England. This attitude spilled over into the colonies of America, where many actors, having spent their abilities on the London stages, came seeking greater luck and profit.

### Molière's Troupe and the Comédie Française

In historical overview we can trace a lineage of ensemble acting organizations. The lineage begins with Molière's troupe, once called the *Illustre Theatre*, which had influence both in Germany and France. Certain eighteenth-century and nineteenth-century German troupes were direct descendants of the Molière ensemble: Conrad Ekhof's companies in Hamburg and Gotha; Schroeder's in Hamburg; Goethe's in Weimar. These troupes predated the famous ensemble of the duke of Saxe-Meiningen, which had its own effect on the late nineteenth-century and early twentieth-century companies of Antoine in France, Brahm in Germany, and Stanislavsky in Russia. Stanislavsky ultimately created a model of ensemble acting that was emulated in America in the 1930s by the Group Theatre. The fervor of the latter in turn influenced many idealistic theatres, including the Open Theatre (1963–1973), and many operating regional America theatres, not the least of which is the American Conservatory Theatre (ACT) of San Francisco.

The first of this lineage of ensembles, Molière's troupe, existed in the mid-seventeenth century in France. Here is a description of the troupe from Cole and Chinoy's *Actors on Acting*:

Apart from the tremendous interest and controversy aroused by Molière's many plays, people flocked to see the excellent *ensemble* acting of his group. In addition to the skillful artistry of Moliere himself, they could see Charles Varlet La Grange (1639–1692), the invaluable record keeper, playing lovers; Philbert Grassot Du Croisy (1639–1695) creating Tartuffe; the intelligent Madeleine Bejart (1640–1700), who became Molière's wife; and later the talented young Michel Baron. A contemporary noted of the performance of *L'Ecole*

4

*des femmes*, "Never was a comedy so well performed or with so much art, each actor knows how many steps he has to take, and every glance is counted."[3]

Similarities between Molière's troupe and Shakespeare's King's Men are obvious. Both had the advantage of a playwright working for them. (Molière's troupe seemed better fit to perform comedy, having failed at tragic performance, and in particular it was best at performing Molière's style of comedy.) Under Molière's leadership the troupe flourished and gained respect in the court of Louis XIV, which ensured its survival in a society that looked upon professional acting with contempt. The King's Men also had court patronage. Under the protection of the court, Molière and his actors performed with the security of knowing that they were honored and free from societal pressure. "In their internal organization . . . the actor's model was the French bourgeois family, which has been defined as one of the tightest and most protective social units that the world has ever produced. The company formed a collection of individuals with well-defined relationships united for mutual assurance and financial security, with a group sense that transcended personal idiosyncracies."[4]

Molière was very much influenced by the Italian *Commèdia dell'Árte* troupes that were touring France at this time. Similarly, his plays were influenced by the *Commèdia* actors' cohesiveness and unselfishness as a model for his own company. A *Commèdia* actor "had to practice a kind of self-abnegation and refrain from indulging his own conceits or overplaying his part to the detriment of other *roles*. The actors of the Italian troupes of necessity developed a spirit of camaraderie in their playing, and they achieved such understanding and mutual co-operation as was not found in the companies playing ordinary drama."[5] Molière was apt to instruct his company likewise, warning them against the "excessive and unnatural, stressing the ability of his actors to present characters quite opposed to their personality, and outlining the little details with which they could build their characterizations."[6]

Thus a style of acting was created that helped maintain the company's identity. As with Shakespeare, the acting style of Molière's troupe reflected the personal understanding of the playwright. The company was based on a family unit, and enjoyed the protection of the court. All these elements together created an ensemble acting company: "There can be no greater tribute to this group cohesiveness than the willingness and ability of Molière's company to continue to function, with barely a missed performance, after the death of the man who had been their guide and inspiration for many years."[7] Molière's death came in 1673 after he performed in his play, *Le Malade imaginaire*. A man of the theatre, his death was dramatic, but his company lived on:

In 1680 Louis XIV created the "Theatre Francaise" by ordering the amalgamation of the Bourgogne with the old Moliere troupe, which had been kept intact by Armande Moliere and La Grange. On the foundation of Moliere's company the "Theatre Francaise" commenced the longest continuous history of any national theatrical institution. France had what no other country had—a permanent company of actors. Despite occasional nepotism or squabbles over position and power, the "Comedie Francaise" was a house essentially run by actors on a democratic basis, with the major actors, the societaires, sharing the responsibilities and the fortunes of the theatre."[8]

The *Comédie*, still in existence, has been the breeding grounds for most of France's finest actors over the past three hundred years. Its internal organization is still based on the family concept. The ensemble distinguishes its members as either *pensionnaires* (temporary) or *sociétaires* (permanent), both of whom join in the decisions of artistic control, membership, and retirement. Each actor owns a share of the company and each gets a sum of money after retirement.

Along with this organization has come a certain style of acting, one designed for successfully performing the French classics. (The style has been characterized as rhetorical with a minimum of gesture.) Despite the difficulties that have accompanied the continuance of the *Comédie*, it is still seen as the standard for the theatre of France. The survival of the ensemble is, in part, due to the respect the organization has for the actors and their craft.

## Ekhof

As a model of ensemble work, the *Comédie Française* was soon to be emulated. Several companies in Germany attempted to copy this organization in the early eighteenth century: "Most failed miserably, but Schönemann, the shrewd manager of Ekhof's troupe, eventually managed to seduce the Duke of Mecklinburg-Schwerin to grant his company a temporary home at court, in 1751, and financial support. It was exemplary that a German acting company was given such a privilege. The sense of security prompted Ekhof, the leading actor, to propose the academy. If one wanted to compete with the French, one had to adapt their artistic standards, possibly surpass them."[9]

Conrad Ekhof founded the academy for the purpose of reforming German theatre, which had no tradition of its own and which was as fragmented and scattered as the country's many small dukedoms. As a reformer, Ekhof was the innovator of acting with artistic clarity. Debates on artistic issues were the first step toward creating the academy. Ekhof addressed this statement to the assembly: "The art of acting is this: to imitate nature through art: to approach it (nature) so closely that apparent truth must be accepted as truth, that events which have happened are represented as realistically (*natürlich*) as if they would happen now. In order to gain expertise in the art, we must demand vivid imagination, steadfast judgement, inexhaustible diligence, and persistent training."[10]

Germany is indebted to Ekhof for its first set of theatre laws. The laws, formulated by 1754, lasted into the nineteenth century. There were three sections with a total of ten rules, and they included such simple edicts as one directing each actor to "dress according to the character played."[11] Rule number nine had particular relevance to ensemble acting: "Each actor or actress shall treat his or her colleague without any arrogance, egotism, provocation, intrigue, in short, with courtesy; but instead be honest to everyone, openminded, and helpful, as friendship, decency, and reason demand, on penalty according to majority vote."[12]

Ekhof was not immediately successful in reforming German theatre—at least, not with his own academy, which dissolved in 1754. However, his concern for the artistic unity of whole productions had a long-lasting impact on eighteenth- and nineteenth-century German and Austrian theatre.

Ekhof was to become the leading actor of Ackermann's company and did much to further the ensemble ideal with that troupe: "There is evidence that Ekhof had much to do with the orientation toward ensemble play and 'orchestration staging' which became the trademark of the troupe, the 'Hamburg Style.' Ekhof was a leading member from 1764 to 1769, with interruptions. The 'natural' acting style developed by Ackermann and his insistence on *breaking the possession of parts* in his company in favor of casting according to talent and situation, ideally suited Ekhof."[13]

Shortly before his death, Ekhof was able to implement his rules of discipline and ensemble style acting. He became *directeur* of the first resident court theatre at Gotha. On 17 July 1775, Ekhof's theatre was organized by decree. The duties of the ensemble company were enumerated; some are stated here:

2. Everyone has to accept the role assigned to him without argument and relinquish such upon request.

3. Those who perform at night, have to be at the theatre at least half an hour before curtain time; likewise they have to be at rehearsal before the time given. Whoever is late without valid excuse, such as illness or proof that he was not informed pays 4 Gr. fine.

7. All improvising is forbidden, and fined with 4 to 8 Gr.

9. Obstinancy or rebellion against the directors will be either fined or more severely punished.

10. The maximum fine is 16 to 20 Gr., the minimum 4 Gr. which the directors can set and collect. Should any actor persist, in spite of warning and fines, either to being negligent, rebellious, or disobedient, he will be fined and the cause of his dismissal published in the public press.[14]

These stern rules were necessary to maintain a unified and working group of professional actors. In one sense Ekhof was trying to create an ensemble quickly through a highly disciplinary set of standards. Up to this time the acting companies of Germany had no such dicta to follow.

## Schroeder

Ekhof's strong centralized power in a directorship and his rules for maintaining an ensemble were furthered by Friedrich Ludwig Schroeder (1744–1816). The actor-director Schroeder, stepson of Ackermann, became head of the company after Ackermann's death in 1771:

Whether in Hamburg or Vienna, where he spent four years at the famous Burgtheatre, Schroeder trained his co-actors. He was one of the first actor-managers to have a strong sense of the necessity for unified productions. By his strict and demanding standards he developed the finest troupe in Germany. Indeed his sternness was said to have caused the suicide of his half-sister, the promising young actress Charlotte Ackermann (1757–1774). But out of his personal brilliance and his understanding of the theatrical ensemble came the finest period of realistic playing almost a century before the development of German realism.[15]

Schroeder followed Ekhof's principle of "the orchestration of staging." The principle embraced such simple rules as the wearing of costumes appropriate to the characters and prohibitions against laughing onstage at inappropriate times, and against actors going onstage with their servants.

Schroeder devised his own set of rules for the Hamburg Theatre, consisting of seventeen articles. Most of the articles were copies of those written at the Gotha theatre, but one section dealt with the playing of walk-on roles, an art neglected before this time:

It is sometimes necessary that silent parts are cast with actors. Nobody can be excluded, because nobody can be diminished by that. But these are the conditions:

1. In performance where only a few silent persons are needed, the actors playing leading roles have preference before those who play supporting roles.

2. If an actor has a demanding role in the first play, he can be dispensed from a silent part in the second play unless it is absolutely essential.

3. An actor can be excused from a silent part in the first play if he has to begin the second, and if he needs for such a role added costuming, a new hairdo, or time for make-up. But for these excep-

tions nobody can refuse a silent part, and whoever comes late for rehearsing of such parts or even performance, or who misses scenes, or stays away altogether, pays one quarter of the penalty of the actors in speaking roles.[16]

Schroeder's clarity ensured that his company would understand his demands on them. This clarity along with Schroeder's desire for artistic unity helped to create a unified company with defined relationships.

Schroeder was greatly influenced by the introduction of Shakespeare and the new German *Sturm und Drang* dramatists in Germany. He was the first to create a style of acting with his company that would be appropriate for the demands of these plays.

As the dramaturgy of the Hamburg Theatre spread so did many of Schroeder's ideas of staging and organization. "Goethe, we know, corresponded with Schroeder to obtain laws as a basis for the Weimar operations."[17]

To summarize, some of the ideals of organization of both Ekhof's Gotha company and Schroeder's company in Hamburg were the desire for ensemble acting, unified art work on stage, and a strongly governed group of theatre artists. Ekhof was the explorer in this realm, relying on the French *Comédie* model. Schroeder used Ekhof's work as his base and improved upon it, making it more specifically German. In one sense, both were striving for a new aesthetic in the art of the theatre, and for both the use of a strongly dictated organization seemed the only route. "The intended 'Total-effekt' of a most perfected aesthetic pleasure can be accomplished only through the most intimate union of all its parts in harmony—for every theatrical production."[18]

### Goethe at Weimar

The new aesthetic of unified performance was to manifest itself in two later German companies. The first resided at the court of Weimar, the second at the court of Saxe-Meiningen.

Weimar experienced its best years from 1798 until 1805. That was the period when Goethe, the universal genius, and Schiller, the great poet, worked together. Goethe had been *In-*

*tendent* of the court theatre from 1791, but never really showed much interest in the theatre until 1796. Marvin Carlson wrote,

Goethe's interest in the theatre was strongly stimulated in 1796 by the guest appearance in Weimar of August Wilhelm Iffland (1759–1814), the first major actor to visit the little theatre. To prepare his company for this event Goethe for the first time carefully and personally supervised their rehearsals . . . . Goethe informed his actors that the great Iffland should serve as an example to them, but he wished them in turn to demonstrate how well they could work together in supporting him. His double emphasis was significant. Clearly Goethe was impressed by Iffland's versatility if not his depth; he played fourteen widely varied roles during his brief visit. At the same time he recognized that none of his own company possessed even the latent ability for such achievement, and wisely emphasized with them the development of an ensemble which placed less demand on any individual actor.[19]

Most of Goethe's actors, while they were paid, were little better than amateurs. The theatre at Weimar had for long been of secondary importance both to the court and to Goethe. As Goethe's desire to harmonize staging increased, so did his output of plays. When Schiller was engaged by the court, Goethe had a counterpart to help balance his autocratic personality. Schiller was described as easy going and likeable, Goethe as stern, cold, and demanding. Yet between the two an ensemble of "average" actors was created. Goethe's style was soon to rival the so-called Hamburg style, and the two continued to be the competing styles of German acting throughout the nineteenth century. "Goethe gave particular attention to stage groupings and carefully rehearsed even the most insignificant actors to achieve the most effective total impact. In all concerns, we can see the beginning of the staging ideals which would reach their full fruition later in the century with the Meininger."[20]

Goethe invented a mechanized style of acting for his company. In essence, the style artificially created an ensemble by the use of Goethe's total dictatorship. The dictatorship may not have been intrinsically satisfying for the actors, but it may have created a sense of security. An actor could trust that everyone else in performance would be performing in precisely the same style. Goethe devised *Rules for Acting* to achieve this precision of performance from his actors:

dictated in 1803 . . .[the rules] set forth 91 commands for the actors' physical and vocal control. Exact arm, hand, and head positions were described, as well as specific methods of delivering lines. All punctuation marks were scrupulously observed and given relative weights— one beat pause for a comma, two for a semicolon, four for a colon, six for an exclamation point, eight for a question mark, ten for a period. Movements were controlled with similar care on a stage marked out in squares for absolute precision. (Pious) Wolfe (one of Goethe's actors) insists that the acting remained natural and convincing, but not surprisingly, his opinion was not shared by most observers. In any case, Goethe was not interested in natural convincing acting. Harmony, grace and dignity were his chief concerns; his principle was: 'Beauty first, then truth' (*Erst schön, dann wahr*).[21]

The new aesthetic of staging had a long-lasting impact, integrating many of Schroeder's ideals of performance. Goethe served his function as absolute dictator, convinced that his judgment was better than that of his actors. He, like Ekhof and Molière, had the financial backing of a patron, and was thus able to dictate his desires.

## The Duke of Saxe-Meiningen

In the German lineage, the court of Saxe-Meiningen had a lasting impact on the pictorial unity (that being stage groupings, settings, and costumes). The company was artistically controlled by a triumvirate: Duke George (who ruled in Meiningen from 1864 to 1914), his wife, Ellen Franz, and Ludwig Chronegk, a former comic actor. Together they consolidated a company that was to become the model for many troupes throughout Europe. The duke himself recorded little about his procedures, but one of his actors, Max Grube, wrote *The Story of the Meininger*, which recounts the working atmosphere of the ensemble. Wrote Grube,

A remarkable artistic trinity had now been effected—a ruling Prince, a former actress, and a Jew. And it was indeed truly a trinity, for almost never did a difference of opinion arise, except, of course, about things that were tried on the stage. With such cordial co-operation a division of labor was established—though only in the most general terms.

The Duke, in whose hands the supervision obviously remained, determined the outlines of the production and the forms of the presentation; Chronegk worked out the details; and Frau von Heldberg took as her province everything of a really dramatic nature.[22]

The duke was well-educated and of an artistic bent. His many extant designs for costumes and settings attest to his talents. He was also a historian and his designs reflect his desire for historical accuracy in his theatrical art. His control over all the elements of production helped to earn him the title of the first *regisseur*, or director, in the modern sense of the word.

The choices he made in the overall pictures of his productions also extended to the placement of his actors, where his mastery of group scenes gained him as much fame as his antiquarianism. Grube described this gift:

I accord the greatest recognition to this master [Reinhardt], but even in the finest shadings in the mass scene, he did not surpass the Meininger. That has not been possible, nor will it be; because the masses were not produced by "supers" but, instead, by young artists—gifted beginners—men and women.

Even this was not enough; every member of the company was obliged to work as an extra. *Mitmachen* (co-operation) does not adequately express this—rank and salary, although both might be significant—allowed no exception. Whenever they had no part in the play, the first hero and the first heroine had to stand beside the untrained beginner in the bristling throng of folk. As we may well understand, these methods were not at first acceptable, but the longer an artist remained with the Meininger, the more he perceived that on this groundwork of equality, the whole structure of the Meininger was erected and maintained.[23]

*Mitmachen* created a community of actors where class differences disappeared and the entire theatrical experience was unified. The duke and Chronegk together helped to construct this atmosphere. Heroic actors and bit players were treated alike in a true participatory theatre. "As a rule, orders, rather than suggestions were given by those in charge, as is more or less the case on every well-run stage; nevertheless, suggestions by the players were never ignored. Whoever believed that he had hit upon a good idea could take it to Chronegk, or for that matter directly to the Duke. If it seemed a good one, the idea would be subject to a test at once." [24]

The duke's company had the advantage of an abundance of rehearsal time to spend on each production, and twelve-hour rehearsals were normal. The audiences in his theatre were predictable, which made the prolific artistic output of the Meininger all the more amazing. The 1866–1867 season offered *Hamlet*, *Intrigue and Love*, *Don Carlos*, *Faust*, *The Robbers*, *Oedipus* (twice), *Oedipus at Colonus* (three times), *Antigone*, *Lear*, *Medea*, *Iphigenia*, *Emilia Galotti*, *Othello*, *Richard II*, and *Maria Stuart*. Taking into consideration that the theatre operated only six months of the year, and the performances were given only twice weekly, this is indeed a prodigious output. [25]

The duke of Saxe-Meiningen's company had several important features which allowed it to function as an ensemble. The first and probably most important feature was an overriding artistic ideal to which the whole organization could subscribe. This ideal consisted of the duke's desire for historical accuracy through the use of mass spectacle, costumes, and settings. This meticulous work was reflected in the precise placement of the actors on the stage and in the use of all the company's actors for this purpose, regardless of experience, class, or status of parts performed. The company was not in competition with any other, and this monopoly situation allowed for experimentation. As employees of the duke the actors were guaranteed financial security; thus, they had fewer worries and could devote endless hours to rehearsals. All these elements contributed to the strong impression that the well-drilled ensemble was eventually to make throughout Europe after it was invited to tour: "when Stanislavsky visited a Meininger rehearsal in Moscow in 1885, he was resolved to imitate the autocratic directing methods of Ludwig Chronegk, and that in Brussels in 1888 Andre Antoine was overwhelmed by the extraordinary realism in the Meininger crowd scenes." [26]

## *Antoine and the* Théâtre Libre

By the end of the 1880s a model was available for other theatre groups to follow. The highly disciplined acting and the unity of productions of the Meininger had made an impression on Andre Antoine (1858–1943) and his *Théâtre Libre* in Paris. Antoine's organization in turn affected another German theatre, run by Otto Brahm (1856–1912) at the *Freie Buhne* and later the *Deutsches Theatre.* These two men and their organizations shared naturalism as an artistic ideal. Both companies eventually acquired naturalist playwrights who contributed to their success.

Soon after Antoine decided to do new plays, whereupon he gathered a few actors and gave amateur performances. The novelty of his approach gained favorable reviews and later financial support through private subscription. John Henderson writes, "Antoine describes how he rejected the possibility of looking for financial help from a patron, and of forming an amateur society supported by subscription, in each case on the grounds of the need to have a completely free choice in the matter of plays to be produced. The only arrangement compatible with this indispensable freedom seemed to be the system of subscription performances or *abonnements,* by which it was eventually found possible to have an assured regular audience."[27]

Antoine could run his theatre as he saw fit. The style of acting and the type of plays he favored—both naturalistic— had a chance to develop without the threat of any other guiding hand. Still, the *Théâtre Libre* was shortlived; it survived from 1885 to the summer of 1893, only eight years. The company's early demise may have been due to the concentrated leadership of Antoine; it may also have been due, at least in part, to the fact that it remained nonprofessional. Many of Antoine's best actors were engaged elsewhere, and thus, Antoine became a victim of his own success. A posthumous eulogy to the *Théâtre Libre* was given by Jacques Copeau in his manifesto of 1913 for his own ensemble company, the *Vieux Colombier:*

Even theatrical companies subsidized by the State are today suffering from a lack of guidance and discipline, from greediness for profits, and the absence of a common ideal. As for the Boulevard theatres, they belong to the great "stars" who force their directors to make ruinous expenditures, throw stage productions out of balance, attract the audience's attention to themselves rather than to the play, and cheapen the playwright's talent by using their plays only as vehicles for their own stardom.

The last integrated company we saw in France was that of the *Theatre Libre*. The members had a faith they all shared. And a director who brilliantly exploited their common sentiments.[28]

Antoine's theatre set a standard and soon other independent theatres sprang up, using it as their model. The most organized ensemble that followed the *Théâtre Libre* was Otto Brahm's German *Freie Buhne*.

### Otto Brahm and the Freie Buhne

Brahm dedicated an experimental theatre in the *Freie Buhne* to naturalistic drama and encouraged a new style of acting. Oscar Brockett and Robert Findlay describe the effort:

Though the *Freie Buhne* was inspired by the *Theatre Libre*, it differed from it in many respects. First, it was founded by design rather than by accident. Second, it was run by a group. Its elected president and dominant figure was Otto Brahm, a drama critic, but he was advised and assisted by a governing council of ten members, an arrangement which differed markedly from Antoine's autocratic control of the *Theatre Libre*. Third, it employed professional actors altogether. Consequently, it worked around the schedules of other Berlin Theatres and presented its offerings on Sunday afternoons at the well-equipped Lessing Theatre and with actors employed at the Lessing, and the Berliner Theatre. Fourth, the major emphasis was upon the plays, with lesser concern for production.[29]

Brahm's biographer Maxim Newmark noted the change in the historical context: "By the 1880s, except for the Meininger and Bayreuth, royalty had largely exhausted its role as a patron of the theatrical arts in Germany, and future development of the theatre was to proceed along commercial (*unternehmerbetrieb*) and social (*gesellschaftbetrieb*) lines."[30]

The *Freie Buhne* filled the need for a socially oriented theatre, a theatre that was meant to be an educating tool for the masses. Brahm believed in *Geschmachsbildung* or an aesthetic education. He wrote, "The theatre must learn from its public, it must draw upon vital sources from all the degrees of its social and temporal milieu. Then it must assimilate this influence and transfigure it through the medium of art." [31]

Brahm took the position of *Intendent* at the *Deutsches Theatre* in 1894 hoping to gather about himself a permanent company. What he sought was a company that would play not only new material as the *Freie Buhne* did, but that would present *Antigone* based on the same artistic conception of realism. Here are Brahm's words on this approach:

We no longer wish merely to play "effective scenes" but rather wish to present complete characters with the whole conglomerate of qualities with which they are endowed. We don't want to be anything else but human beings who find the emotions of the characters to be represented from within and who express these with a simple, natural voice regardless of whether that voice is beautiful and resonant, regardless of whether the accompanying gesture is gracious or not, and regardless of whether it fits in with the conception of stock types. One problem is to adapt the representation to the simplicity of nature and to show the picture of a complete human being to the audience. [32]

His design for an acting company led him to seek the position of producer at the *Deutsches Theatre*. The ensemble was his ideal, as it had been Antoine's and Saxe-Meiningen's. Although Brahm had his own perspective, Toby Cole and Helen Kirch Chinoy point out that "unlike the last, who achieved coordinated effects at the expense of the individual actor, Brahm tried to create the ensemble through individual talents." [33]

Brahm worked toward his goals with a more mature idea of how to go about creating an ensemble than had his German predecessors. He did not shun actors of high quality or experience. Instead, he somehow molded the company together with these actors under his own artistic style, his "Brahm style" of acting.

## The Moscow Art Theatre

The influence of Antoine and the German director Brahm was limited, but, wrote Mark Slonim, "The Meiningen Company made a great impression on the general public in 1885 and 1890 (the years that they toured Europe), and their guest performances in Russia were a sensation."[34] Constantin Stanislavsky was very impressed by the work of the troupe and sought to use the style of Chronegk with his own group of amateur actors. Vladimir Nemirovitch-Dantchenko, Stanislavsky's contemporary, also wished to form a theatre group based on a more naturalistic and disciplined style of acting than was found in Russia at the turn of the century. The two had a famous eighteen-hour conversation in a Moscow restaurant. In his autobiography, Nemirovitch-Dantchenko recalled that they discussed "all the rules of life behind the scenes, the whole discipline, mutual relations, rights, and responsibilities—everything contributing to forging the unity so essential to our endeavor. In this manner was formed the group of theatrical workers which would eventually be called the collective."[35]

The first problem facing these artists was how to combine their two sets of actors, namely Dantchenko's students and Stanislavsky's amateurs. After that was settled their concerns turned to more practical matters, such as securing a theatre and getting financial backing.

The Moscow Art Theatre was started in 1898 with a company of thirty-nine, limited financial resources, and hardly any technical equipment. At the beginning of the twentieth century it grew into a large flourishing, well-organized and perfectly directed institution with a company of one hundred and a large staff. Strict discipline imposed upon everybody from top to bottom, from directors to stagehands, maintained a rigorous order within the theatre . . . . Instead of bureaucratic red tape and a formal hierarchy, which undermined the Imperial Theatre, it was ruled by a community spirit and comradeship based on a unity of vision and a sense of responsibility freely accepted by all as participants in the "common cause."[36]

This "common cause" was the theatre's creed that all the actors would be treated with equality, similar to the arrangement at the Meininger. The difference, however, was that for Dantchenko and Stanislavsky the actors' craft was of the highest value. Wrote Dantchenko, "It is necessary to watch the actor's will and direct it, without his being conscious of it; to be able without inflicting humiliation but with love and friendliness to mimic: 'This is how you are doing it; is this what you intended?' so that the actor may see himself face to face, as in a mirror."[37]

The actual birth of the company, according to Dantchenko, was on 27 June 1898 at a small farmhouse in the village of Pushkino. "It was there that the whole company first gathered; it was there that the first introductory word was uttered; it was there at the first rehearsals that our babe gave vent to its first cry."[38]

The isolation of the company at its inception helped to create the communal nature of this tightly knit ensemble. "They themselves had to clear the stage and auditorium, prepare their samovars, and take turns housekeeping. Nothing lowered their spirits. Even marriages were soon arranged—something like a dozen within the first half-year."[39] This spirit was aided by the company's enthusiasm; they showed devotion to the whole undertaking, to the work itself, without petty vanity and with tremendous faith.[40]

Stanislavsky and Dantchenko believed in a "no-star" form of repertory; anything less smacked of commercialism to them. Wrote Slonim, "Stanislavsky challenged the usual routine of building a performance around a great actor or actress, be it such an outstanding figure as Savina of the Alexandrinsky, or Yermolova of the Maly Theatre. When he announced 'there are no small parts, there are only small actors,' and later began casting plays in a fashion the old hands called fantastic, he was only following his main idea and was giving his actors the opportunity to experience various artistic possibilities."[41]

In the tradition of the Meininger, after playing a leading role in one play the actors of the Moscow Art Theatre would play extras in crowd scenes of the next play.

At the Moscow Art Theatre there is more done with individuals, the director and a single artist rehearsing alone together, discussing lines and trying movements, than at other Moscow theatres or than most New York directors do. Where the production is based on the principle of a collective of harmonized individual creations, with every part considered as important as the whole (the perfection of the whole being attainable only when every part makes its own perfect contribution) as opposed to the principle of the solo creation of the master regisseur who regards the perfect creation of the whole as attainable only through his own ability, such practice is quite inevitably necessary.[42]

Stanislavsky, who started as an autocratic director with a group of amateurs, matured and changed as his theatre succeeded. His style of directing became less authoritarian and more concerned with the actor's process of creation. Thus, to create his ensemble he combined the styles of Meininger and Brahm with his respect for the talent of individuals.

As the *Comédie Française* was referred to as "the House of Molière," so was the Moscow Art Theatre called "the House of Chekhov." While Stanislavsky was developing his actor techniques Chekhov was supplying the material that fit the Moscow Theatre's new style. And, like the *Comédie*, the Moscow Art Theatre is still functioning, outliving both their organizers and their playwrights. The "good sense" of their ensemble ideals has transcended time and political change.

### The United States

The United States, which has historically been considered an artistic backroad, has also had its experiments in unified production and permanent ensemble companies. In the mid-nineteenth century the Olympic Theatre in New York, managed by William Mitchell, had a "first rate comedy company presenting light entertainments at low prices to a mixed audience."[43] The company did without stars, but never reached the high ideals of an ensemble repertory. But in 1843 a permanent company of actors was formed by W. H. Smith at the Boston Museum: "There for nearly fifty years, a competent company with only one or two visiting stars a season presented a judicious mixture of standard plays and contemporary novelities."[44]

### Augustine Daly

These early attempts at permanence were tainted by the traditional inferiority of American theatre as compared to British theatre at this time in history. Not until the 1870s did a dominant figure in American theatre emerge. His name was Augustine Daly: "It may be said that others before Daly displayed some of the characteristics of the all-powerful producer-director. This claim has been made for Dion Boucicault and John E. Owens. But Daly is the first to stand clearly as a *regisseur*." [45]

Daly parallels the development of the Meininger in time. But his company existed in a competitive atmosphere where star actors were very important. Still Daly "maintained a permanent company, but almost from the beginning he aimed at the long-run, using his company's repertory mainly as a stopgap to keep his theatre open while a new production was in preparation. A new production in Daly's hands required time." [46] Daly succeeded both in New York and in London, modeling his company after his own design.

### David Belasco

By the end of the nineteenth century the new awareness of naturalism was sweeping through Europe. Another *regisseur*, David Belasco, emerged in the United States to fit the requirements of this new form. He attempted to train actors to fit the demands of the specific plays he wished to produce. Like Daly, Belasco was not interested in using star actors; instead he was concerned with the entire production and its total effect. Belasco sought to remedy the lack of training for American actors. He wrote,

talent must come to the American stage untutored. Since he is denied the preparatory course of study which would be considered necessary for the successful practice of any other artistic profession, the actor, to a great extent, is a victim of the influences and circumstances which attend his first entrance into the theatre. His fortunes, especially in the early period of his career, are nearly always the result of accident, not of discipline. That is why personality counts so much on our stage today. It also explains why so many among even our popular actors seem unable to progress beyond the constant performance of types of character which fall within a very limited range of techniques, or are identical with their own temperament and natures. [47]

In essence, Belasco was a pioneer with a new style of theatre. He spent many hours developing every production and felt that the same attention should be paid to actors and how they fit into the production, as to setting, costumes, and lighting.

## The Art Theatres

The need for a theatre that could be called American saw fruition at the start of the twentieth century. Art theatres sprung up in New York that were to have long-lasting effects upon the country's drama. The Provincetown Players, The Neighborhood Players, and The Washington Square Theatre all attempted to produce plays not being done in the Broadway theatres. These early ventures were bound to fail because of the economic strain of running a theatre in New York City.

A theatre formed by some of the former Washington Square artists had more success; it was called the Theatre Guild. Still, the Theatre Guild was only one theatre in a city that should have supported several like it. A former actress of the Guild, Eva Le Gallienne, attempted to create a repertory company in New York in 1926. She gathered "a group of aspiring young actors and a few veterans who preferred the artistic excitement and the modest financial security of repertory in a permanent company to the artistic tedium and financial bonanza of Broadway and the long run, and opened the Civic Repertory Theatre, October 26, with the performance of Chekhov's *The Three Sisters*."[48]

Eva Le Gallienne's Civic Repertory Theatre survived seven seasons before succumbing to financial pressures. Le Gallienne had to bail out her theatre several times with the assistance of Otto Kahn, a theatre impresario; she also tried to raise an endowment fund that would provide a financial cushion. "Le Gallienne's company was noteworthy for its wide-range selection of fine plays, its permanent troupe, and its use of a true repertory system."[49]

## The Group Theatre

The ensemble of the greatest importance in the American theatre (which was also connected with the Theatre Guild) was the Group Theatre started by Harold Clurman, Lee Strasberg, and Cheryl Crawford in 1931. The ensemble was founded in Stanislavsky's acting techniques, known to Strasberg, along with

Clurman's feeling that theatre should have social relevance. The need for continued actor training also shaped their work. Clurman discusses the need for training in his book on the Group Theatre:

Young actors, Strasberg and I declared, had no opportunity at the Theatre Guild, or elsewhere, to be trained while they were rehearsing. It was taken for granted by the Guild, as well as by commercial managers, that every actor was ready to perform as required, but the actor's individual problem as a growing craftsman was neglected. There were two reasons for this neglect: theatre organizations, like other business firms, were concerned solely with marketing their product; furthermore the problem itself was neither realized nor understood by most managers or directors. In our group we would pay careful attention to the actor's development. Rehearsals themselves would constitute schooling.[50]

Clurman's remarks echoed the concern with the lack of actor training in America that Belasco wrote about earlier in the century. But the Group Theatre was unique in wishing to create a company with methods for acting that would aid in the expression of social problems. Clurman wrote,

New technical methods, no matter how intriguing in themselves, had a very minor value unless they were related to a content that was humanly valuable. To what human beings, one might ask, were theatre ideas valuable. First, to the theatre artists themselves—to the actors, since they were the theatre's crucial factors; actors were citizens of a community before they took on their dubious connection with "art." Second, theatre ideas were to be important to an audience of which the actors were a focus, for it is the audience (seen as a "community") that has given birth to its artistry.[51]

The Group Theatre began work in 1931 with a theatre company based on a no-star system. The founders agreed that what was needed was unified artistic production and brought with them their own particular understanding of the Stanislavsky "method": "For this is what we decided to do: to go away to some country place with twenty-eight actors and rehearse two plays till they were ready for production in New York. We would pay no salaries, but we would provide meals, living quarters, laundry expenses. The three directors—that is what Cheryl Crawford, Lee Strasberg, and I now constituted ourselves—had chosen a company from among the people we had come in contact with during our winter meetings. A good many, indeed, a majority—remained with us for years, some to the very last days of our functioning."[52]

This sojourn to Brookfield Center, Connecticut, gave the company time to prepare a working relationship based on the equality of the actors. In New York, after they opened their first play, *House of Connelly* by Paul Green, the Group initiated innovative policies. They listed actors' names alphabetically in all programs. They paid salaries to all actors even if an actor was not performing in a current production. "In other words being assigned a better part in a Group production did not necessarily entail receiving more money. The actor's value was determined by his status in the Group as a permanent organization committed to the production of a number of plays every season."[53]

In the effort toward being socially relevant, the members of the Group found several playwrights to write specifically for them. Their greatest successes were the plays of one of their actors, Clifford Odets. Still, the Group Theatre was not able to sustain itself (it closed in 1941) in the competitive atmosphere of New York. Clurman explains: "The Group Theatre was a failure because, as no individual can exist alone, *no group can exist alone*. For a group to live a healthy life and mature to a full consummation of its potentiality, it must be sustained by other groups—not only of moneyed men or civic support, but equally conscious groups in the press, in the audience and generally in large and comparatively stable segments of society. When this fails to happen regardless of its spirit or capacity, it will wither just as an organ that is not nourished by the blood's circulation through the body."[54]

Furthermore, Clurman asserts, the Group failed "because its premise went against the American grain. The Group aimed to cultivate the individual through a collective approach to the individual's problems; and America's culture is fundamentally individualistic."[55]

## The Open Theatre

Despite the failure of the Group Theatre, other companies have organized subsequently; most have high ideals, and most have failed. Joseph Chaikin's Open Theatre lasted for ten years, from 1963 until 1973. This ensemble came closest to creating a new theatrical aesthetic in the United States, and had a considerable impact on the American theatre scene. Here, too, the organizers felt a need for a collective of artists that would approach acting problems as a community. Joseph Chaikin's recollection below epitomizes the present state of actor training in America and echoes the familiar Belasco statement about our professional theatre:

I had to come up with a full-blown character [the] afternoon of the first morning of work, which means of course, a stock character. I was terrified that I'd be fired. It just seemed to me such a breakthrough, such an opportunity to have this job. In fact, I didn't come up with a character in the afternoon but [the director] gave me 'till the next morning. During the course of the night I didn't sleep. I was walking around with funny walks. None of this had to do with what I had been studying at all. It was all a new requirement . . . I came up with something the second day. But I actually think the real reason he kept me was because it was at that point too late to replace me.[56]

This statement reaffirms the realities of present-day American theatre. Box-office success in New York and its "provincial" road houses to a large extent still depends upon proven star actors or hit Broadway shows.

The idea of an ensemble acting company is a managerial philosophy that has been applied to varying companies throughout history. William Ball, the creator and present general director of the American Conservatory Theatre of San Francisco, asserts, "By creating an *ensemble* company, you can present all forms of dramatic works. Nothing is too difficult to bring off because communication among the actors is rapid. These people become used to each other; *ensemble* acting, therefore, has the greatest potential."[57]

In summary, we can discern a number of elements of ensemble acting that have recurred in companies over the history of such efforts:

1. A permanent company of actors.
2. A consistency in acting style.
3. A commitment of the actors to the ideal.
4. Equality in and cooperation among members of the acting company.
5. Unified productions created either by a particular playwright or by the company's *regisseur*.
6. Financial security to allow for growth and experimentation toward the furthering of the art.
7. Often, but not always, a no-star system of acting whereby small and large roles alike are shared by all in the acting company.
8. An overriding ideal often based on the societal factors of the company's environment and engendered by the company's management.

# 2

# The American
# Conservatory Theatre:
# The Evolution of a Concept

The American Conservatory Theatre was an itinerant troupe for two years before it settled in San Francisco in January 1967. During this tenuous period ACT initiated, shaped, and clung fast to its goal of creating an ensemble. Wrote Julius Novick in *Beyond Broadway*, "The initial impetus for the group was for a structure that had continuity separate and independent from location, so the artists could perpetuate their own work whether or not a board of directors happened to subscribe to it."[1]

The company began in 1965 in Pittsburgh, under the direction of its conceptual artist William Ball. Ball's reputation had peaked after a successful production of *Tartuffe* at the Lincoln Center in 1965. Ball's theatre ideal was influenced by his theatrical experiences and his close colleagues, including Ellis Rabb, Allen Fletcher, Margaret Webster, and Edward Hastings, Jr.

Ball's large and somewhat contradictory goal was to create a national theatre that would not be in the nation's theatre center, New York City. The obvious conflict inherent in that goal naturally created a severely strained situation: maintaining an acting company of any quality while convincing the actors that their theatrical careers would not suffer if they left New York, were equally difficult tasks. Much credit is due Bill Ball and to his tenacity, foresight, and charismatic powers of persuasion. He fulfilled his own goal of creating an ensemble theatre while finding a way to keep his actors satisfied with inhabiting the regional theatre world.

Decentralization of the American theatre was under way by the mid-1960s, and ACT was about to make its mark. However, the credit for the creation of the regional theatre movement goes to a bold man from the Ford Foundation, as Bill Ball noted in a 1971 interview:

I credit the major force behind decentralized theatre to McNeil Lowry of the Ford Foundation. He started seventeen years ago to give grants to actors in regional theatres. He also made substantial grants to struggling professional theatres in Houston and Washington. The support that Mr. Lowry gave those theatres on matching grants gave them a new kind of life in the community. The communities saw that the Ford Foundation felt there was worth in their theatrical work and they came up with matches for those grants. More than any one single force in the theatre, I think it is the Ford Foundation which has inseminated the cultural scene with decentralized theatre and made it work.[2]

### The Pittsburgh Playhouse

To be precise, ACT, which had been an idea of Ball and others in New York, started on 15 July 1965, when it made its debut performance to enthusiastic reviews. A Rockefeller Foundation grant of $115,000, with additional monies being raised from other sources, was the initial financial backing for the company's existence. "According to Mr. Ball, his aim in founding the ACT was to establish 'an artistically creative, fertile ground free from the pressures of intense financial operations.'"[3]

Ken Costigan, former director of the Pittsburgh Playhouse, explained the Playhouse's point of view:

Well, there's a lot of scuttlebut about why Bill Ball was brought in. I think the problem was a problem which, at that time, was happening everywhere. It was in the early sixties. The Guthrie had just begun to build up and was making lots of noise. Regional theatre was billed as the savior of the American Theatre, and the people here at the Playhouse, from what I can gather, had decided they should jump on the bandwagon. They'd been around for quite a number of years, had certain good facilities, the money was here, and the one problem was that they were beginning to lose some of their audience to T.V. Then, too, a lot of people began to flee to the suburbs, so many of the people they had had for an audience slowly left; and I think they felt, behind their minds, that in order to keep up with things, they had to change the policy very radically and bring in the big guns. At that time Bill Ball was debating whether to go to the Lincoln Center. He had just made big news in New York in *Tartuffe*.[4]

*Tartuffe* had been well received in New York and had given Ball more exposure as a successful director, but his production was surrounded by internal upheaval at the Lincoln Center. Ball told of the frustration he experienced directing at the Lincoln Center, which became a primary reason for his decision not to base ACT in New York.

The conditions were so awful that I nearly had a nervous breakdown. I brought a tape recorder to hear the sound cues, and the union people said I couldn't turn it on; it was going to cost me two days' salary for sixteen men. The sets were delivered without doorknobs. In the middle of the rehearsal the board of directors fired [Robert] White-head and [Elia] Kazan. This great effort of two years, the great hope of the Lincoln Center was dissolving, and they told me to go back to rehearsal, as though nothing had happened and you could go right on creating theatre. Here I'd come all this distance to what I thought were the highest professional standards, and what did I find? A profession? No! It was madness.[5]

Out of this frustration Ball wrote a theatrical manifesto that eventually influenced the Rockefeller Foundation to fund his creation of ACT in Pittsburgh. With the Rockefeller Foundation's pledge a theatre was created that fit the declarations of this determined director. ACT was not intended to be a commercial success, as was demanded of a theatre in New York. Rather, ACT was to be a cultural institution of high artistic ideals, in its structure not unlike a museum, library, or an opera company.

After conceptualizing the theatre company the next great need was to create funding sources that would accommodate a national theatre's expenses. Ellis Rabb, former head of the now-defunct Association for Producing Artists (APA), and once Ball's roommate at Carnegie, pointed out in a 1970 interview the need to create an "establishment" or "institutionalized theatre":

What this country needs more I think, than almost anything else is a form of really vibrant and vital Establishment to have something to buffet against so that anti-establishment people in the theatre saying: "Oh, no! That's all bad. We must do something new and more dynamic and more revolutionary." They have something to fight against. I mean, the National Theatre of Great Britain—there stands Sir Laurence Olivier. And maybe some young directors and actors say: "Oh! We don't agree." But at least they have something to disagree with. There is no point in being anti-Establishment in this country. There is no Establishment unless you want to consider the David Merrick/Broadway thing the Establishment. I don't think that it is what I would call an Establishment Theatre. I can easily see in France a movement against the Comedie Francaise, you know, a great war, a revolution taking place because there it is and there is something, you know, and it should be so that if somebody else comes along with a more dynamic idea than the Comedie Francaise or the National Theatre of Great Britain, maybe with a great battle they will win. But there the structure stands—the economic structure and the buildings.[6]

Rabb's influence upon Ball's thinking can be seen clearly in the organization and goals of ACT. The form of ACT, not as a commercial venture but as a cultural asset needing public assistance to survive, was a reflection of Rabb's philosophy. As Ball suggested, the time had long since passed when

everybody involved in cultural aspects of American life should realize that the theatre is—right along with the ballet, museums, the opera—a cultural institution that needs support; financial support and Foundation support. A theatre cannot live on box-office take alone. It can't sustain itself. Because if we rely only on what happens at the box office you are obliged to do very popular works and sell-out. And with support in the form of subsidy and contributions and with subscription audiences we are allowed a certain security, artistically. And in that security we can do the kind of plays that are worthy of the cultural life of the community. I think that civilizations are known for the cultural life that they have created as well as the wars they have won. And our hope is that this period of time in American culture is a time when we achieve the finest in the performing arts.[7]

ACT's basic premises were set in 1965: a theatre national in artistic intention, regional in its setting, and nonprofit in its financial structure. "Ball founded the American Conservatory

Theatre Foundation as a response to existing conditions in the theatrical profession and as a positive step toward a fuller, richer future for the art of the theatre in our country. His wide experience as a director had made him painfully aware of shortcomings inherent in the New York commercial theatre and present to some degree in resident companies. At the same time he realized his ideas for the kind of theatre that would transcend these shortcomings would be valid only if they were embodied in a vital, active, living organization of artists—a theatre committed to the actor's art."[8]

ACT began its fledgling six-month season in Pittsburgh, performing from July to December of 1965. Joseph Zeigler recorded the event: "The ancient Pittsburgh Playhouse, a rich community theatre, had a mammoth physical plant that seemed a natural setting for such a venture, and there were rumblings about a connection being formulated between the Playhouse and Carnegie Tech. Ball, securing initial support from the Rockefeller Foundation, proffered his genius as the guiding force of ACT at the Pittsburgh Playhouse. The board of the theatre, realizing that the city was far behind others in the regional theatre movement, jumped at the chance, and in July of 1965 ACT was born in Pittsburgh."[9]

## The Mission of ACT

The American Conservatory Theatre had three definable goals, two of which followed the first and most important goal of creating an ensemble acting company. The two subsequent goals were to establish a repertory theatre in a conservatory atmosphere. When ACT first began in 1965 its statement of purpose identified the following mission:

The United States is the only country in the civilized world without a national conservatory of theatre art, and there is no immediate likelihood of one being created within our existing theatrical structures.

The commercial theatre is so heavily burdened with the pressure of immediate projects that it cannot be expected to provide development and training for theatre artists.

Such training as exists in universities and professional schools

31

often suffers from inadequate standards and is often limited by the highly individualistic stamp of one teacher or method.

There is no consistently available link for young professionals of these schools and the competitive commercial theatre.[10]

Consequently, the American Conservatory Theatre resolved to found:

A non-profit, tax exempt educational institution resembling the European concept of Conservatory—adapted so that development and performances are integral and inseparable parts of the professional's creative life. Training and production shall be indigenous, as the one to the other, not working as separate programs with separate personnel. All participants in the conservatory—as in a ballet company— will always be in training.

To bring together the finest directors, authors, playwrights, actors and educators in the theatre arts to provide comprehensive advanced training to the large professional company and to make that aggregate training available to representatives of regional theatres and educators in university and professional schools of drama.[11]

Through the commingling of a training institute and a repertory theatre the hope was that the actor would have a fertile ground on which to grow artistically. Ball found that "many American actors, even those with considerable reputations, frequently were deficient in the performing skills provided by basic theatre training. They lacked the technique, range and versatility which make it possible for an actor to work creatively in plays from a variety of historical periods in a multiplicity of theatrical styles. He noted that many successful careers were based on what was essentially a single skill or facility, a dependability in one kind of role which led to a fear on the part of the actor attempting anything new or difficult from his established mode."[12]

The lack of indigenous actor-training was a complaint voiced by many American twentieth-century directors, including David Belasco, as noted earlier. Ball's ambition was to create a conservatory, not unlike the original Moscow Art Theatre or the present *Comédie Française*, where a transfer of training to the professional stage could take place.

A self-definition of ACT emerged in 1965 and was printed in the company's statement of purpose. This document attested to the commitment that would help to create this modern American ensemble:

The American Conservatory Theatre combines the concept of resident repertory theatre with the classical concept of continuous training, study and practice as an integral and inseparable part of the performer's life.

The American Conservatory Theatre is simultaneously an educational and performing organization. This purpose in the first three years is to provide actors, craftsmen, directors and designers with a triple-pronged program. Each participant in the program will

1. develop his own artistic potential through study
2. teach the younger professionals
3. perform with repertoire

As the project is aimed at broadening the expressive ability of the actor and director, all available techniques for acting and directing will be used as sources. An eclectic program will be explored with a wide range of theory and experiment, while performance will serve to apply and test techniques.

The training program of the Conservatory will be concurrent with the program of presentations. Training will be woven into the rehearsal pattern by stage managers specifically engaged for the purpose of preparing the daily schedule and assignment of personnel (*Estudientenlieder*). Our goal is to awaken in the theatre artist his maximum versatility and expressiveness.[13]

## Ensemble Acting Company

Another of Ball's complaints about the commercial American theatre was that he repeatedly found himself "in the position of attempting to mold a group of strangers into an acting ensemble within the impossibly brief period of rehearsals for a single production."[14] Dennis Powers writes of Ball's intention to change this condition: "A.C.T. was founded in Pittsburgh to dig out, collect, test and use the kind of knowledge Ball talks about in order to create a theatre for which there is no precedent in this country. In forming the company, Ball brought together some of the nation's finest talents representing all aspects of theatre performance, production, training and administration." [15]

Indeed, the goal of ACT was as revolutionary as it was ambitious. Yet there was a need for such a conservatory approach in this country, and the timing for such a venture never seemed better. Decentralization of the American theatre was peaking, backed by substantial grants by notable foundations. ACT had its chance to join other new regional theatres and took hold of the opportunity with great energy.

Edward Hastings, one of the charter members of the company, explained the desire to create ACT as a model theatre: "The idea [of A.C.T.] was born really from the sort of bitchery that actors and directors get into about what's wrong with the theatre, particularly the theatre they're working in. So Bill decided to do something about it, and that's really how we all got involved at the very beginning—from complaining." [16]

Ball elaborated on the reasons for ACT's structure and ideals in an interview with Joan Sadler, a member of ACT's supporting foundation, the California Association for ACT (formerly called the California Theatre Foundation):

In the commercial theatre a group of strangers come together and work very rapidly and intensely for four weeks of rehearsals. After a play opens these people separate and once again go their individual ways. A.C.T. is based on the proposition that if you put actors together for a long period of time, they can affect each other's work through the *continuity* of their work and also by knowing that they have *job security*. If actors have these things and don't have to worry about reviews or the temperament of the director, all they have to do is go to work. Then these artists can concentrate on acting, they can constantly act well without fear. [17]

To those unfamiliar with the theatre, job security might seem to be an unimportant issue; at that time, however, an actor at ACT was being offered a contract for one season, to be used in several plays. This eliminated the need to compete on the open market (where there are always more talented actors than parts available). Said Ball, "A.C.T. is a theatre company for actors that is here essentially to provide those actors with everything they need. We attempt to create an atmosphere in which an actor's full potential can be realized . . . . Actors must also continue to refine their craft and be in constant training; they also need friendship, growth, nourishment, challenges, and a *sense of community.*"[18] A theatre for actors would become ACT's banner. Here, and reiterated in other documents, ACT was defined as a community. This meant that the actors worked together as a whole, not merely as individuals. Stated Ball,

At A.C.T. we are a *community.* Some artists are fortunate because they can create a sculpture and work alone in a studio like a painter. A theatre artist cannot exist or succeed alone. There are no soloists in our business. We are all *interdependent.* We call ourselves a community art: Our success is based on the relationship of one artist to another, or one craftsman to another. A.C.T. is a *group* of two hundred people bound together in service of one idea. We support each other and we know without each other we are lost. Nobody can be a success in theatre alone, and this gives us *mutual respect.* Carpenters, prop people, the wig mistress, the dresser backstage, the actors, the administrators, the secretary, the teacher, are all interwoven together into one texture. We use what might be called a sense of the universal consciousness in this group of two-hundred people. Everything that is expressed within this group is useful, meaningful, and pertinent to the life of the group.[19]

One of ACT's objectives was to imbue all company members with the sense that their work was a significant part of ACT's survival. Therefore, all members of the company were intradependent and supported each other. One aspect of this supportive community stressed by Ball was the right to fail:

In the learning process we know that no one ever learned anything by having continuous success. The way we learn is by experiencing failure, through the process of failure we learn. Failure is a necessary, healthy and valuable ingredient to the creative process. Critics and producers try to avoid failure at all costs. In the art form of the theatre, we know that failure is part of the creative process. We attempt to build upon anything that fails because it is a necessary and helpful component of our work. Failure is a doorway, once you pass through that doorway, ahead is greater knowledge, understanding and achievement. It is most essential that artists have no fear of taking risks in their art form. . . . We ask actors to perform parts they don't believe they have the potential to perform. An actor might initially think they could never be believable in a particular role because it may be an older character, or a comedy part, or athletic, or involve dancing or playing the piano. An actor must then run the risk of failure. And frequently, because of unschooled criticism, an actor may read notices in a newspaper saying that they have failed. But that's all right, we would congratulate the actor because he is now going to be more successful and more expressive because he has taken the risk and is more capable for it. That actor's vocabulary of expression has been expanded.[20]

Ball took this idea of "right to fail" a step further to what he called *positation*, and the idea permeated the organization.

At A.C.T. we inhibit the use of negative words because they are based on negative behavior. If one uses such words you are turning off and turning down opportunity. We try to say "Yes" to every idea that occurs, even if it seems like a bad idea, but a creative idea. Intuition is perfect, it wants to be expressive. The nature of creativity is to be right and pour outward. In this process, maybe the first thought is clumsy, but once you try to work with these ideas, the intuition and the imagination pours out everything that they have to offer.

One must nurture the imagination. The process of forcing oneself onward brings into play the thought that "necessity is the mother of invention." If an actor gives me an idea that isn't appropriate, it necessitates me to be inventive about the idea and nurture it. Then I must come up with another idea to match the actor. Two things are accomplished: First, I am forced to be more creative, and second, the actor is encouraged because I used his idea. The end result is that all our ideas become better.

When ideas begin to travel your intuition becomes sharper. We all long to be witnessed, to be seen clearly, truly and justly. The individual artists must learn to be trusting of one another. Intuition is like a flower, you can't force anything to be beautiful. A flower is like nature, it naturally seeks to be beautiful. You don't pull or pluck, or pound at a flower. You whisper quietly to the roots, and it will do what it wants to do. It becomes more beautiful for you than you could ever force it to be by all your requests, threats or intimidations. What we do is nurture and encourage every idea. No imagination ever got out of control and ruined the situation, it's never so expansive that it becomes obtrusive.[21]

## Conservatory and Repertory

ACT's ensemble acting company was founded on a repertory performance schedule in a conservatory environment. ACT, since its first days in Pittsburgh, clung fast to the Continental style of repertory performance.

Ball began formulating plans for a new kind of theatre company, keeping in mind the best aspects of the English and continental companies he had visited as well as the different needs of American actors. Essential to his vision were a policy of rotating repertory performances which would challenge the actor by having him play three, four or even five widely differing roles in the course of a single week; ongoing comprehensive training for members at each level of the acting company to stimulate artistic growth and development on a continuing basis and to make possible the full realization of each actor's creative potential; continuity of employment which would provide the basic security that engenders full attention to the actor's work and liberates his imagination to explore all facets of that work; and an organizational structure in which the artists would have a voice in determining policies and goals; a theatre where selection of plays for the repertory, training, use of facilities, scheduling of season and mode of operation would evolve with a concern for the actor's growth and progress.[22]

A key corollary was the conviction that an artist must continuously grow, and that a theatre, like a ballet company, must always be involved in the discipline and creativity of training.[23] Ball thought that it was necessary for an actor to play many different parts:

In New York an actor may perform the same role for three or four years, and do nothing regarding their personal growth. It's very difficult to keep from growing stale in that situation, but even worse is that the actor's creative energies and forces are languishing and probably dying. If an actor is to be an artist, he must be creative every day. The idea is to give the actor many roles so that every part feeds off the other roles. Stimulation keeps the creative juices flowing . . . at A.C.T. we make tremendous demands on each actor, and they are eager to give and fulfill those demands. Essentially, we are like a ballet company, when we sweat we know we're healthy.[24]

In keeping with the spirit of these remarks, the early years of ACT saw tremendous demands placed on actors. During their first full season twenty-seven plays were produced in repertory. The excitement generated by the demands of repertory kept the company vibrant and successful.

The company was also kept successful by its ability to inspire its audience. As Ball stated,

We need potential champions of humankind. We need to be able to witness the success of human beings in a pure, innocent, and complete state. All of us need models to admire; admiration is something that almost disappeared in human life. We must have something to admire that awakens our human sense of awe, wonder, delight, enjoyment, and exuberance. We all need something to awaken us, something that comes from inside ourselves. If we lose our ability of awe and admiration, then we dissolve into a terrible torment of ugliness. This is what the arts can do. The arts give us the possibility to admire something outside of ourselves. . . . This is the essential element of what A.C.T. has to offer.[25]

This intangible ability to awe one's audience was central to ACT's reputation in its beginning, both in Pittsburgh and in San Francisco. The first ACT season in Pittsburgh had the additional laudable quality of being a double repertory: "To allow them the widest possible opportunity for experimentation and expression, Ball instituted the revolutionary policy of performing simultaneously in two theatres every night. The double theatre system, he reasoned, would reinforce financial stability without a corresponding increase in operating costs."[26]

The Pittsburgh Playhouse's two theatres, which ACT used, were the Craft Theatre, with 540 seats, and the Hamlet, with 340 seats. The ambitious double repertory was based on the assumption that ACT could stun its audiences by presenting three or perhaps even four times as many productions as any theatre in the United States while it expanded the number of creative opportunities it offered to every member of the company.

On 15 July 1965, ACT opened its premiere season at the Craft Theatre with Ball's production of Molière's *Tartuffe*. (This was the same production he had presented at the Lincoln Center to good reviews, in which some of his favorite New York actors, including Michael O'Sullivan and Richard Dysart, and some former Carnegie students, including the versatile young talent René Auberjonois, appeared.) On 28 July of that year Luigi Pirandello's play *Six Characters in Search of an Author*, also directed by Ball, opened at the Hamlet Theatre. Both theatres remained in operation for the six-month season, offering a total of fourteen productions in rotating, or Continental style, repertory.

Another show in the ACT repertoire was the operatic-style production of Edward Albee's baffling play, *Tiny Alice*, which created the ACT reputation for visual and physical theatre presentation. Along with *Tiny Alice* were *The Rose Tattoo*, *King Lear*, *Death of a Salesman*, *The Apollo of Bellac*, *Antigone*, *In White America*, *Noah*, *The Servant of Two Masters*, *The Devil's Disciple*, *Under Milkwood*, and *Beyond the Fringe*.

The obviously eclectic play selection was greeted with praise by local critics. Julius Novick noted, "In Pittsburgh, said the *Post Gazette*, the theatre never had it so good. Mr. Ball and his American Conservatory Theatre have restored it to an eminence nobody hereabouts ever hoped for or dreamed of." [27]

### The First Crisis

Although the acclaim was great, ACT and the Playhouse suffered from internal squabbling and from lack of support. The initial venture was doomed. Richard Hoover, then general manager of the Playhouse, said that "it was simply too unwieldy for three corporations [Carnegie, the Playhouse, and ACT] to produce plays together, and what was to be a three-year venture ended after only six months." [28] Author Dennis Powers agreed: "The result was a decision on the part of the Conservatory officials to leave A.C.T.'s first home and seek another which might offer more freedom for the Conservatory to determine its own future and maintain the standards Ball had set for it." [29]

The company teetered on the edge of extinction, but the

39

Rockefeller Foundation awarded ACT a grant of $160,000 for the company to travel to New York and train for ten weeks. During this time bookings were made to play at the University of Michigan; in Connecticut; in Ravinia, Illinois (outside Chicago); and at Stanford in Palo Alto, California, for the spring and summer of 1966. Joseph Zeigler, commenting on the challenging booking pattern, said, "with his ability to turn the company's insecurity into not only philosophy but also promotion, Ball announced that the nomadic approach was deliberate—in order to find a community interested in supporting his company, and worthy of it."[30]

# 3

# A Theatre in Search of a City

Although New York City has traditionally been the theatrical center of the United States, and terms such as "Broadway" and "long-runs" are synonymous with success to actors all over the nation, by the mid-1960s the quality of theatre on Broadway had severely deteriorated, and efforts were being made to change the situation. Two alternatives to Broadway were Ellis Rabb's APA and the Lincoln Center project. However, the greatest change to come out of the Broadway backlash was the growth of professional theatres outside the New York City area. The new—and to some, heretical—regional movement was seen as a revolution in American theatrical history. Regionalism was, however, based on some sound philosophical arguments. James B. McKenzie, ACT's first executive producer, explained: "Any revolution is caused by a couple of points. In this case it was money—money combined with disenchantment with New York. If you look at the New York scene in those years, it was brutal—the techniques of hiring actors, the budgets which reduced the time of rehearsals, which cut down on any consideration for the actor's life. So, a lot of actors were desperately searching to find another way of life. At the same time, the commercial road was in bad trouble."[1]

The high costs of producing theatre in New York created another problem: there was no room for the development of a cohesive group of actors. Cohesive acting, or ensemble playing, seemed to be almost unattainable. Instead, the use of recognized star actors with a supporting cast performing in musical comedies was the general Broadway offering. Walter Kerr wrote in the *New York Times* in 1967 of the hope for an actual company of actors:

Good acting companies are not brought into being by monuments. They are created by being free to work *where it doesn't matter much if they fail.* In New York such a company would be most likely to emerge from a loft or a Cafe La Mamma. More probably—because New York with its many professional distractions, generally doesn't permit actors to stay together long enough to play together—the next good acting company we get will come from the sub-road, from the catch-as-catch-can university campus performances, from the summer stock used as a kind of survival kit, from wandering the by-ways—in however gypsy-like a fashion—until harmony and cohesiveness come along as a result of a kind of companionable endurance test.[2]

The insurmountable odds against the survival of an acting company in New York destroyed Ellis Rabb's APA in 1969, after ten years of touring countrywide and performing in New York. Bill Ball did not want his ACT actors burdened with the need to succeed in New York. He chose Pittsburgh as ACT's new home, then took the ensemble on the road until he was able to find an environment that could sustain it. Ball had discussed being stationed in New York with Rabb:

We talked, because we were very close friends, many times about values. He felt that it was absolutely essential to have residency in New York City. I had exactly the opposite feeling, that it was, in the long run, destructive and something that I would not agree upon, that I would not take a company to New York. He felt that it was very important to play in Los Angeles because of its talent pool and exposure there. I felt, on the other hand, it was very important not to— and still to this day I specifically don't want talent scouts raiding my company. I also don't want actors who are looking for exposure in television and film. They can get that on their own, if they want. . . . There are certain things that Ellis did that are different from our company.[3]

Ball's reasons for refusing to be based in New York would eventually be expressed by points seven and eight of ACT's statement of purpose: (7) "The Metropolitan theatre audience consists mainly of hit-followers; the minority of thoughtful theatre lovers is offered little in the way of a sustained meaningful répertoire; (8) "A handful of drama critics find themselves in a position to shape the canons of theatre art and the tastes of the entire nation; that their mere opinion may make or break the self-esteem, progress, and longevity of an artist or company."[4]

Such is the power of criticism in New York, where a play often fails to make it past opening night. The probability of a company surviving in such an environment on a permanent basis is slight.

### A Structure for Independence

With the signing of ACT's articles of nonprofit incorporation by William Ball, Jules Fisher, Edward Hastings, Jr., Kristen Linkletter, and Robert Whitehead, the structure that made possible the creation of the acting company came into being. (The reasons for establishing ACT as a nonprofit organization are explored in detail in chap. 5.) On 27 May 1965, Charles A. Church from the Department of Treasury sent to ACT acknowledgement of its nonprofit corporate status. The letter said, "On the basis of your stated purpose and the understanding that your operations will continue as evidenced to date or will conform to those proposed in your ruling application, we have concluded that you are exempt from Federal income tax as an organization described in section 501(c) (3) of the Internal Revenue Code."[5]

Thus began the organization known as the American Conservatory Theatre. ACT's nonprofit status made the company an entity unto itself. In other words, ACT could both produce plays on its own and be hired to perform its repertoire. ACT would have complete control of productions, scheduling, location, and the hiring and firing of artists and administrators. Jim McKenzie explained the independence the structure allowed:

ACT, a Delaware corporation, began with a thirteen-member board of trustees selected from the theatre world of New York City. Its first season was at the Pittsburgh Playhouse in Pittsburgh, Pennsylvania.

43

The directors in charge of the Playhouse wanted some involvement with the governance of ACT as it became apparent that Ball's group could well become Pittsburgh's permanent resident theatre company. Ball could not countenance any control of ACT by other parties. He allowed the Playhouse directors the front of house; i.e., audience services, but insisted that the ACT Foundation remain a separate entity, and the artists and related staff be employees of ACT.

At the end of the first season, the Pittsburgh board demanded control of some ACT policies. Ball thought that a steadily expanding umbrella of local power would overwhelm him. He feared a repeat of the Kazan-Whitehead debacle at the Lincoln Center and resolved to avoid forever the possibility of "civilian" control of ACT.

His concept of artistic control of a nonprofit theatre was unique. Unable to resolve the issue of control, Ball gave up substantial subsidy promises from the Mellon Foundation and other Pittsburgh philanthropists and moved the company back to New York, preferring to face an uncertain future rather than compromise his belief in self-governance. He resolved that if he could not keep his dream intact, he would close the company entirely and return to the commercial theatre.[6]

The most worrisome of Ball's problems in creating ACT was the traditional gap in understanding between a lay board of directors from the community and the arts institution. Therefore, he wrote ACT's by-laws specifically to prevent the company's having to depend on a board of this type: "Experience and observation indicate that organizational patterns set by nonprofit performing arts organizations for their governance have more often than not inhibited the functioning and the imagination of their artistic leadership. Most arts institutes in this country are governed by lay community boards which, however enthusiastic and well-intentioned often lack the experience and life commitment needed to understand fully the artist."[7]

The memory of the dismissals at the Lincoln Center in 1965 helped Ball to shape the idea of ACT as an independent production corporation. Whitehead, a commercial producer previous to his work with the Lincoln Repertory, saw the board as a limited partner that barred investors from direct participation in administrative or artistic choices. Because of its financial responsibility to the theatre, the board of the Lincoln Center panicked when the theatre incurred expected deficits after the first two years of operation. Thus, both parties were unhappy with the situation. As Kazan and Whitehead were nearing the end of their tenure, the board was in effect choking off cash flow by no longer actively raising funds to erase the deficit and thus allowing the company to survive.

The entanglement of three producers in Pittsburgh—those from the Carnegie Institute, the Pittsburgh Playhouse, and ACT—confirmed for Ball that a separation from the source of subsidy was essential for continuity. McKenzie explained the need for the separation:

By 1966, scarcely a decade into the new regional theatre movement, Ball was familiar with at least twenty situations which echoed the Lincoln Center artistic massacre. Even his closest friends, Julius Rudel and Ellis Rabb, had been deposed from artistic directorships by nontheatrical boards of directors. Bill's need for autonomy in his own company strengthened each time another artistic director was fired. His mandate was for adequate company support by a community of philanthropists who would not be allowed financial, artistic, or political control in any area of ACT. All decisions including his own contract, would be made by the ACT board of theatrical professionals, who had no obligation to provide funding.[8]

The independence of ACT from its support structure was a luxury unmatched in community-supported regional theatre. In one sense, this arrangement insulated the company from tampering by power-conscious businessmen and socialites. Edward Hastings, ACT's original executive director, recalled,

the company was always for the actors. There was no outside entity that came in and said, "Okay, you guys, we're going to hire you to do this." It came from within. Sure, some of the actors were contacted after the fact. But nonetheless, what they were being asked to do they were being asked to do by their fellows. Not that the company was ever a co-op, because it wasn't. There was always this notion that what was being done was being done for the actors, but for the art of the actors, not necessarily the comfort of the actor, for his ultimate expression. . . . There was no group saying, "We gave you ten million dollars and you have to make our theatre beautiful." That wasn't why the thing was being done. You felt that.[9]

One of the activities of the ACT Foundation Board was to raise funds from national foundations. This board became the connecting pin to the Ford Foundation, the Rockefeller Foundation, and the newly created National Endowment for the Arts, and it consisted of theatre professionals. The first ACT Foundation Board included Julius Rudel, Robert Whitehead, Jules Fisher, Henry C. Boettcher, James McKenzie, Marian Searchinger, Evelyn Daw Smith, Edith Markson, Edward Hastings, William Ball, Allen Fletcher, and Morton Leavy. ACT's self-study document describes the structure and function of the board:

Several of the A.C.T. Board are also administrators of the Company and Conservatory, thereby consolidating the Board/Management relationship. William Ball, General Manager, serves as President of the Board. . . . Although the A.C.T. Board has ultimate responsibility for setting and implementing A.C.T. and Conservatory artistic and fiscal policy, a conscious attempt is made to avoid the imposition of formal structures (which can too often be constrictive and stultifying) on the policy-making process. There is a basic commitment to responsive flexibility which enables A.C.T. administrators to react to needs and opportunities which arise, often spontaneously, from existing programs.[10]

The ACT administrators constituted an executive committee, a position that gave them the power to react quickly to any problem that might occur. The executive committee exercised this power in its decision to leave Pittsburgh.

When the Pittsburgh season was aborted, ACT fled to New York, held an "in-training" session, and barely kept itself together. It was at that point that the road tour was mounted that included stops in Palo Alto, California, and Ravinia, Illinois, cities Ball hoped would offer their support to establish ACT as a resident national theatre.

*San Francisco and the Chamber of Commerce, 1966*

ACT received offers from interested parties in San Francisco and Chicago after the aborted Pittsburgh season, but neither city seemed able to find the adequate funds to subsidize the expense of the large company. The city fathers of San Francisco saw ACT perform *Charley's Aunt*, directed by Edward Hastings during the 1966 Stanford engagement. Cyril Magnin, at the time the president of the Chamber of Commerce (COC) of San Francisco, recalled, "On a summer evening in 1966, I received a telephone call from the representative of the American Conservatory Theatre asking whether I, as President of the San Francisco Chamber of Commerce, would discuss with him the possibility of bringing A.C.T. permanently to the San Francisco Bay Area. He explained that the company was presenting a summer season at Stanford University and that the reception had been fantastically good."[11]

The phone conversation prompted the chamber to rent a bus and go to Stanford University to see the performance of *Charley's Aunt*. Their recent disenchantment with and loss of the Actor's Workshop Theatre found them in need of a resident company.

*The Actor's Workshop, ACT's Predecessor*

The Actor's Workshop, formed by Herbert Blau and Jules Irving in 1952, was San Francisco's first regional theatre company. It folded in 1965 owing to a lack of local funding support. The Workshop "put San Francisco on the theatrical map," said McKenzie.[12] When it folded (with the final curtain on 23 July 1965), Frederick Gardner of *The Nation* magazine wrote, "The Actor's Workshop lies dead in a pool of red ink. For years, the *Chronicle*, San Francisco's pro-enlightenment newspaper, warned that the demise of the Workshop would mean 'a loss of cultural face.' The head of the city's Arts Commission said, 'It would place us on a cultural par with Salinas.'"[13]

The Workshop, which brought San Francisco its first taste of Genet, Brecht, and Beckett, closed because it never drew a sizable and consistent audience to fill the Marines' Theatre, and because the city and the former mayor, John Shelley, chose not to bail it out financially. Blau and Irving, the founders, left San Francisco for New York and a chance to manage Lincoln Center's theatre. Ironically, the local government's desire to build a complex similar to the Lincoln Center in the downtown area of San Francisco had resulted in the failure in support for the Workshop. Wrote Gardener, "Mayor Shelley won't do anything on behalf of culture except promote a Lincoln Center type of construction project that few artists want. Governor Brown was 'actively unfriendly,' according to Marc Estren, when the Workshop made a last-ditch appeal for his help. Estren says he would like to see Ronald Reagan elected on the theory that things must get worse before they get better." [14]

The reasoning seemed simple: San Francisco was considered a major American cultural center. ACT offered San Francisco a complement to its well-established opera company, symphony, and art museum (the DeYoung Museum). ACT's timing couldn't have been better. Magnin wrote:

It was one of those marvelous coincidences that brought A.C.T. to the Bay Area . . . when San Francisco's only resident theatre company, the Actor's Workshop was folding to a $75,000.00 loss.

The directorship of A.C.T. had gotten wind of the demise of the Actor's Workshop and sent a man named Bill Baer to see me and chamber of commerce headman Bill Dauer. Baer came flying into my office, anxiety written all over his face. He pointed out the obvious— that San Francisco didn't have a rep company, but now it had a vacant theatre with no company to fill it. He felt it was our civic duty to fill the vacuum and hopefully, to fill it with A.C.T. [15]

The COC was excited about ACT, but no definite terms were set during the summer of 1966. Before ACT took to the road to honor its engagement with the Ravinia Festival, the company was invited by Mortimer Fleishhacker, a COC member, to a pool party at his home. It was there that ACT actors made a lasting friendship with the man credited with giving the greatest Bay Area support to ACT. Magnin described the link between Fleishhacker and ACT:

In the course of our negotiations we went to see A.C.T. several times. Morty Fleishhacker especially liked the Pirandello play, *Six Characters in Search of an Author*, and invited the company to his home for a party. The Fleishhackers had a swimming pool, and during the course of the evening one of the company, Robin Gammel, decided to take a skinny dip, doffed his clothes and dived in. Instead of being horrified, Janet Fleishhacker was so amused that her guests were free enough to act themselves, the incident was forgotten with a good laugh and a comfortable, familial link was established.[16]

Ball was not with the company during the Stanford engagement, but the COC members were impressed by the performance of the company alone; the company sold itself, in effect, without the help of its founder and artistic force. In fact, Ball had not met the Fleishhackers, and in his eyes he was facing the seemingly imminent dissolution of his company, for he knew that existing funds would run out by the end of the 1966 summer tour.

Ball asked the company members where they would prefer to take residence, in San Francisco or in Chicago. Their answer was San Francisco. On the eve of their last day, Ball asked his company who in San Francisco had been especially nice to them. The answer came back that the Fleishhackers had thrown a pool party for them. When Ball inquired further, he learned that the Fleishhackers were members of the family after whom the San Francisco Zoo was named, and that they had holdings in Crocker Bank, one of the largest banks in California. He also discovered that the Fleishhackers had two pools: an Olympic-size swimming pool and a reflection pool with a Roman colonnade at the far end. Ball recalled his reaction to this news:

I said take a wire to Mortimer Fleishhacker. I didn't know him from Adam, but the Roman colonnade did it for me. "Will you support ACT in San Francisco beginning October for twenty weeks for the amount of $250,000? Answer by return collect wire." The next morning was the end of our company. I got a wire back from this man I had never known. The first word of the wire was "Yes." The rest of the wire was, "We will support ACT in San Francisco next year according to the terms of your wire," from Mortimer Fleishhacker. I had never met him.[17]

With this fateful answer in hand, ACT began to set up its twenty-two-week 1967 season. The pledged subsidy was actually $200,000. On 26 September 1966, the first agreement was signed between the sponsors and ACT, which included the following statement: "The sponsors recognize the high artistic quality of the American Conservatory Theatre and believe that having it as a repertory company in San Francisco will make an important contribution to the cultural and educational life of the community. The sponsors also recognize that at this time the American Conservatory Theatre is not in a position to operate in San Francisco without substantial support. The purpose of this agreement is to provide that support."[18]

According to Jim McKenzie, the first agreement did not take the form of a contract, and was merely a pledge of support. ACT was seen as the recipient of a grant from the COC and its civic leaders. The internal workings of ACT as a theatre were to remain strictly in the domain of the ACT Foundation Board—that is, Ball and his chosen directors.

Of the initial grant, $35,000 came directly from Mortimer Fleishhacker, Cyril Magnin, and Melvin Swig (a San Francisco hotel magnate). Magnin recalled: "It is no small chore taking on a repertory company. We promised to raise $200,000—the amount needed to support A.C.T.'s first season in San Francisco. Morty, Mel, and I primed the pump with $35,000 of our own and then went on every radio and television show that would have us to pitch for city-wide support. By September we had raised nearly $50,000 in pledges and advanced ticket sales, and by opening night, January 21, 1967, we had raised $202,000."[19]

ACT opened its first San Francisco season with *Tartuffe*, "our funniest and biggest work," said Ball. Stanley Eichelbaum, of the *San Francisco Examiner*, wrote the next day in his review: "A.C.T.'s splendid opening with *Tartuffe* may very well be remembered as the single most important event in this city's theatrical history. The electricity alone made it the most sparkling and exciting triumph and an auspicious start for what we all hope will be a long, lasting relationship."[20]

## San Francisco

On 21 January 1967, ACT opened its first season in San Francisco. Using both the Geary (a large commercial touring house) and the Marines' Memorial (formerly the Actor's Workshop Theatre), ACT presented an impressive sixteen-production program in rotating repertory over a twenty-two-week period.

John Wasserman of the San Francisco *Chronicle* wrote of ACT's debut: "Well, it was all worth it—all the hassle and manipulating, all the frantic phone calls and almost fanatic dedication involved in bringing the American Conservatory Theatre to San Francisco. The company opened *Tartuffe* Saturday night at the Geary and it was a screaming, bellowing, unbelievable triumph."[21] This initial season ran through 18 June 1967. Sixteen different plays were presented for a total of 296 performances. "The season drew a total of 222,685 paid admissions. The Geary with its seating capacity of 1448, accounted for 154,501 of the season's theatregoers, with the 640-seat Marines' drawing the remaining 68,184 people."[22]

The box office receipts totaled $799,150, with the top weekend ticket price being six dollars. The average seating was 68 percent of the capacity for the two theatres. The larger Geary averaged 62 percent, while the smaller Marines' averaged 86 percent of the capacity.

That first season's plays included the startling production of *Tartuffe*, one of the audience's favorites, with 42,558 paid admissions. Dylan Thomas' *Under Milkwood* ran for twelve performances to 76 percent of the capacity at the Geary. The rest of the season at the Geary featured *Man and Superman, Arsenic and Old Lace, Our Town, Tiny Alice, Dear Liar, Death of a Salesman*, and *The Torch Bearers*.

At the Marines' Theatre's repertory *Charley's Aunt* was the most popular show, playing twenty-three performances to 99 percent of the capacity, a total of 14,345 people. The other shows at the Marines' that rounded out ACT's very eclectic first season were *Long Day's Journey into Night, Six Characters in Search of an Author, Beyond the Fringe, Endgame, The Seagull*, and "A.C.T. one-acts" (*The Zoo Story* and *Krapp's Last Tape*).

The forty-seven acting members of the conservatory played a total of 187 characters during the twenty-two-week period, an average of four roles per actor. Jay Doyle and Paul Shenar doubled that average to appear in eight different roles each, more than any other ACT performer. Actors Richard A. Dysart, Scott Hylands, and Ray Reinhardt were seen in seven productions each, and René Auberjonois, Ken Ruta, and Patrick Tovatt were in six.

ACT actresses were not quite as busy. Of the 187 roles, only sixty (not counting Madame Pace in *Six Characters*, played by Doyle) were for women. DeAnn Mears and Barbara Colby played more roles than any other actresses in the conservatory, with five roles each.

These roles only account for actual performance roles. All ACT actors were either double-cast or understudied in many roles. As ACT's program of the first year stated, "It is the custom of the Conservatory to rehearse more than one actor in a role. Unless otherwise announced prior to curtain, the first name on the program will designate the actor playing the performance."[23] The cast list of *Tartuffe* was as follows:

CAST
*(in order of appearance)*

| | |
|---|---|
| Tartuffe | René Auberjonois |
| | Patrick Tovatt |
| Madame Pernelle | Josephine Nichols |
| | Ruth Kobart |
| Dorine | Judith Mihalyi |
| | Ann Weldon |
| Marianne | Deborah Sussel |
| | Charline Polite |
| Elmire | DeAnn Mears |
| | Michael Learned |
| Damis | Ray Laine |
| | David Dukes |
| Cleante | James Ragan |
| | Peter Donat |

| | |
|---|---|
| Valere | Paul Shenar |
| | Mark Schell |
| Orgon | Ramon Bieri |
| | Robert Gerringer |
| Monsieur Loyal | Phillip Kerr |
| | Jay Doyle |

The total commitment on the part of the actors to the repertory performances was stretched even further by what were called "out-rep" productions. That first six-month season included twenty-eight performances in thirteen cities throughout California. The most performed play was Jerome Kilty's *Dear Liar,* based on the correspondence of George Bernard Shaw and Mrs. Patrick Campbell. Michael O'Sullivan played Shaw and Sada Thompson portrayed Mrs. Campbell.

### Chicago or San Francisco?

As the first San Francisco season came to an end, ACT again had to establish a home base. During the summer of 1967, the company was once again forced to go on the road. Clearly, the initial conception of ACT as a national company—one that would transcend a particular region and resist becoming a New York City troupe—was a noble one, but one difficult to realize.

That summer ACT raised the battle cry to find a home with community support. Two cities were most desirable to the troupe, San Francisco and Chicago. Chicago had traditionally been seen as the cultural center of the Midwest and a good theatre town, while San Francisco was seen as the cultural capital of the West. The grand scheme was for ACT to have a home in both cities.

The plan for the upcoming 1967–1968 season included six months in San Francisco followed by six months in Chicago. The *New York Times* discussed the possibility: "The Conservatory is negotiating with the Action Committee for Theatre in Chicago to play there, also to use two houses for 20 weeks from February 5, 1968 to June 23, 1968. Contracts are expected to be signed this month. The Committee chairman is Edward R.

Kenefick, a vice president of the Columbia Broadcasting System and general manager of WBBM–TV in Chicago. He said $100,000 in donations had been collected for the $300,000 budget."[24]

The Chicago Action Committee for Theatre was the counterpart of the committee from the COC of San Francisco. Their initial pledge was greater than San Francisco's by $100,000. It seemed that the reality of a two-city repertory was imminent.

In the end, however, Ball and ACT opted to stay in San Francisco. The official reason was stated in the *New York Times*: "Reports indicated that the Chicago engagement was called off because Actor's Equity, the performers union, had insisted the players be paid $7.50 per diem for expenses whenever the company was on tour. Ben Irving, Equity's assistant secretary, asserted that because San Francisco was the troupe's 'home base as a resident theatre,' the Chicago season was a tour. He went on to explain: 'William Ball, General Director of A.C.T., had asked us to waive that requirement, which we declined to do.'"[25]

The per diem argument was a valid reason for terminating the arrangements for making Chicago a second home for ACT's company. But Ball was also influenced in the decision by the massive effort involved in a second city repertory. The negotiations with the Chicago Action Committee were more difficult than those with the original COC members, and it was the latter who subsequently formed San Francisco's California Theatre Foundation. William Bushnell, ACT's first managing director, explained:

In the final analysis, it was a very scary proposition to try to make it happen. There were certain, perhaps sensory, feelings out of Chicago that the control of factors in Chicago as related to their financial commitment would have been more difficult for Bill to deal with than they were in San Francisco. That was a principal factor. . . . It was a hard negotiation with Chicago, as opposed to the fact that San Francisco was a pretty easy negotiation. At the time, I think that it was an originally fascinating idea, [but] the more it was negotiated and the closer it came to a potential reality, the more perceived problems began to put themselves on the table—*per diem*, obviously, being one of them. Where does an actor actually have a home if he is spending six months a year rocking back and forth across the country? . . . [There was no model on which to base any of this.] There were a lot of questions as to whether our budget estimates were realistic. There was, at that point particularly, with Mort Fleishhacker a real sense that we had a very real supporter. That it certainly is comfortable living in San Francisco, a lot more comfortable in San Francisco than Chicago in the winter time. To a certain extent, at that point, it was perceived that a good part of the season would be: Chicago in the winter and San Francisco in the summer . . . there were myriad elements that came into it.[26]

Yet the perceived problems were not insurmountable. The board-separation problem that ACT faced in Pittsburgh seemed to have been settled with the Chicago Action Committee. In fact, the only reason ACT decided on San Francisco as its home may have been that the first season was in San Francisco, preceding the first planned six months in Chicago. Hastings explained:

They accepted that [the independent ACT Foundation] in Chicago too. It was just luck, really. The idea could have succeeded anywhere. That's sort of an heretical thing to say. I really do believe that the energy that was abundant in Chicago was different than the San Francisco energy, but it was good. They were really muscular in Chicago. . . . In San Francisco there was a certain ease to the audience and to the committee to support ACT. They had done it a lot with opera and symphony and KQED [the public television station]. But in Chicago, the people that were behind it were a little "greener," but they were very energetic. . . .

I think it would have worked. It was a different combination— of a great art work and a great art patron [San Francisco] versus a more *bourgeois*, a new rich patron [Chicago]. But I think they both made good patrons and good supporters. . . . The only lucky part of it was the plans for the first six months would be in San Francisco and the second in Chicago. . . . I think if the first six months were in Chicago, we'd still be in Chicago. . . . It was the flip of the coin. . . . San Francisco knew how to do these things and that was clear.[27]

Though the Chicago stay was possible, ACT decided not to go. The enormous amount of work involved and the complications that may have occurred were the major factors contributing to the decision. Bushnell explained:

What happened with [the Chicago plans] was Bill decided that was not something that he wanted to do. My perception was that situation was in place and do-able from the financial point of view as far as what they had been asked to do and what they had been asked to commit. In retrospect . . . you could sit back and say that it may very well have been an idea that was too grandiose, before its time.

In point of fact, as far as the city of Chicago and a woman named Hope Abelson were concerned, they had a deal. We, to a great extent, backed away from a verbal-commitment deal that would have enabled the company to at least attempt the two-city rep.[28]

Bushnell's reference was to Hope Abelson, a Chicago-based producer, who had just successfully produced *The Royal Hunt of the Sun* at the New York American National Theatre Association (ANTA) Theatre (1965). She was a reputable and capable producer who was in a good position to aid ACT's possible success in Chicago had the company followed up on the two-city plan.

### San Francisco: a Home and a Success

Thus, ACT and Ball chose San Francisco over Chicago as its home. As McKenzie stated, "We are here because we want to be here." The COC was very much in favor of keeping ACT to itself.

On 6 September 1967, ACT announced that San Francisco was to become its permanent home, ending the negotiations to make ACT a two-city repertory. ACT planned to produce a forty-week season at the Geary and Marines' theatres. The newly created CTF promised to underwrite their season. Mortimer Fleishhacker announced: "As we see it, there is a good opportunity for us to serve as host for the entire nation with the very best in American Theatre. Reviewers everywhere have given acclaim to the performances of A.C.T. and the unusual stimulation generated by the Conservatory program. A.C.T. will now become the first theatre institute to provide such advanced professional training and performance programs on a year-round basis."[29]

At that time the CTF pledged $400,000 in contributions

for ACT's projected budget of $1.5 million and the conservatory's budget of $800,000. An additional $500,000 in subsidy was to be obtained from national sources outside the Bay Area. The balance of ACT's funding was to come from subscriptions and box-office revenues. Fleishhacker explained at the time that "an additional factor is the elimination of any possibility that A.C.T. might be shared with other communities. A.C.T. has now become a full-time Bay Area enterprise. It takes its place alongside our other important artistic institutions, to round out the cultural and entertainment scene with well supported and well attended theatre."

Melvin Swig, president of CTF, said, "We're not talking about one year; we expect to go on and on."[30] And Ball was quoted as saying, "We'll make it work; it was like taking a stone off our backs."[31]

The next season's plan included the production of thirty-one plays in repertory. The effect of thirty-one plays would be as stunning as the sixteen-play repertory had been during the first twenty-two weeks, since they were to be staged over forty weeks. The number of productions was unparalleled in both seasons. As Julius Novick wrote in his book, *Beyond Broadway*, "There was no attempt to start slowly and build support gradually; the A.C.T. came to San Francisco under conditions that made it, by almost any measure I can think of, larger than any other remotely comparable theatre in this country."[32]

Bill Ball explained his reasons for planning these large numbers of plays both in that first full season and in the preceding twenty-two week season of 1967:

We produce so many plays that we dazzle.... In other words, my goal was I wanted to occupy the drama page of every newspaper for ten days in a row—every day it was a different review. They might not like one or two plays, but at least for ten days that city would be aware of our presence. In addition to which I was not sure that we could sell two performances in a row. But I knew that if we got all the shows open and ran them in repertory and kept them far enough apart, we would get a backed-up audience. Because, if we came in and ran a show for two weeks, we would have done forty people a night.

The idea was to have so much, such a splashy repertory that it was an undeniable experience. We had to dazzle our audience and overwhelm them, essentially.[33]

Dazzle they did. All the reviews were favorable from the opening night, and all three of San Francisco's major critics gave good notices (Paine Knickerbocker of the *Chronicle*; Stanley Eichelbaum of the *Examiner*; and Gerald Nachman of the *Oakland Tribune*). Eichelbaum epitomized the wonder with which the local critics viewed ACT: "I was stunned by their work. It was the most imaginative, the most remarkable by a rep company that I had seen. It reminded me of an European-trained company, something like the Royal Shakespeare (of England) because they had an ensemble feeling that the Actor's Workshop never had. There was a level of professionalism that was wonderful. They did very imaginative staging. The other thing about A.C.T. that was so exceptional was the number of productions they had on the boards, and the versatility of the company showed up so exceptionally. Anyone who saw them had to be impressed."[34]

ACT seemed to blend in with San Francisco almost instantaneously. San Francisco, called America's favorite city, has always been hailed for its charm and beauty. Cyril Magnin described San Francisco: "San Francisco has been triply blessed: we have a spectacular blend of mountains and sea. Built on seven hills, San Francisco has vistas unparalleled in the United States. Our weather is temperate and can produce those glorious sun-washed days that make our beautiful city sparkle and shimmer like a casket full of jewels. And there is a pervasive attitude of 'do your own thing,' a *laissez faire*, that allows people . . . to grow and develop . . . it prefers that if you say you can do something or are something, that you deliver what you promise."[35]

The 1950s saw San Francisco's beatnik and jazz scenes grow and bring national attention with them. Out of this free environment came several notable American writers, including Ginsberg, Ferlinghetti, Corso, Kerouac, and McClure. Novelist Ken Kesey wrote during the 1960s about the hippie and love generation, ushering in a new era in San Francisco's identity. In spite of such cultural expansiveness, however, the feeling persisted outside the immediate area that San Francisco was little more than a good road stop for traveling companies.[36]

ACT had to survive in a city that at worst was called "a terrible town for theatre,"[37] and at best, "ambiguous."[38] In spite of its dubious theatrical reputation, however, the population's patronizing and chauvinistic attitudes about its city's beauty and culture seemed to promise a good reception. Wrote Mike Steele of the *Minneapolis Tribune*: "It's a city of theatricality. Every street corner is a stage and every fourth person seems to be either a manic actor out of Genet or a street musician out of work. It's the obvious city for the American Conservatory Theatre, A.C.T. for short, America's most flamboyant and regional theatre and one of its best. It reflects San Francisco exactly, erratically brilliant, vain, diverse, perverse and very exciting."[39]

ACT rocked San Francisco with the diversity of its repertory and the flamboyance of its staging. It did so with a company that played with a unity of spirit not seen before in San Francisco. "It was like bringing Broadway to San Francisco," said Eichelbaum.[40] "The City's response to A.C.T. has been 'marvelous,' Ball remarked recently, citing 13,000 season subscribers, an impressive figure compared to the Actor's Workshop peak of 5,200. Such popularity is due in part to a repertory aimed at attracting rather than alienating (*a la* Blau) large audiences."[41]

In 1965, the Workshop's deficit was $75,000. A year later, the same city that turned its back on the Workshop offered to underwrite ACT for $200,000. The dramatic turnaround was explained by what the local community saw in ACT as compared with what it saw in the Workshop:

It was woozily suggested that A.C.T. won backing from an establishment that felt "guilt" over letting the Actor's Workshop die. Guilt had nothing to do with it; A.C.T. simply served up the kind of theatre the Establishment wanted—the Workshop didn't. Herbert Blau and Jules Irving were artistic and political revolutionaries who gave San Francisco its first *Mother Courage*, *Waiting for Godot* and Pinter years before they were "in." Ball's stagecraft is apolitical, operatic, and *safe*.

Blau courted the academicians and disdained anyone outside the faculty; Ball romanced the Right People. Costumes, scenery and light shows meant nothing to the Workshop, they are the glory of A.C.T.[42]

Since the success of ACT, the Workshop has had a post mortem success of its own. But some say in retrospect that the reputation of its actual product was inflated and that only an occasional hit among the many failures allowed the somewhat anti-establishment company to survive. Said Eichelbaum,

We were used to at best a semi-professional resident troupe. The Actor's Workshop, although they brought us some exceptional material in the way of plays . . . they were very uneven in terms of their acting company.

The Actor's Workshop complained bitterly about not having audiences. The public was just hard, hard, hard to draw into their theatre. I felt they had a point. It was hard to get people to see Genet and Pinter and Beckett back then. San Francisco, it seemed to me, didn't have the intellectual vitality that it might have had back in the late fifties and early sixties.[43]

The Workshop served as the local standard for theatre and drew a small house. Its competition came from road show houses that produced touring Broadway hits. Yet the Workshop may have simply been too far ahead of its time to be a commercial or nonprofit success in the Marines' Theatre. Bob Goldsby, a director both with the Workshop and with ACT, suggested, "There is a very small audience for alternative theatre. It doesn't change much . . . . There is a whole series of reasons why it does or doesn't grow: the weather; the lack of publications in the arts; no feedback. There's no real intellectual publications to feed off of, like there is in any major cosmopolitan city. There's no habit of it here. ACT got involved and there is an audience there. Because Bill understood what people liked to go see, he really did."[44]

In 1965, while San Francisco was serving as host to ACT, changes were occurring in the city government. Mayor Shelley decided not to run for re-election, and his successor was to be Joseph Alioto, an attorney who had served as the head of the city's redevelopment agency. San Francisco was beginning to feel the same urban blight and suburban flight that most American cities suffered through during the 1960s. Alioto took it upon himself to give San Francisco a much-needed facelift. He proclaimed, "Some cities may have run out of time. But, I don't think San Francisco has."[45]

Until Alioto was elected in the fall of 1967, the hope still ran high for the development of the downtown performing arts complex. The idea was to maintain a theatre along with the symphony (which had no home of its own) and the ballet. Mayor Shelley had backed the complex, but most of the San Francisco cultural critics saw the proposal as typical of those realized in many other communities, where money was lavished on real estate while the arts groups that inhabited the buildings were ignored. One of those critics was Dean Wallace, art and music editor of the *Chronicle*. He wrote, "San Francisco is rapidly becoming known from coast to coast as the place where everyone talks about culture and nobody does anything about it. . . . Sometimes it seems as though our city is engaged in a desperate struggle to remain second-rate—and not quite making it."[46]

On the heels of such criticism, the initiative to build the arts center was defeated by referendum. At the same time, the business community saw the sense in having certain tourist attractions in the city. With the election of Alioto and his crusade to revitalize San Francisco, interest began to reawaken in the survival of the arts. ACT, a true professional company now committed to making its home in San Francisco, could fill the gap left vacant by the Actor's Workshop. Thus, the arrival of ACT in town allowed the city fathers to call San Francisco a "city of the world" once again. Culture was seen as something that was commercially desirable and ACT fitted the bill.

### Building an Audience

ACT was "winging it" in San Francisco. As previously noted, Ball thought that the company had to dazzle the audience to survive.[46] With the failure of the Workshop, San Francisco had a poor track record. There was no model for ACT to follow. In general, ACT took the recommendations of the Rockefeller

Foundation. One of its suggestions was to make theatre afford-able for a large number of people: "The panel is motivated by the conviction that the arts are not for a privileged few, but for the many, that their place is not on the periphery of society, but at its center, that they are not just a form of recreation, but are of central importance to our well-being and happiness. In this panel's view, this status will not be widely achieved unless artis-tic excellence is the constant goal of every artist and every arts organization, and mediocrity is recognized as the ever-present enemy of true progress in the development of the arts."[47]

One of ACT's aims was written in its purpose statement: "to build and rely completely upon a subscription audience, offering a meaningful repertoire at a popular, accessible price scale."[48] Even with the top ticket price at six dollars, the imme-diate success of ACT was nevertheless astonishing, as Julius Novick remarks:

How to explain such an immediate, massive popular response? Guilt over the death of the Actor's Workshop may have had something to do with it. . . . But where the Workshop had tended to keep the San Francisco audience at arm's length, the A.C.T. embraced it enthusias-tically.

[Ball] was similarly accommodating as to repertory of the plays. Many people found the Workshop's repertory too formidable for their tastes, but Mr. Ball is such an eclectic that he can produce, with no loss of integrity, plays that Blau and Irving could not have done with-out feeling that they had sold out. "To succeed," said Ball, "a theatre must have an audience!" ("Give an audience a chance, and it will certainly be wrong."—Herbert Blau) "We try to pick plays with enough variety to reach a wider range of audiences."[49]

ACT's and Ball's "showmanship" educated a larger audi-ence than the Workshop, and provided the Bay Area with "a large, on-going center of high level of professionalism that lives and works in the area where it performs."[50] Ball was not afraid to produce plays that would draw. The economic pressures of filling approximately two thousand seats daily made it nearly prohibitive to do anything else. Moreover, he was able to gauge what would succeed. Goldsby explained Ball's uncanny and suc-cessful combination of plays for San Francisco audiences: "ACT brought a kind of fun and entertainment without anything else around it. It wasn't serious, it wasn't intellectual, it wasn't political. It was just a fun evening. San Francisco likes to go out and have fun. So, the things that are successful here, they are just entertainment. The "old white way," the old Broadway idea, only this time it's done with classics instead of with musicals and new plays as it was on Broadway."[51]

The entertainment that Goldsby referred to was connected to the positation attitude held by Ball. The heavily intellectual material presented by the Workshop in large doses was only sparingly introduced into ACT's overall seasonal offerings. As Ball explained,

The first criterion of the plays we do is that they are full of lasting merit. We do plays that are classical. Secondly, we want to do plays that are in the support of illuminated life. We believe in life and humankind and we believe that plays should be a reflection of the beauty of life. We tend not to do plays that are hopelessly bad news. Most of those plays are not even true. . . . We like to do plays with truth in them and exuberance and filled with life because that's the way people are. We like great variety among the plays. We like to do great classics, great plays that have been popular in London and New York, plays of curiosity. We like to include new plays, although this is a theatre for actors, not a theatre for playwrights.[52]

Ball's positive outlook combined with his energetic staging created tremendous excitement in all ACT offerings. A footnote to this excitement was that during the first season, the musician's local union had demanded that musicians be paid nightly at the Geary Theatre, even if they were not needed for the play. Ball, not very pleased with this demand, posted the paid musicians outside the theatre nightly to play a fanfare, an arrangement that added to the celebration of the evening. The theatricality of ACT brought immediate results from its audiences: as Eichelbaum described it, "standing ovations, screaming bravos, it began to seem as if they were employing a claque."[53]

## Subscription

The first season was an immediate success, drawing the highly educated and professional sector. But as it began to chart its second full season for 1968–1969, the company began to sense how difficult it would be to keep this audience and maintain subscription rates: "The company launched its second 40-week season in December, 1968 with less than 10,000 season tickets sold. Artistic successes and a few box office hits among the 15 new shows and revivals on the schedule were overshadowed by dwindling audiences as the overlong season wore on." [54]

One reason given for the poor subscription show and the 40-percent-of-capacity houses in 1968 was that the subscription program was confusing. According to McKenzie, the subscription "was all screwed up and poorly administrated." [55]

The subscription campaign is exemplified in the following press release: "A.C.T. season subscribers will receive a subscription book containing coupons for the plays they have selected from the 16-play repertory. The coupons may then be exchanged for reserved seat tickets to any of these plays throughout the season. In this way, the subscriber is free to select performance dates, without being tied to a specific night of the week." [56]

This confusing subscription scheme was replaced by McKenzie in 1969. He insisted on a more uniform subscription system, whereby subscribers would select one day in the week when they would see the season's plays, and the same seat would be reserved for them at every performance on that day. The new system was termed "Tuesday Subscription," because when, for example, nine plays were in repertory, there would be nine Tuesdays with different plays. Thus, subscribers who bought season tickets and picked a Tuesday as their day would immediately receive those Tuesday dates. The system extended to other days of the week over the entire season. McKenzie's experience with summer stock came into play in the maturing of this aspect of ACT's subscription campaign.

Another reason for the dramatic decline in attendance was cited by Joseph Zeigler in his book, *Regional Theatre*.

However, as in other cities where a theatre burst upon the scene rather than evolving slowly, A.C.T. and San Francisco did not enjoy a permanent honeymoon. The company's spiralling spending almost immediately incurred large deficits. . . . Audience interest, too—as in

Minneapolis with the Guthrie—fell off after the first [full] splashy season and A.C.T.'s practice of regularly repeating old productions, sometimes gave it a *déjà vu* appearance. Characteristically, San Francisco had over reacted to the chic vitality of A.C.T., making it inevitable that seasons after the first would seem a letdown. Still, A.C.T.'s expansiveness spilled over the stage, even if for fewer people.[57]

Given the dropoff in audience response and its threat to ACT's survival, the 1969 season was postponed while certain permanent adjustments were made in the company's repertory. First, the subscription technique was simplified as described above. Second, the numbers of shows offered was reduced to nine. Third, fewer revivals were remounted in the new twenty-week season planned for the early part of 1970. Eight of the twenty-seven 1967–1968 plays were revivals: *Dear Liar, Under Milkwood, Tartuffe, Tiny Alice, Our Town, Long Day's Journey into Night, Charley's Aunt,* and *Endgame.* In the 1970 shortened season there were only two revivals from the previous season: *Rosencrantz and Guildenstern Are Dead* and *Six Characters in Search of an Author.* Eichelbaum summed up San Francisco's strong response to ACT changes: "It has also been the shortest (only twenty weeks as against last year's thirty-five) and the one with the fewest productions. Nine plays entered the repertory—a sharp drop from last year's fifteen—and four were significant box-office hits, including 'The Importance of Being Earnest' and 'The Tempest' which had mixed notices. They tell me attendance is the best it's ever been. The audience level rose to 70 percent of capacity, considerably greater than last year, when it fell disastrously below 50 percent."[58]

ACT slowly built a steady audience during the next two seasons (1970–1971 and 1971–1972), and 13,035 subscriptions were sold for the 1972–1973 season, well exceeding the goal of 11,000. ACT boasted of 90-percent-of-capacity houses for that year, and the season's length stabilized at approximately thirty weeks. The 1971–1972 season, in comparison, had been twenty-eight weeks long and had drawn 173,966 people and 10,300 subscriptions for an average capacity of 71 percent.

The 1971 season—one of recuperation—was considered one of the best, and it was called "the brightest and most encouraging" theatrical year for ACT. What was once called "splashy" was now being called "carefully conceived."[59] Eichelbaum wrote, "The American Conservatory Theatre is stronger, healthier and more confident than at any other time in its oft-threatened career. The company had weathered its fifth season without a single financial or artistic crisis and they tell me they are 'cautiously optimistic' about the future, which is the rosiest outlook we've ever had from them."[60]

### *"Safe" Repertory*

All the strategy seemed to be well-planned and, as some criticized, "safe." Of the critics of ACT's play selections, Grover Sales, writer for the *San Francisco Magazine*, led the charge when he wrote in 1972, "In looking over the list of A.C.T.'s 50-odd offerings, one is immediately struck with an airy lack of relevance to a society in turmoil. Its five-year foray into present realities was limited to the tepid *In White America*, an impossible *Blood Knot* and *Little Murders* that, while credible fell glaringly short of the movie version."[61]

These arguments regarding ACT's "relevance" often translated into the charge that the company failed to take chances with new works at either of its theatres. Historically, one type of ensemble was created by or worked in close cooperation with a playwright. The *Commèdia* actors, of course, created their own plays *extempore*. And, as described in chapter 1, other ensembles built their style of performance around their playwrights: Shakespeare; Molière; Goethe and Schiller; the naturalistic schools of Chekhov and MAT; Hauptman and Brahm; Odets and the Group Theatre. But ACT had not been conceived in this way. It was created to allow actors to grow and pass on the techniques of acting that would be useful for younger actors.

It is true that ACT put on new plays sparingly. ACT produced only five new plays during its first five San Francisco seasons. Two of these were the moderate successes of Jerome Kilty: *Don't Shoot Mable, It's Your Husband*, and *Long Live Life*. (Kilty was in residence at the time as both a director and actor.) However, it was never ACT's intent to be a launching pad for playwrights. Tyrone Guthrie's attitude toward play selection for a repertory seemed more appropriate for ACT:

Suppose a repertory theatre to have a more intelligent and purposeful policy and to conduct its affairs more efficiently than any of the management at present operating. Its mere existence will not automatically call into being a crop of dramatic masterpieces. I see no reason to believe that, even in the present conditions of anarchy, there are any produceable author's desks. There are some, no doubt, but these mute, inglorious Miltons, Molieres, Maughams or Millers are not more likely to be offered expression and glory by a repertory theatre than by the multitude of private producers who in New York, to do them justice, have a creditable record of enterprise.

The principal public service that I can foresee for a repertory theatre is that in any given season at least three or four classical masterpieces would be in its program.[62]

Bill Ball echoes this sentiment in aspiring to create a "standard," staid repertory theatre that produces, first of all, classics. "Every time we do a play it should reflect a different aspect of the state of literature so that [the subscribers] never get the feeling that they are getting the same thing. I like to feel that we are giving plays in a way and in order that if someone were coming to our theatre for seven or eight years, they would feel as though they had a complete theatrical education. That there was nothing left out of their show-going. That they would know as much about theatre as anyone else in the world."[63]

As ACT became more settled and established a strong subscription base, it had more freedom to try plays that might not have been successful during its first few seasons. Hastings recalled, "It has taken a while for us to get the audience to where they come and they know they're going to have an adventure that will please them, you know. And now they're willing to take some chances."[64]

Ball admitted that the strength of a theatre rested on its strong subscription audience. With such an audience, a theatre had maneuverability and could sometimes "fail" with certain plays. "One of the nice things about repertory is that you have a subscription audience and they're a generous audience, an audience that likes to be entertained. An audience that if they see a 'flop,' they'll compare it with other works they have seen and they'll say, 'Oh, well, we'll ride this flop with them because they have done so much good work.' You have to have the latitude to make mistakes. And sometimes with the best will in the world everything can go wrong with a production. Our audiences are generous in understanding that."[65]

### ACT and the Growth of Local Theatre

In 1972, ACT gained relative security with a strong subscription base. It maintained the level of subscription at more than fifteen thousand for the next decade. Some critics claimed that ACT had lost some of its daring in order to maintain its audience. Charles R. Lyons, professor at the University of California at Davis, wrote of the 1970–1971 season, "A.C.T. is not the perfect repertory company which so many voices predicted it would become; neither has it fallen as far behind its original promise as others claim. A.C.T. may have chosen to be too popular, not to be an experimental and art theatre which would satisfy the most demanding. However, A.C.T.'s eclecticism is working in San Francisco. As long as A.C.T. brings productions as compelling and revealing as this season's Saroyan, Ibsen and Shakespeare, our complaints should be voiced quietly."[66]

While ACT stuck to an eclectic but popular schedule of plays, other theatres seized the opportunity to produce new playwrights. On the other hand, so much money was needed to keep the big theatres operating that many of the smaller theatres in the Bay Area felt choked off from financial sources that may have otherwise been available to them.

Like the Broadway stage of New York, A.C.T. has spawned a local off-Broadway theatrical culture in the area. Those theatres which have emerged as contenders for the attention of this newly-found audiences are, in part, benefitting from the success of A.C.T. This is not because they are following in the larger company's footsteps. In fact, some theatres are founded on an admittedly profound disgust for the traditional type of drama which A.C.T. represents. However, all theatres are benefitting from the improving theatrical climate, for the positive response to A.C.T. has become a positive response to theatre in general. It is fortunate that theatres are not like automobile dealerships: they do not compete for clientele, they create it for each other and share it. A.C.T. has, by no means, created all of it, but it has done a great deal towards giving the local community a sense of both interest and pride in its local theatre. And what was once a willingness to "try" theatre now seems to be an ever growing eagerness for more.[67]

To a certain degree, the presence of ACT nurtured the growth of other theatres; however, no other theatre ever seriously threatened ACT's position. The Bay Area sustained only one Equity theatre company besides ACT—the Berkeley Repertory Company. That company grew slowly and its house never exceeded four hundred seats. Other theatres that have had various degrees of success were the Julian Theatre, the Magic Theatre, the Eureka Theatre, and the Berkeley Stage Company. The other notable San Francisco company that gained international repute was the political-action-oriented San Francisco Mime Troupe. The Mime Troupe started as an ancillary program of the Workshop, and never really had a theatre of its own, but over the years it earned fame on the strength of its improvisation and its touring. Still, no Bay Area theatre was ever in competition with ACT for its funds or audience.

ACT may well have succeeded in Chicago, or in Pittsburgh, but through a series of events ACT found its home in San Francisco, a city noted for its laissez faire and progressive attitudes. What ACT offered San Francisco audiences was its consistently professional entertaining productions of ensemble playing. It fared much better with this approach than the Actor's Workshop was able to with its more avant-garde theatre.

As with Goethe's theatre and the Meininger, ACT had no true competitor in its locale. Thus, ACT was able to maintain both its company and its commitment to ensemble, repertory, and conservatory theatre. Moreover, though ACT came to feel increasingly at home in San Francisco, it nevertheless kept its national significance as a regional theatre.

# 4

# The *Regisseur* and His Staff

Just as ACT's ensemble acting company was the basis for the entire organization, so was the sharing of responsibility among all within the ACT umbrella the basis of Ball's management. He likened the organization to a family: "I like to work with people I know . . . . Besides, I have a family of two-hundred and fifty people dependent on me."[1] The "family" concept set up a complex matrix of organizational flow and responsibility:

At A.C.T. tasks are not necessarily divided into highly specialized jobs because there is no one best way to direct a show or design a set. Creativity and teamwork should be the keynote of an artistic organization. Likewise, abstract rules cannot be universally applied to guarantee top quality performance in a job. Instead, internal professional standards provide the guide for action until a direct review is conducted by a superior. Because this type of artistic organization requires total dedication from their personnel, the full range of human experience is drawn upon. Relationships in A.C.T. are better visualized as relationships in an extended family than as typical bureaucratic interchange.[2]

One aspect of ACT's structure has remained constant: the ultimate artistic and organizational leadership of ACT by William Ball. Since the beginning, Ball has been the head of the ACT Foundation's executive committee. The other key members of the management that landed in San Francisco for negotiations on 31 October 1966, after the Stanford stand, were Wil-

liam Bushnell, managing director from 1966 to 1969; Edward
Hastings, executive director and long-time working companion
of Ball; and John Seig, production director. In 1967, Robert
Goldsby was added with the title of associate director. Two
other people who were to play important parts in the support
structure of Ball's ACT were board members James B. McKenzie
and Allen Fletcher.

## William Ball

William Ball began his theatrical career as a designer and actor
before directing. His first theatre job was with the late Margaret
Webster, who, along with Eva Le Gallienne, cofounded the
American Repertory Theatre in 1946. Ball recalled Margaret
Webster: "I was an apprentice and paint bucket washer. I was
planning to be a designer at the time, but she encouraged me to
go into acting and directing. She was a brilliantly artistic woman
and she taught everyone she ever worked with. She could put
into words a lot of things that other people were thinking. I
learned from her how to speak to a theatre company. But most
of all, I learned her professional attitude—everything about her
was professional."[3]

Of Ball, Webster wrote,

When I first knew Ball, he was (forgive me, Bill) a blonde fat boy from
high school rather sluggishly painting in a summer stock company I
was running—not a beach-party affair, but a serious theatre, doing
Chekhov and Shakespeare and such expensive items. He didn't paint
scenery very well. But, he agreed, not with much enthusiasm, to be
drafted to play the sewer man in the *Madwoman of Chaillot* with the
apprentice students.

Having seen his performance, I told him to stop doing whatever
he had planned to do and go and be an actor. I can honestly affirm
that he is the only person, male or female, to whom I have ever given
such appallingly rash advice.

Our paths crossed a few times after this. Once I was able to
facilitate his getting a Fulbright Scholarship to study classical theater
in London. Once I persuaded him to stick with a job as Assistant Stage
Manager which he loathed because of the inefficiency of the management and the behavior of the company—or some of it. I convinced
him that he would benefit from learning what brought about these

very usual phenomena, so that they shouldn't happen under his own management in, for instance, Pittsburgh. I am very proud of him.[4]

The impact of Margaret Webster's no-nonsense approach had a lasting effect on the way Ball approached his ACT company. Ball characterized Webster's style of directing "as going from thought to word to energy."[5] In many respects Ball's approach was a throwback to the earlier era in American theatre in which a strong actor-manager, or *regisseur*, had complete autocratic control of his company.

From the time of Ball's early professional directing experiences, critics marvelled at his ability to create ensemble-style playing. In 1969 George Oppenheimer of *Newsday* wrote, "'His actors are engaged in some of the finest ensemble acting since the days of the Group Theatre and the Theatre Guild.' I wrote this eleven years ago on my first encounter with the work of William Ball. The occasion was his staging of Chekhov's *Ivanov*. This was the first time to my knowledge, that this little-known play had been done in New York and thanks greatly to Mr. Ball, it seemed not too far below the level of Chekhov's major works."[6]

William Ball was born in Chicago on 29 April 1931. He attended Iona Preparatory School in New York state and spent two years in Fordham University in the Bronx, where he began his acting career in student productions. He transferred to Carnegie Institute of Technology in Pittsburgh in 1950, and appeared at the Pittsburgh Playhouse as Richard in *Ah, Wilderness!* From 1950 to 1953, Ball spent his summers with the Shakespeare Festival in Ashland, Oregon, where his roles included Mark Antony in *Julius Caesar*, Feste in *Twelfth Night*, Lorenzo in *The Merchant of Venice*, Ariel in *The Tempest*, and Claudio in *Much Ado About Nothing*.

In 1953, after receiving his bachelor of arts degree in acting and design from the Carnegie Institute, he spent one year in England on a Fulbright scholarship, where he studied English repertory theatre. He returned to the Carnegie Institute to earn his master of arts degree in directing. One of his teachers there was Allen Fletcher, who later became the director of the conservatory at ACT.

In 1955 Ball played Hamlet in Fletcher's production at the San Diego Shakespeare Festival. That year he began a one-year NBC/RCA director's fellowship awarded by the Carnegie Institute. That was the first of the several awards he was to receive in the next few years.

Ball acted in several Off-Broadway productions; he played Acaste in *The Misanthrope* (1956), the voice of Rosencrantz in Siobhan McKenna's experimental *Hamlet* (1957), Nicholas Devise in *The Lady's Not for Burning* (1957), and Horner in *The Country Wife* (1957). He acted at the Arena Stage in Washington, D.C., during the 1957–1958 season, playing Dubedat in *The Doctor's Dilemma*. He was the stage manager in *Back to Methuselah* on Broadway in 1958.

All this acting experience gave Ball a first-hand knowledge of the plight of the American professional actor. John Adams described the use Ball made of that knowledge: "His thesis is a simple one—acting is not a profession as it is generally practiced today, because actors do not have either the knowledge or the complete complement of tools to measure up to the standards of other professions such as doctors, lawyers or scientists. Ball bluntly placed the load upon the 'profession' of acting as it exists today to bring itself up to the levels of the other professions. An actor should be complete, capable of eliciting any emotion imaginable upon the stage."[7]

Ball's decision to direct arose from his frustration with the state of American acting in the late 1950s. His goal was to create better and more versatile American actors. "Our profession is untutored!" he charged. "We have no technique. Because of Broadway we've become frightened and lazy. Take the way we use our voices. Even an amateur musician can tell you there are 88 keys on the piano; an artist knows there are six colors in the pinwheel. But ask a group of theatre people: How many inflections are in American speech? They don't know."[8]

Ball reiterated this position in a 1976 interview:

After four or five miserable years of acting, I saw the damage most directors did to actors by robbing them of their self-esteem and inhibiting the natural flow by placing obstacles in their paths. Since I decided very early I was going to spend my life in theatre, I decided to make it a positive experience. So I made choices that would lead to happiness, rejecting the schools of discouragement that predominated in theatre, as in life.

As a former actor, I understood the need for a director to make actors feel used. An actor should be constantly called upon to exercise his talent. Most sit around for months or years and then are suddenly hired for a part that lasts maybe eight weeks. To maintain his craft, the actor must sweat to keep up his creative flow, in teaching, rehearsing, understudying, and performing. When he's used the actor experiences the ever-increasing sense of revitalization.[9]

Bill Ball began his meteoric professional career as director with his New York debut of *Ivanov* at the Renata Theatre; the date was 7 October 1958. Brooks Atkinson of the New York *Times* wrote of the show that the production was "poignant and comic, *Ivanov* is an achievement of the first order." Ball won the *Village Voice* Obie and the Vernon Rice award as the best Off-Broadway director of 1958. His later work included staging *Once More With Feeling* for the Houston Alley Theatre and *A Month in the Country* at the Arena Stage in Washington, D.C. He returned to the San Diego Shakespeare Festival to stage *Henry IV* (parts 1 and 2), *The Merchant of Venice*, and *Twelfth Night*. At the American Shakespeare Festival in Stratford, Connecticut, he staged *The Tempest*. He directed several productions for the New York City Opera Company, including *Cosi fan Tutti*, *The Inspector General*, *A Midsummer Night's Dream* by Benjamin Britten, *Don Giovanni*, and *Porgy and Bess*.

In 1961 he directed a revival of Dylan Thomas' verse narrative, *Under Milkwood*, at the Circle-in-the-Square. This production won him a special Lola D'Annunzio citation for contribution to the Off-Broadway theatre. Of Ball's production of Pirandello's *Six Characters in Search of An Author* at the Martinique, Off-Broadway, Howard Taubman wrote in the *New York Times* on 11 March 1963, "William Ball deserves full marks for his imaginative direction. The essential theatricality of the play is conveyed without sacrificing its human values." Ball restaged this play in 1964 in London with Ralph Richardson leading the cast.

Ball made his Canadian debut at the Stratford Theatre in

Ontario in 1964, with Gilbert and Sullivan's *Yeoman of the Guard*. He collaborated with Lee Hoiby as librettist for *Natalia Petrovna*, under a commission from the Ford Foundation for the New York City Center. In 1965 he directed *Tartuffe* for the Lincoln Center, winning a nomination for an Antoinette Perry (Tony) award.

Ball had built a considerable reputation for himself by the time he was thirty-four years old. The American regional theatre movement was maturing while he was gaining acclaim. Because he had gained recognition quickly and had achieved much at a young age, Ball developed the reputation of an *enfant terrible*. "Dating back to his *wunderkind* directional debut in New York . . . Ball has been tagged with a series of billboard epithets, attempts to comprehend him in a single stroke. 'Absolutely shameless . . . the finest director in America,' wrote critic Martin Gottfried. 'A borderline genius,' says a former student. 'A benevolent dictator,' according to Ray Reinhardt, the company's longest continuous performer." [10]

Ball claims to have found his vocation at ten years of age while doing a play in his backyard:

It was one of those backyard plays kids put on for their neighborhood. To this day I can remember Georgie Harrigan who played the king, sitting in a child's rocking chair. When it came time to answer whether he would give his daughter's hand in marriage,—all he had to say was "Yes!"—he began to rock back and forth furiously. His face turned red, he broke out in a cold sweat, his teeth started to rattle, his eyes bugged out. It was the worst case of stage fright in the world. Then all of a sudden he came right out with his line: "Well, it's not easy to be a king, you know." That was the beginning of my career as a director. [11]

### The Regisseur

Ball was the *regisseur*, the force behind ACT. He shaped the company and its workings to his liking and taste. He was in the eminent position of power in the organization. Fran Fanshel wrote in the San Francisco *Chronicle*,

Although Bill Ball will tell you that A.C.T. is 200 people working in concert to create a vision of a theatre, everyone else will tell you that

A.C.T. is Bill Ball. Employment at A.C.T. involves a personal and artistic commitment to Ball. The strength of allegiance to Bill Ball is impressive, not one of the many former or present A.C.T. members interviewed would agree to be quoted saying anything harshly critical of him. Although this is understandable considering Ball's position of power in the theatre world, it seems that most actors and directors declined to voice negative opinions more from reluctance to hurt his feelings than from fear of burning their bridges. Ball seems to inspire a protective response in those who know him, based either on grudging admiration or sincere affection for a shy, vulnerable man who some call a genius.[12]

For one person to hold so much authority was unique in noncommercial theatre. Regardless of this authority, however, the concept of a cooperative company ruled over by a single individual was not easily realized at ACT in San Francisco. The total commitment to the concept of ACT and to the person of Bill Ball, who at times was unavailable, created uncertainties and tensions as ACT grew during the first three years. Robert Goldsby explained:

In the first year Ball was a mysterious figure. We didn't see much of him. So, I don't know what he did. He was presumably in charge of everything. But, whether he actually was, to what extent he was there or not there was very hard to say. He certainly was not there the way that Seig or Bushnell were. However, he was in the first six months, certainly, very much the head of everything. When we were developing the conservatory, for example, there's no doubt that it was Bill's idea. He signalled what he wanted, how many people he wanted. He had a list of forty different subjects that could be taught. He wanted two hundred students and forty subjects and go for it. And we did. It was a large and daring and unusual idea, and it was certainly all Bill's idea. How to do it was our problem. As a notion of a major company getting involved in a major training program, there's nothing like it anywhere.[13]

[The quotes from Bushnell, Hastings, McKenzie and Goldsby throughout this chapter are drawn from the personal interviews cited in notes 13, 14, 15, and 18 of this chapter.] Ball's freedom to maneuver in the early years, and the centralization of his power as *regisseur* of the company, came in no

*James B. McKenzie, executive producer of the American Conservatory Theatre.*

*The first reading of* Twelfth Night, *by William Shakespeare, at the ACT rehearsal space on Geary Street in 1967.*

*The ACT in residence at the Pittsburgh Playhouse during the 1965–19 season. William Ball is on the stage.*

*McNeill Lowry, acting president of the Ford Foundation, with William Ball on 26 October 1967.*

*The managers of the American Conservatory Theatre in 1967. From left to right: William Bushnell, William Ball, Edward Hastings, Jr., John Seig, and Robert Bonaventura.*

*William Ball and Edward Hastings in* 1967.

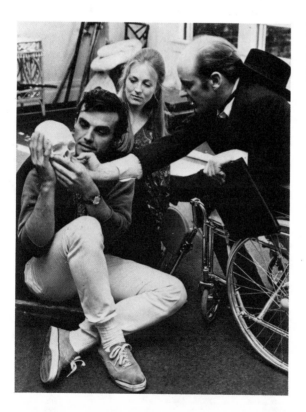

Hamlet *in rehearsal in* 1968. From left to right: *Paul Shenar, Izetta Smith, and William Ball.*

The opening night marquee for the American Conservatory Theater at the Pittsburgh Playhouse in 1966.

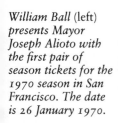

William Ball (left) presents Mayor Joseph Alioto with the first pair of season tickets for the 1970 season in San Francisco. The date is 26 January 1970.

The "heralds" of ACT, union musicians who were not needed for the plays, were employed by the company to perform outside the theatre in 1967.

*The late Mortimer Fleishhacker, the man credited with financially "bailing out" ACT during its first three years in San Francisco. Fleishhacker was one of the staunchest supporters of Ball's ensemble ideal.*

*Ball wearing his famous gaucho hat in 1967.*

*Marc Singer in ACT's production of* The Taming of the Shrew, *staged by William Ball and broadcast on Educational Television.*

ACT's acting company for the 1967–1968 season.

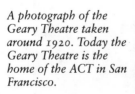

A photograph of the Geary Theatre taken around 1920. Today the Geary Theatre is the home of the ACT in San Francisco.

*Allen Fletcher in rehearsal.*

*ACT actor Jay Doyle running from the Geary Theatre to the Marines' Memorial Theatre during a hectic double repertory evening.*

*ACT members with Arthur Miller during "An Evening with Arthur Miller." From left to right: Robert Goldsby, Peter Donat, Angela Paton, Arthur Miller, William Paterson.*

Michael O'Sullivan (left) and Harry Frazier in A Flea in Her Ear. The play was presented in costumes of black and white.

Michael Learned in the ACT production of Albee's A Delicate Balance.

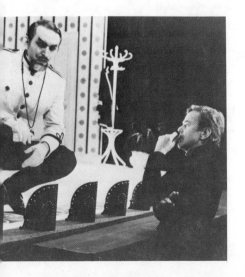

Director Gower Champion talks to actor Ray Reinhardt during the staging of A Flea in Her Ear.

*Ray Reinhardt as Claudius in the ACT production of* Hamlet.

*Robin Gammel* (left) *and René Auberjonois in ACT's production of* Under Milkwood, *written by Dylan Thomas and staged by William Ball.*

*DeAnn Mears as Blanche in ACT's production of* A Streetcar Named Desire.

*Paul Shenar in the monumental ACT production of Albee's* Tiny Alice, *staged by William Ball.*

*ACT's opening show,* Tartuffe, *with (from left to right) Ramon Bieri, René Auberjonois, and DeAnn Mears. The play was directed by William Ball.*

*ACT's production of* Arsenic and Old Lace, *with (from left) Richard Dysart, Ruth Kobart, and Carol Teitel.*

Six Characters in Search of an Author, *by Pirandello,*
*staged at ACT by William Ball.* From left to right:
*Jennifer Nebesky, Frank Kelleher, Barbara Colby,*
*Josephine Nichols, Paul Shenar (rear), and Richard*
*Dysart.*

*Sada Thompson and Michael*
*O'Sullivan in ACT's*
*production of* Dear Liar.

Little Murders, *a play directed by Nagle Jackson for ACT. From left to right: Mark Bramhall, G. Wood, Michael Learned, John Schuck, and Angela Paton.*

*Marsha Mason and Paul Shenar in the 1972 production of* Private Lives.

*ACT's entry in the ANTA festival in 1969 was Chekhov's* Three Sisters, *directed by William Ball. From left to right: Angela Paton, William Paterson, Michael Learned, and Kitty Winn.*

*Ellis Rabb directs ACT's production of* The Merchant of Venice, *called "boldly up to date" by the critics. Peter Donat is at center, and Ken Ruta is at right.*

*Peter Donat* (center) *in ACT's production of* Hadrian VII.

*ACT's original production of*
Glory! Hallelujah! *with Ramon*
*Bieri and Michael Learned.*

small measure through his direct connection with the Ford Foundation. As Jim McKenzie explained,

the original concept of ACT was created entirely by William Ball. He was an award winning director in New York's lively Off-Broadway theatre scene. He had a successful directorial and acting record in the already existing regional theatres as well as summer Shakespearean theatres across North America. Many influential theatre people, including Mac Lowry of the Ford Foundation, had been impressed by his work. Bill was shocked by the firings at the Lincoln Center of Elia Kazan and Robert Whitehead, the more so because he was directing a Lincoln Center production at the time. He said, "The only way I would start a theatre of my own would be under the following conditions."

His conditions, listed succinctly in twenty-six items, became the declaration on which ACT was based. He sent his statement to the Ford Foundation and the Rockefeller Foundation. Both approved of it and eventually gave massive support to the idea. He garnered further support from the Carnegie Institute of Technology and others on the same premise. Sponsors were asked to gamble on an individual rather than on a company or an institution. Ball had already proven, albeit he was young, that he had clear vision, drive, and dedication and more important, talent.

The original ACT company was composed of actors who had already been directed by Ball. Almost all of them went on to lustrous careers in the theatre, and all gave up promising careers in New York to follow his genius to Pittsburgh in 1965.[14]

Ball assumed certain rights as the general director and conceptual artist of ACT. "The Hierarchy worked to the extent that Bill as general director had the right, certainly, to make any and all decisions that he chose to make," said Bushnell.[15] Of these decisions two key ones have consistently been in his domain: the casting of the actors and the selection of the plays for the season. Goldsby pointed out,

The decision about plays . . . [was] always made, finally, by Bill. I had very little to do with that selection. I suspect that [it was] done pretty much entirely by Ball. He also obviously chose who was going to direct, who was going to design and who was cast.

The casting was a big issue in the company. So far as I could tell, Bushnell or Seig could lobby for certain actors, or argue that if they contracted DeAnn Mears, they had to do certain things for her. It was a very complicated business, sixty actors and twenty-six plays and hundreds of parts. Everybody wanted the best part. It must have been murder. But it was Ball who really had the authority—who said "so and so" will play "such and such." That's the way it worked.

For example, as director in the company I was more or less told what play I was going to direct and who was in it, and who would be my designer. I didn't have any choice about that the first year. Nor did I have any quarrel with it. . . . It was Ball who was making those pivotal casting decisions.[16]

The directors of ACT were not voiceless, explained Allen Fletcher: "Every director of those of us who normally direct, makes suggestions for plays he or she personally would like to do." Still, he said, Ball made the final decision on any suggestions from his directors and production people: "The basic philosophy was Bill's and decisions have always been made by Bill, except in those periods when he's been ill, just, physically unable to do it. Then Ed and I would do it together, or one of us. But there has always been a lot of discussion between Bill and Ed and myself."[17]

Ed Hastings thought that Ball was "infinitely approachable" and that he was always there if anyone wanted him.[18]

### Seasons of Discontent and William Bushnell

Not everyone at ACT was satisfied all the time with the handling of policy or the company. From the beginning, ACT felt the growing pains of changing from an itinerant group with hopes in 1965 to becoming a full-fledged resident company in 1967.

William Bushnell was hired as managing director in 1966 and flew with Ball to San Francisco on 31 October 1966. They were faced with the unenviable task of organizing a double repertory company consisting of forty-seven actors and countless production people. Bushnell recalled the start: "I got all the responsibilities immediately [as managing director]. I was brought in specifically in that slot, because when ACT, in its wanderings, had reached a point when this San Francisco situation was going to become real, the net situation was the fact that, what existed was an acting company, some plays and there was really no administration or production unit whatsoever. There was no management."

Bushnell had been a Ford Foundation fellow in its theatre management training program and never doubted that he had come to ACT with the foundation's blessing. He had been the executive director of Baltimore's resident professional theatre, Center Stage, where, as Ed Hastings explained, "he ran the company. The absentee director just let him do it." The problems that Bushnell was to face, according to Hastings, were based on Ball's complete final say on all questions of policy. Neither Bushnell—nor any secondary person, for that matter—could expect that his judgments would always mesh with Ball's tastes. Said Hastings,

If the secondary person doesn't do it the way [Ball] wants to do it, then Bill will change it. Make it change, so that the secondary person has to learn to edit. That is autocratic in that sense. On the other hand, Bill is somebody who allows everybody to do their job. As long as they do it the way he likes it. He doesn't muck around. He doesn't come in to a director and say, "You should have a different curtain call or blue, blue hair!" He never does that, he never does that. . . . Because he believes that once he's hired a person, he gives them the freedom to do the job—but within the objectives of that job. Those are always determined in terms of the overall master plan. That's particularly hard if there's an absence.

Bushnell was a cornerstone of the original San Francisco company. He had been contacted by Edith Markson, who was a member of the ACT Board of Trustees with close ties to the Ford Foundation. When he was hired he was put in charge of finances, promotion, front-of-house, and the entire management of the theatre. He was "one of four people who made all the decisions with regard to the guidance and direction of the company." Bushnell and the production director, Seig, were eager to work with ACT and to see it succeed. "It was a concept that we were enthusiastically interested in creating," said Bushnell. Years later, Jim McKenzie said Seig and Bushnell were "key people" in the creation of ACT in San Francisco. Bushnell spoke of his responsibilities as managing director:

In practical terms, the day-to-day operation of the company was effectively done by John Seig and myself, with each of us focusing on our own particular areas, but then a great deal of interchange between the two of us. Ed had less to do with the day-to-day function of the company. He was often an arbiter. He was someone who could have a certain kind of perspective, because he didn't have a lot of day-to-day responsibilities. He was also, in effect, a director of plays.

It involved a great deal of meeting and interpreting what those decisions were and implementation of them. Though, in effect, the implementation of all decisions made were my responsibility and John's responsibility. I had a great deal to do with the liaisoning with what at that point was called the California Theatre Foundation. Plus the negotiations of all labor contracts. That area John Seig and I worked very closely on, in terms of firing, hiring, and also in discussions. Input, as far as scheduling was concerned, both in terms of selection and in terms of actual scheduling. . . . It was a twelve-to-fourteen-to-sixteen-hour regimen, seven days a week.

Goldsby recalled Bushnell as being in charge of everything that "wasn't production," and Seig as being in charge of everything "that was production," while Ed Hastings "floated around wherever extra help was needed." These three men managed the theatre in the first three seasons from 1967 to 1969. Bushnell took care of all budgeting and contracting. "The company ran on a very close relationship between Seig and Bushnell," said Goldsby. "They would talk a lot. They worked, I would say, from eight or nine in the morning until one the next day, seven days a week. They were always there. It was a back-breaking, total commitment. The only other two people I saw that worked like that were Blau and Irving, who ran the San Francisco Actor's Workshop."

Bill Ball recalled that when he was searching for a staff he tried to get as many of the "best people" he could find: "We had a very, very dedicated staff; there were eighty-seven of us. And we worked ferociously. . . . We had a very energetic and very committed staff. I've always been very fortunate. But, there was a time we had some trouble."

The "trouble" Ball referred to was an incident in 1969 involving Bill Bushnell, one that had endangered Ball's absolute control of ACT. At that time ACT had grown rapidly, and Ball, owing to illness, had not been available to help make the day-to-day decisions that were necessary to run the large company. Thus the company was running itself without input from its leader. Bushnell had clashed with Ball over the internal management of the company, and, more seriously, over the ultimate artistic direction of the company, a conflict that resulted in Bushnell's dismissal from ACT. Bushnell described the confrontation:

I don't know that there was any one particular bone of contention. In many ways it was probably deep-seated differences ultimately in philosophies about how you go about managing and operating a company of that size and that complexity.

Also big problems in terms of once you gave your word to somebody, how did you deal with that at that point. Whether or not once you have an operation of that size and complexity you can continue to operate in what was in effect; at that time Bill had wanted to operate on what is known as crisis management. That's fine for the first six months, nine months, twelve months, what have you. That becomes a little old hat after that.

The principal crisis . . . which brought my relationship with Bill to a head, and at least from my perspective was the straw that broke the camel's back, had to do with the production of *Three Sisters.* . . . When it came time to rehearse that play which Bill was to direct, he simply didn't show for rehearsals. . . . I eventually had to create a reverse crisis, which then forced that issue to a head and he came to rehearsals and directed an excellent production of *Three Sisters.* But out of that he got a great deal of confidence, that he perhaps didn't have before it, in terms of what he could or couldn't do, and he felt that he was strong enough to let me go. It was inevitable at some point anyway. That was simply the issue that brought it to a head. Because it was becoming more and more difficult for us to work together. Our perceptions about how you ran that operation simply were not on parallel tracks. We were on tracks that were running away from each other and the further down the road we went, the further apart we got.

### Robert Goldsby

Robert Goldsby, who had been teaching at the University of California at Berkeley, was hired by Bill Ball for ACT's 1967 season. His original position was associate director. He was named as the first head of the conservatory program and eventually created the base for the present training program.

Goldsby came to ACT with considerable directing experience, having worked in New York and with San Francisco's Actor's Workshop. In his second season at ACT he directed *A Streetcar Named Desire*, which was generally acclaimed. In his third and last season with ACT, from 1968 to 1969, he directed *The Staircase*, by Charles Dyer, and a controversial production of *The Architect and the Emperor of Assyria*, by Arrabal. Goldsby, who described himself as "more method" and "more emotional" than Ball, also became a party to this dark period in the first years of ACT. He, too, felt that a change would be necessary if ACT was to survive the erratic behavior of its artistic director. He described the *Three Sisters* incident from his own perspective:

The actors and Bush and everybody finally talked Ball into doing it, and they said they would support him and help him and get him back to work again. So they did. They were all very nice to him and very supportive of him, and he did a superb job of the play. As soon as it opened, he fired Bushnell. . . . That, I suppose from his point of view, had been coming for a long time. He wanted to take control of the company again. Bush had obviously moved in, was making all the decisions that Bill wanted to make. They didn't get along temperamentally. Bush was stuck trying to do Bill's plan, this huge operating theatre. They were losing money. The deficit was enormous. So all of a sudden Bush was told, tomorrow get out. We had this month of thrashing about. He had already hired McKenzie. Nobody knew about any of this. There was no reason why we should've. From Bill's point of view, why should he tell anybody? It was his company. Well, of course, by then . . . we didn't believe it was his company . . . we basically thought it was our company, that it was a group effort.

## James B. McKenzie

James McKenzie was one of the two people hired to take Bushnell's place. The other was Charles Dillingham. Jim McKenzie was no stranger either to theatre or to ACT. In many respects he came to represent what Bushnell called a father figure to ACT. There can be no doubt that his commercial theatre experiences helped to stabilize and strengthen ACT's position as the largest active regional theatre in the United States.

On Thursday, 19 March 1969, ACT sent out a press release that formally announced McKenzie's appointment as executive producer of ACT, calling the position a new one created by the board of directors.

By age forty-two McKenzie had been involved in more than eight hundred plays on Broadway, on national and international tours, in repertory, and in summer and winter theatres. He was president of the Council of Stock Theatres and of the Producing Managers Guild. Previous to being hired by ACT, McKenzie had been producer of the Westport Country Playhouse in Connecticut, the Bucks County Playhouse in Pennsylvania, the Peninsula Players in Wisconsin, the Mineola Theatre in New York, and the Royal Poinciana Playhouse. He was also, as he puts it, "Lawrence Langner's protégé." (Lawrence Langner, of course, is the monumental figure in modern American theatre who helped to create several companies, including the Theatre Guild and Eva Le Gallienne's theatre.)

Ball asked McKenzie to join the ACT Board of Trustees as treasurer after McKenzie saw the company during one of its "in-training" sessions in New York and "fell in love" with it. Besides having solid commercial experience, McKenzie had started the Milwaukee Repertory Theatre in 1952, which was one of the first efforts at a nonprofit regional theatre. It was in Milwaukee that he met Bill Ball and Edith Markson.

McKenzie was treasurer of the board of trustees in March of 1969 when he was asked by Ball to come to San Francisco to replace Bushnell and solve the management problems. He found the company to be in serious financial trouble, as well as in the throes of a conceptual crisis in management. He explained:

My assignment was to initiate any action necessary to solve the problems. The financial and emotional crises were very real and very critical. Cash flow was not even meeting net payroll costs, and the administrative department was not speaking to or in any way relating to the artistic leaders. Revolution was eminent at ACT.

This situation was so unstable that I didn't even unpack or relocate from my hotel room adjacent to the theatre for over six weeks, expecting that each day would be the last.

William Ball conceived ACT as his own personal dream, and demanded that he control it within his own vision of the perfect regional theatre. His attitude could only result in a feudal kingdom with complete loyalty to Ball and his often unusual ideas were a basic precept to the employment of any person.

Some key staff members had been trained in the more conventional nonprofit theatre of bureaucracy and had great trouble in following the leader instead of making group decisions. The "conventionalists" had lined up a good portion of the company behind them, and were insisting that Ball's powers be limited and that group wisdom prevail in many areas.

Many of the original (Pittsburgh) company members however, respected Ball's genius so much that they vowed to stay and defend him in any extremity. I chose to join the latter group, because of great admiration for Ball's theatrical genius and the concurrence of his thoughts with my personal philosophy regarding theatre management.

The schism climaxed at a full company meeting in the Geary Theatre in the spring of 1969. Ball asked for complete loyalty, financial sacrifices and instant response from each of the 150 members of the company. Shortly thereafter we accepted the resignations of the "conventionalists," reduced the size of the company, cut short the playing season, and postponed the opening of the next season until we could find the proper financial footing. Our funding organization, the California Theatre Foundation, eventually agreed to support the next season and the crisis was over. ACT began to breathe again.

This "schism" is what Goldsby was referring to when he said that many of the actors thought that ACT was their company too, not merely Bill Ball's. Some of the company members felt betrayed; the general consensus was that the company was more important than any individual, and that Ball was no longer in control of the company. Goldsby explained:

We fought it. We collected signatures on a telegram. I think we had 95 percent of the company sign this telegram that we sent to McNeil Lowry, saying we respectfully request Mr. Ball direct, but that he not tear the company apart and fire everybody. Lowry and [Edith] Markson (who had been very close to McNeil Lowry for years) sided with

84

Bill, and to make a long story short, Lowry got to [Mortimer] Fleish-hacker and more or less said, if you don't support Ball, I'll pull out the Ford Foundation. Seig and I stayed on because ACT was involved in a tour to New York and we thought we owed it to the actors to help keep the company alive so it could honor its obligation to play in New York.

While the control of the company was a very important issue at this time, there were other issues which Bushnell and Ball did not agree upon. Bushnell predicted that ACT would have the strongest acting company by far in residence in any city in the nation because of the conditions and beliefs under which Ball had formed ACT. However, he maintained that, in addition to building and maintaining the company, ACT had to be both flexible with its own actors, serving as a "mother" company to them while encouraging new playwrights by offering to produce their works. Bushnell was an advocate of ACT's "company ideal." Said Bushnell, "The desire is to keep the company going. I had no desire then nor any other time not to see the company keep going in some way, shape, or form. It provides some gainful employment for an awful lot of artists. The prime philosophical differences beyond all the management problems that Bill and I had . . . had a lot to do with repertory. My interest was and is in developing new American plays and not, in effect, presenting Dramatic Literature 101 each year."

Bushnell thought that no real power struggle existed between himself and Ball, merely differences of opinion. Despite his position, he never questioned the notion that ACT was Ball's company.

On the day Bushnell was fired, Ball appeared reluctant to tell him of his decision. Bushnell recounted his dismissal:

I was the one that had to push him to the point of saying, "frankly Bill, what you're talking about is you want to fire me and you're going to have to say it out loud. Because I'm not taking an extended vacation; I'm not going on a leave of absence. I helped you devise the concepts. If we have no ground on which we can figure out how to work together, then you're going to have to fire me and you have the right to do that."

The power struggle, if there was any, was effectively an uprising within the company that was not orchestrated by me, because I simply stepped out of it.

While this chapter with Bushnell was drawing to a close, ACT was invited to perform in the American National Theatre Association (ANTA) festival in New York during the early fall of 1969. Three productions were selected: *Three Sisters*, *Tiny Alice* (both Ball's), and *A Flea in Her Ear*, directed by Gower Champion. All three were big, splashy shows that Ball thought would show the strength of the ACT acting company.

The cast of *Three Sisters* was as follows:

| | |
|---|---|
| Olga Prozorov | Angela Paton |
| Marya Prozorov | Michael Learned |
| Irene Prozorov | Kitty Winn |
| Andrei Prozorov | Jay Doyle |
| Fyodor Kulygin | Harry Frazier |
| Antisa, the nurse | Ruth Kobart |
| Baron Tusenbach | Paul Shenar |
| Ivan Chebutykin | William Paterson |
| Vasily Solyony | Robert Lanchaster |
| Lt. Col. Vershinin | Ken Ruta |
| Aleksel Fedotik | Philip Kerr |
| Vladimir Dodo | James Milton |
| Ferapoint | Michael O'Sullivan |

This outstanding company is one that Bill Ball still points to with pride, calling its members "strong actors." The company had weathered the upheaval of the spring of 1969 and the New York booking was generally well received, in spite of some last-minute changes in the production of Albee's *Tiny Alice*. But the 1969–1970 season had to be postponed: reorganization took place, the cash shortfall of five hundred thousand dollars needed to be raised, and the company's future seemed to be dangling.

Bill Ball had regained his former position as sole decision-maker on ACT policy in the classical *regisseur* sense of director, a position that was never again to be challenged in the history of ACT. Bob Goldsby, at the time the conservatory's director, resigned in 1969, and only staunch supporters of both Bill Ball and ACT remained as managers. John Seig also resigned, and was replaced by Benjamin Moore, a Yale graduate. Goldsby recalled his own resignation:

They cancelled the opening. The season was going to be later. I had a session with Bill in New York about what I was going to do the next year. Of course, I had been instrumental in this whole revolution, so our relationship was pretty frigid. But he needed me to run the conservatory, so he didn't want to get rid of me at the moment. . . .

I said I wanted some lead time, so I can work on a good play over a period of months. I didn't want to go in and do a play in six weeks. I've directed many plays, I can do that, but I don't want to do that anymore. Bill agreed with me and said I could do *The Tempest* and *Saint Joan*. . . . Well, the summer wore on and wore on and then I found out the casting of Ariel was to be a boy I had had as a student. In my view this boy was totally inexperienced and untalented, and to put him in such a role would be cruel and unusual punishment not only to the audience and his fellow actors, but to the boy himself.

Also, *Saint Joan* was supposed to start rehearsals in about two weeks. I still hadn't been given the play officially, so I quit. I wrote a letter that said, "All right, I waited long enough; I'm not waiting any more. I had only one stipulation, that I have some lead time to rehearse, and since you won't give me the time to rehearse, and you don't have another director, and you're not telling me I can direct, then I'm just being strung out. I don't want to do it anymore, so goodbye."[19]

### Edward Hastings

Goldsby felt justified in leaving ACT, and in fact, his staying on would have probably increased the tensions that were finally dissipating after Bushnell's dismissal. Others had been active in this uprising as well, and many of them left shortly thereafter or never renewed their contracts with ACT. All these conflicts served to strengthen Ball's position as *regisseur* of the company. Allen Fletcher was hired as the conservatory director shortly after Goldsby resigned. Goldsby later felt that Ball was justified in seeking this change; the free-spirited company was finally on its feet and there was no need for managers or directors who had an entrepreneurial spirit. Many of the people hired in that year of 1970 remained for the next decade as ACT changed and stabilized its position in San Francisco. And through it all, one man remained as an in-house support structure—Ed Hastings, ACT's executive director.

Hastings was the sounding board of the company and was always able to talk with Ball. He described his role as a "giant band-aid." Ball recalled, "He was the second person I spoke to about the company when I decided to form it." Hastings, who has been described as likeable and easy to talk with by company members, was the key liaison between ACT's management and the company in general. He was always available and willing to work to solve problems on a day-to-day basis. He had the ability to console Ball, who described himself as very stubborn. Ball summed up his relationship with Hastings:

Well, in the early days, we were very close and we wouldn't make a move without consulting him. He invariably told me I was wrong. But, I could always tell by how loudly he protested, whether I was really wrong or whether he was counseling me to be cautious. In order to get anything done, you have to be a little mad. To get something done you essentially have to break the established order. I had the role of the glazed-eyed madman who was breaking the established order. He had the role of the West Hartford diplomat advising me, "There, there, be calm; there, there, be moderate; there, there, choose the most modified path of action." In a sense, it was good. If he didn't yell very loud I figured I was all right. But, if he yelled very loud I usually modified my behavior. He was a good, very good friend to have, and gave a balance to us.

Hastings never threatened Ball's position as head of the company, because he also believed in the principles of ACT's charter. He had been one of the cosigners of the articles of incorporation, and in fact had been a supporter of Ball's work before ACT was developed. Early in their friendship, when Hastings was the stage manager of an Off-Broadway run of *The Lady's Not for Burning*, the cast was complete except for the character of Nicholas Devise, and Hastings suggested Ball for the part. Ball got that role. Later, Hastings managed both of Ball's Off-Broadway successes, *The Country Wife* and *Ivanov*. Hastings' reputation as a stage manager grew, and he took an assignment with David Merrick's production of *Ross*, starring John Mills. He also directed the touring production of *Oliver!* His friendship with Ball started nearly ten years before ACT became a reality; he and Ball had had several discussions with Ellis Rabb, when the APA was beginning, about how a theatre should be run and organized. There was never any doubt that Hastings was a staunch supporter of the ACT concept. Recalled Hastings,

A lot of us had come from the universities to descend on New York— Bill and Ellis Rabb, who had been roommates at Carnegie Tech, in addition to myself. It was a time when many rep companies from other countries were visiting our shores—the *Comédie Française*, the Old Vic, some German companies—and it started everybody thinking. We didn't really have any rep companies here in the United States. Stock companies, yes, regional theatres and performing planned schedules, yes, but no companies actually working in repertoire, the way the opera or the ballet functions. So, what could we do about it?

Bill and Ellis had beer and wine sessions that went on until two or three in the morning. Ellis started his own company, APA in New York by then. . . . They discussed the problems pro and con, and with Allen Fletcher, their former teacher, they worked together in Shakespeare festivals around the country.

To Hastings, ACT was a product of these "bitch" sessions where hopes and frustrations were aired. He believed in the ACT principles of employing a full-time, permanent group of actors and training them: "I think the most important thing that held the company together was not managerial, really. It was the idea of what an actor was or is, and what an actor needs, even though it wasn't always possible to deliver that ideal. Everything about the company was in relation to the actor."

According to Hastings, the ensemble ideal above everything else helped to form a strong bond within the company. The actors could focus both their attention and their energies on their work. Said Hastings, "When I say making an actor's company, I don't mean making it comfortable for the actors. I mean trying to find out what it is that actors do and how to make that do-able, the best way to make it happen, time after time. So, almost everybody who was first involved were actors. The directors, many of them, were actors. I was an actor. Bill was an actor. It was always that emphasis on devising a process and the company would be the expression of that process. That's what made it all cohere."

Ed Hastings has been termed Bill Ball's right-hand man, but he thought that his role was an extension of his original direc-tor-to-stage manager role. That role has always been of major importance to the smooth running of a theatre. In one sense, the relationship between Hastings and Ball had a historical parallel in that of the duke of Saxe-Meiningen and his aid Chronegk. The duke sent his messages to the company often through the interpretation of Chronegk, a man more versed in the expres-sions of theatrical management. But unlike Chronegk, Hastings was never a task master or disciplinarian. He was a capable administrator with a sympathetic ear, who took up the slack wherever and whenever he was needed. In this respect, a more apt comparison might be the Schiller and Goethe relationship, who together forged an ensemble suited specifically to their style of writing.

History offers many examples of theatre people who joined forces to run an ensemble. Usually the pair consisted of one forceful, creative genius, and one practical, supportive, and often less temperamental individual, who in his own right might have been a creative genius. Besides the pairs noted above, other notable couples were Lee Strasberg and Harold Clurman and Stanislavsky and Dantchenko. Hastings described his role as the practical half of ACT's duo:

The first year I was the production manager. I did not direct the season in Pittsburgh. There was Bill, there was a business manager, and me. Bill was directing two or three plays. The business manager was doing things in New York, so he was never there. There I was, the only person that knew everything that was going on. I did a lot of managerial [work], but it was impossible, although I wanted to, to direct. It was obvious that the first season I wouldn't. I was the manager, producer, I suppose.

As far as management policy went, I did everything that Bill didn't want to do or wouldn't or didn't have time to do. That continued to be my role for a long time. We kept getting more and more good people to do things. When we came to San Francisco, I said I wanted to direct and not be the production manager. We got a good production manager [John Seig]. But my role as the person that did all the things that Bill didn't want to do remained. To a certain degree, I did what the production manager didn't want to do, or couldn't do as far as decision making. As far as the management of it was—yes, yes, I suppose a glorified assistant, associate artistic director.

I was called the executive director, because we didn't know what else to call me when I stopped being the production manager. I think that was a fairly apt title. Bill thought it up. I did a little bit of everything. There were times, either when Bill was directing or something, or Bill was off to Europe for a couple of months or something, and I would just do what I could to keep the company functioning. A lot of the time I found myself interpreting for the rest of the world what he was saying. Sometimes, not accurately, but at least pretending that I knew what was going on, when he didn't know exactly what was going on but he was winging it. I would just pretend that it was all policy. It's the way a stage manager works for a director, which is really my first relationship with Bill. So if the director doesn't show up for a rehearsal, the stage manager can keep it going. If someone says there's a deadline, we've got to decide on this poster and the producer is not here, well, the stage manager can say, all right, I think we'll start at 8:35 or whatever. That's where I worked, besides [as] director, which was my goal and my delight.

Hastings' work as the middle man also made him aware of the problem of running the company during Ball's absence. Although he always considered Ball "infinitely approachable," like Bushnell he too at times found his decisions being countermanded:

That's particularly difficult if there's an absence . . . you make certain policy decisions because you have to make them in order to keep things going or to plan or whatever. Then this guy comes back from his rehearsal or his sickbed or his vacation, or whatever it is and says "that's not it, that's not the way I want it," and you have to change it. It is not only bad for his ego and the efficiency of the organization, it's mainly bad for your ego. But it's bad for everything. That drove Bill Bushnell crazy. Finally, he just didn't want to do it that way anymore. He wanted to have more power and get the roles shifted a little bit or equal or something. That was never going to happen.

Bill Bushnell summed up Ed Hastings' role as that of "arbiter" because of his perspective both as a director and interpreter of the decisions that were made. The term also acknowledged the close relationship of Ball and Hastings: "Bill, in effect, has a great deal of trust in Ed. Ed represents [a time] way back before Bill Ball was Bill Ball (he had the name, but he wasn't who we are talking about). Ed is not an ambitious person. He was very non-threatening to Bill. To some degree Bill looked at him as a student. What Ed offered was at times the ability, again, to be one of the people who could have a certain perspective in terms of what was really going on when you were down in the mud-throwing at each other."

Goldsby found Hastings' aid invaluable, owing to the latter's ability to help anyone who was in need. Many ascribed ACT's ability to maintain itself in part to his availability and dedication. As Goldsby recalled, "Hastings was involved in everything. He helped me in the conservatory. He helped Bushnell in P.R. He helped Seig in production. He also directed. He was a guy who could operate as a go-between Ball and the rest of the group, because Ed could talk to Bill, whereas almost from the beginning Bushnell and Ball didn't really have much to do with each other."

The supportive work of Ed Hastings gave stability to ACT in its early and flamboyant years. Hastings' experience and even temper gave a comfortable balance to Bill Ball's intense and, at times, eccentric behavior.

*New Role, New Directors, and Allen Fletcher, 1970–1972*

After the 1969 dismissal, Ball settled into his role as leader and chief administrator of ACT. The ground rules and procedures

had stabilized. Jim McKenzie was supplying the needed expertise in the financial affairs of ACT by reforming its accounting
and subscription plans. Ball regained his health and did away
with the Mexican cowboy hat that he had donned so theatrically
in previous years. The company kept some of its high-quality
performers, and a series of new directors streamed in for the
opening of the truncated 1970 season. Ellis Rabb was one of
the directors; his APA had folded. Ball hired Rabb, first as an
actor playing the messenger in *Oedipus*, and later as a director
for *The Tavern*, by George M. Cohan. Rabb returned for the
1970–1971 season to direct a "boldly up to date" *Merchant of
Venice*.[20]

Another director hired for the short 1970 season was Jack
O'Brien, who had been Rabb's assistant with the APA as well as
a director with the San Diego Globe Theatre. These two directors became available at a time when ACT was in need of strong
directors. ACT also had the good fortune to hire Allen Fletcher
to guide the conservatory after Goldsby's resignation. Fletcher
had been instrumental in the support of both Rabb and Ball. He
had been their teacher at the Carnegie Institute and had worked
with them regionally, both in Connecticut and California.

Fletcher's university experience helped him to mold a very
strong conservatory program. He had just lost his position as
artistic director with the Seattle Repertory (another case of a
strong board overrunning its artistic director) and he had behind
him a great deal of managerial experience in the regional theatre
movement. Fletcher became an original board member of the
ACT Foundation, and Ball credited him with being one of the
great influences on ACT and his own directing career.

Fletcher directed several of ACT's first productions, including *Death of a Salesman*, *Uncle Vanya*, and *Arsenic and Old
Lace*. His ideology of actor training, shaped by a combination
of technical skills and psychological realism, structured what
could be called ACT's acting style.

Thus, by the beginning of the 1970–1971 season several
key changes had taken place. A more consonant group of managers—people who had initially supported ACT and Ball—
were now present as part of the day-to-day operations. An ac-

tive executive committee was on hand, consisting of a staff that included Ball as president and general director, McKenzie as executive producer, Hastings as executive director, Edith Markson as developmental director, and Allen Fletcher as conservatory director. The power was centralized, and Ball assumed leadership of the company with more organizational support and consequently with more conviction that ACT could survive. This staff was to remain intact for the next decade, solidifying ACT's strength as a company and ensuring absolute support for the principles of the ensemble.

## The Responsibility of Leadership

The strength of Ball's position of leadership at ACT was unique in the regional theatre movement. His position could be likened to that of the *regisseur*, not unlike Antoine, Otto Brahm, or Augustine Daly. The inner workings of the company were structured to his tastes; the staff edited their work to his desires. As with previous ensembles, a strong central authority—albeit a paternal or autocratic one—seemed necessary. ACT was formed along these lines of a company with a central director, and not on the central playwright model.

As noted, Ball was never the kind of artistic director who insisted that all the art work be done his way. He only required that the company be run in accordance with his master plan. After finding directors whose viewpoints were consonant with his own regarding organization and principles, he let them do their own directorial work. The issue of the right to fail and the philosophy of positation took precedence at ACT. As Goldsby explained,

I did the world's worst production of *U.S.A.* for the end of the first year. While I was doing the conservatory I was suddenly told that I had to do *U.S.A.* The company was getting ready to go to Ravinia. Then we were supposed to go to Stanford. . . . So, I was supposed to direct *U.S.A.* for Stanford's opening. I ended up with two weeks of scattered rehearsals, maybe an hour a day. I ended up in the Stanford Memorial Auditorium, that seats two thousand people, with about six painted boxes and one five-hour session to set something like one hundred-eighty light cues before an audience came that night.

It was a horror story in a sense. It was a starved production idea; it had no budget. All the money went to produce a Jean Anouilh play that was going to go to Ravinia. We had to share. We were competing for rehearsal. We also had conflicts with casts.

The production of *U.S.A.* was supposed to open at Stanford and go into the Marines'. . . . Well, I wanted to do it with film and this or that. . . . I couldn't do any of that. I ended up being told, just do it the way it is with no money. Pat Tovatt forgot his lines. It was very amateurish and looked lost on this huge stage. But Seig and Bushnell and Ball himself all realized that it wasn't really my fault. I never got put down for it by anybody. I mean we all knew it was lousy; so did everybody else. But Bill never said anything; he didn't care. I mean it was an experiment. He said, "So you have the right to fail and so what." Yet it didn't fail because it was an experiment, but because if had no rehearsal time or design.

Bill explained hs laissez-faire attitude toward directors and his principle of positation, or saying yes to one's intuition: "What happens is, a side result of [positation], that everybody enjoys themselves and the work is better; it's impeccable. That's why I never worry about our plays. It may not be a good play to do; maybe we shouldn't have done that play. But at least when we do a play I know it will be well done because everyone is feeding their absolute fluid creative intuition into it . . . . I don't sit in on rehearsals, sit over directors, but I do hire directors who subscribe to this principle."

By 1971 Ball sat on top of a company that was maturing and about to hit its prime with the 1971–1972 season. Attendance at the Geary Theatre climbed to 90 percent of capacity and nearly twenty thousand people subscribed. There was never any doubt, even during the turbulence of the 1969 season, that the company and its principles were Bill Ball's. As William Bushnell was to say several years later, "there was never a power struggle for control of the company between Bill and myself. At no time was there a question as to whose company A.C.T. was, it was and is Bill Ball's."[21]

# 5

# Means of Survival

The American Conservatory Theatre Foundation was created as a nonprofit organization so that it would not have to function under the "high-risk" circumstances that commercial theatre was subject to. The freedom from the need to succeed commercially would help to ensure ACT's growth and to create theatre of the highest artistic standards.

During the time ACT was being formed, the regional movement of American theatre was also developing. The principles that governed all other theatrical enterprises in the nation played a role in ACT's governance. However, ACT was unique in that it was formed specifically to keep alive the ideal of a true ensemble theatre in the classical mold—one that was ruled by a central *regisseur*, that had consistency of style, and that ensured continuity of employment for its actors.

As a nonprofit theatre, ACT had to rely on subsidy, as was the case for all of the regional theatres in America. All such theatres needed subsidy to survive and grow because box-office income would simply not suffice in allowing regional theatre to maintain a professional company. The public, still used to theatre as a commercial business, viewed subsidizing with a jaundiced eye as regionalism grew. Wrote Dennis Powers: "In past decades—and even as recently as the nineteen-fifties—the ideal of subsidy for our theatres was often regarded as vaguely 'socialistic' or even 'un-American' by a nation steeped in the principles of individual enterprise, self-reliance, and paying your own way."[1]

The effort to create broad community support to help subsidize the professional theatre was based on the comparison between subsidizing museums, opera companies, or libraries and funding theatre companies. A theatrical enterprise, the argument went, would enhance the desirability of a community as these other institutions do, since a community's attractiveness depends, in part, on its cultural activities.

## Philanthropic National Foundations and the Cultural Boom

The 1950s were an era of increased leisure time for many well-educated American citizens. During that decade, the country was awakening to the need for more stimulating and cultural activities that might help to humanize its urban centers: "In the decade since World War II, our society has achieved material advances almost beyond belief. Yet, man increasingly realizes that meeting basic physical needs falls far short of attaining the end objective of life—the emotional, intellectual and aesthetic satisfactions he seeks, and therefore are important, even essential to the human mind and spirit."[2]

The realization that there was an absence of American cultural activity outside of New York City directly influenced the Rockefeller and Ford Foundation's decision to provide seed money for establishing a theatrical regionalism:

In 1959, the Ford Foundation announced a number of three-year grants designed to help resident theatres develop permanent companies. The Alley Theatre [Houston] and the Actor's Workshop of San Francisco each received $156,000, and Arena Stage [Washington, D.C.] received $127,000.... In 1962, the Ford Foundation announced grants totaling $6,100,000 to nine resident theatres.... Ford has since continued its massive support of resident theatres. It has been joined by the Rockefeller Foundation, other foundations, corporations, state arts councils and the Federal government.

The Ford grants in 1959 were for a kind of "demonstration project" to see what could be done if a few theatres had resident companies for three years. The 1962 grants were mostly for the purpose of helping companies to expand activity and increase audiences....

Grants to theatres continue to be mainly for the purpose of stimulating activity, not sustaining it indefinitely. In addition, most grants have been contingent on the theatre's ability to raise matching funds.[3]

ACT was created against the backdrop of this increasing interest in regionalism by the large foundations, specifically the Ford and Rockefeller Foundations.

The standard procedure for performing arts groups that were formed with a nonprofit corporate structure was to institute a board of directors that ruled over the organization. Often, as briefly noted in the preface, members of these boards were lay people from the local business community. Dealing with community boards was a precarious bargaining position for artistic directors, for they had to ask the boards for increasing subsidy support while they often spent large amounts on their own artistic work. In most cases, the artistic directors had been the guiding artists of vision who had molded the artistic ideals on which the theatres were based. These directors were in the best position to understand the needs of their theatres, and the boards were far from that position. Ball explained his feelings about the nonprofit structure:

I said that I wouldn't work in the nonprofit system because the nonprofit system had this basically flawed structure, where a group of businessmen can play games with the creative lives of a group of artists. I said, I do not want to work very hard for three years and then leave myself open to the slight or whims of a group of businessmen who are used to firings. Boards of directors of profit corporations are used to firing people, firing presidents when the profits are not good—and in profit corporations they fire one president every two or three years. . . . The corporation goes on. But in a theatre if you fire an artistic director nothing goes on. Everything collapses. One has to start over from the beginning.

I decided that if I entered into a situation where I gave three years of creative work to an organization, if somebody didn't like it I wanted them to be able to fire not only me, but to fire me with all of the company and equipment I had purchased, all the productions. That if they didn't like what I was doing they could be rid of me, but with me I would take away all of my creative accumulation.[4]

In the absence of either a strong hereditary aristocracy or state patronage, performing arts organizations depended on funds from community business people. Richard Hofstadter described what motivated people in the private sector to give money to efforts in the arts: "Sensitive of their reputation, fearful and resentful of criticism, often arrogant in their power, they can hardly help but be aware that the patronage of learning and art will add to their repute. To speak less cynically, they are also heirs of traditional moral canons of stewardship, they often feel responsible to do good with their money."[5]

In spite of the altruism mixed with egocentric aims of the business world, conflict has always characterized the relationship of business with the arts. Continued Hofstadter,

The contemporary businessman, who is disposed to think of himself as a man of practical achievement and a national benefactor, shouldering enormous responsibilities (as a patron often feels subjected to the impracticality and) hostility of flighty men who have never met a payroll. . . . [On the other hand] the intellectual is well aware of the elaborate apparatus which the businessman uses to mold our civilization to his purposes and his standards. The businessman is everywhere; he fills the coffers of the political parties, he owns or controls the influential press and the agencies of mass culture, he sits on university boards of trustees and local school boards; he mobilizes and finances cultural vigilantes, his voice dominates the rooms in which the real decisions are made.[6]

The convergent forces of business and art combined in the 1960s, the tenor of which was set by John F. Kennedy. In 1963, Kennedy spoke of the need for our cultural growth: "I see little of more importance to the future of our country and our civilization than full recognition of the place of artists. If art is to nourish the roots of our culture, society must set the artist free to follow his vision wherever it takes him. . . . Art is not a form of propaganda, it is a form of truth . . . art establishes the basic human truths which must serve as the touchstones of our judgment."[7]

The need to set the artist free for the good of the society led to the "cultural boom" or "cultural explosion" of the 1960s.

Alvin Toffler, in his book, *The Culture Consumers*, described this phenomenon:

The American attitude toward the arts has completed a 180-degree turn since the end of World War II. From one of apathy, indifference, and even hostility it has become one of eager, if sometimes ignorant enthusiasm. The distance traveled, and the speed of movement, have been startling, even in an age of rapidly shifting values. . . .

Americans have not only, by and large, moved past the subsistence level, they have been changing their entire psychological attitude toward work and leisure, for along with having more money they are beginning to rethink the Puritan ethic that insisted on work and frowned on play, relaxation, and the muses. With the declining need to work, people are liberated to spend, enjoy sensual satisfaction, to search for new and different delights—and they have increasing time to do so.[8]

The newly discovered need to fill Americans' free time prompted President Johnson, in 1966, to sign a multi-million-dollar cultural development program "to make fresher the winds of art in our land."[9] The legislation took the shape of the National Endowment for the Arts (NEA). The endowment's purpose was to help make professional arts available to as many Americans as possible. This goal of democratizing the arts was the banner carried by the regional theatres of the 1950s and 1960s.

In direct conflict with the idea of democratizing the arts was the subsidizing of their high costs without governmental aid, or with little governmental aid. The prevailing attitude in many arts organizations in the early sixties was that through subsidy the government would dictate what should or should not be produced. The old adage of "giving money with strings attached" was seen as a reality. A viable solution for the arts organizations was to seek private support from their communities. In keeping with this assumption, the Rockefeller Panel Report on the Performing Arts put forth the following recommendations in 1965: "no form of governmental aid to the arts would eliminate private initiative, reduce private responsibility for direction, or hamper complete artistic freedom. These must remain in the prerogative of the citizens who direct performing arts institutes and of the artists." [10]

The cooperation of the private sector in the beginning years of regionalism helped some organizations to succeed but contributed to the demise of others. One of the greatest problems was reconciling conflicting personalities in the two groups— that is, garnering support from the private sector for artistic directors who were not business oriented. The Rockefeller Panel recognized this problem when it stated: "It is the characteristic of the performing arts that outstanding success can almost always be traced to some gifted, inspired and driving individual. Organizations can provide no substitute for that individual effort. But they can give it an underpinning." [11] It went on to make the following recommendations: "The arts and artists must be accepted on their own terms, not an unorthodox requirement when we consider the amount of freedom accorded scientists and educators by those who support them." [12]

It was in following this recommendation precisely that Ball forged his concept of separated boards of subsidy and governance. His rationale for having separate boards was based on fear: a real fear of being fired after accumulating several years of work. Ball explained:

I'd seen so many people hurt. I'd been hurt myself. I'd been part of companies where I'd been an actor and I was seeing the management close in on the directors. It was happening left, right, and center. No one was accumulating anything. You can't build a theatre that makes everybody happy in three years. It takes years and years and years to build a theatre.

The organization is based on the principle that the artists who do the work control their own destinies. They create a product, the product is for sale to anyone who wants to buy that product. They can have it if they can afford it. [13]

When the Carnegie Institute and the Pittsburgh Playhouse came to terms both with Ball and with the Rockefeller Foundation, ACT had its first home. But the Playhouse board wanted a larger role in the company's decision making. Bill Ball would have none of it, and thus the first crisis occurred. When Ball took flight to New York to hold "in-training" sessions with his actors, he was given the remainder of the three-year Rockefeller grant, which had been only partially used during ACT's residency in Pittsburgh. This period, a time of wandering, was the most tenuous in ACT's existence.

The Carnegie Institute agreed to apply on behalf of the now sponsorless ACT for the remainder of the three-year Rockefeller grant. The action allowed ACT to survive. Later, in 1966, the NEA allocated a matching grant against the Rockefeller grant. Ball described the Rockefeller move:

We used the first part of the grant at the end of the first year . . . at that end we left, the Tech and ACT essentially agreed in principle that what was going on at the Pittsburgh Playhouse was an adversary role. But the money was coming from Rockefeller. . . . What happened was the amount of the second year was paid in the first six months of the second year, which was perfectly natural for their foundation to do. So that any special considerations that were given to us were that the third-year amount was requested to be paid in the second half of the second year.

Essentially, we received a three-year grant in eighteen months. They were doing their best to help us through a bad period.[14]

ACT and Ball had proven themselves during the first season as worthy of support. Both the Carnegie Institute and the Rockefeller Foundation believed that Ball was an artist who should be helped while he searched for a community to call home. This timely move by the Rockefeller Foundation ensured the life of ACT for the remainder of the 1966 period, when it seemed inevitable that the company would fold. It was clear that if ACT was to settle in a community it would have to be on Ball's terms. He did not waiver in his basic belief that ACT should be independent from its subsidizing support. ACT's independent policy forced it to tour the country in an effort to seek a new residence. A factor that loomed large in Ball's decision to find a permanent home was that additional large-scale funding would then become available to it from the Ford Foundation. Hastings explained:

Representatives from Ford saw the work in Pittsburgh. But they had a rule at that point: you had to be resident in a city for two years before they would give you any money. They had seen the work and they loved it. Unofficially, they said they'd support us if we could get anywhere and live for two years. So that was nice, it was sort of like coming with a dowry. If the marriage survives for two years, the bride will be rich, or reasonably rich. That's what that was. So it was like an endorsement, but it wasn't anything official.

All we had to do was to keep delivering what, artistically, was good and you knew they would come through and so did the city fathers. That was nice and that helped to make it all happen.

But it was all unofficial. I don't know how publically known it was, but certainly it was known that ACT was this big meteor rising, and it was reasonable to suppose that Ford would support it, once we met their requirements. Edith Markson, who was the head of the development and vice president of the board of trustees, had been a field scout for Ford, going out and observing. She knew the people and the workings at the Ford Foundation. So we had that connection. Still, if the work hadn't been good or the community acceptance good, they wouldn't have done anything.[15]

The support of the Ford Foundation was waiting in the wings if ACT could succeed in San Francisco and find that community's support.

ACT embarked upon an expensive course: to create an ensemble repertory company that would be able to stay in residence. This massive undertaking fit in perfectly with the concept that McNeil Lowry had been backing in his capacity as head of the arts division of the Ford Foundation: the residence in regional settings of professional American theatres.

Part of the expense generated by theatre is the labor-intensive aspect of performing. Both the Ford and Rockefeller foundations understood this cost. In its study of the performing arts organizations of the nation, the Ford Foundation explained that "the most obvious fact, and one the theatre shares with other performing arts fields . . . is that in each theatre the largest and least flexible cost is the one for artistic personnel."[16] For this reason the Ford Foundation was willing to give seed money to help create the matching local funds that would sustain a regional theatre's subsidy. The hope was that if a community saw the Ford Foundation's interest in the theatre, then citizens would follow with their private contributions.

The Ford Foundation had previously granted the San Francisco Actor's Workshop money to hire a company of New York professional actors for their theatre. The experiment met with dismal failure because the Workshop had already built a company of San-Francisco-based actors. Nevertheless, the foundation had perceived San Francisco as a strong candidate for theatre-arts support. When ACT was to make its home in San Francisco, the Ford Foundation, headed by McNeil Lowry, became committed supporters of ACT and Ball.

The connecting pin with the Ford Foundation was Edith Markson. Ball and Markson first met and became friends at the Fred Miller Theatre in Milwaukee, and Markson soon became a strong advocate of the young director. She was a good fund-raiser and a friend of McNeil Lowry at the Ford Foundation.

The foundation's role was to become of vital importance in the life of ACT. Bushnell explained the relationship of ACT and Ford:

They played the role of an iron fist wrapped in a velvet glove. There was one person at the Ford Foundation who played a major role, and [that was] McNeil Lowry. . . . Mac played a key role in all of this from the very beginning. Edith Markson was a "field rep" for the Ford Foundation. That may not be a correct title. She may have been, in a sense, like an ambassador without portfolio. . . .

Mac was extremely instrumental in making it clear to Mortimer Fleishhacker that if the city of San Francisco was incapable of providing the funding that ACT needed, that the Ford Foundation might have to reevaluate all of its commitments to other San Francisco arts organizations, like KQED [the public television station], the symphony, and the opera, because they might have to reevaluate San Francisco's ability to be a major league player in the arts world. . . .

They were the major backers of the company. They backed the concept. Mac had a great role to play in the overall emergence of the regional theatres in the resident concept, of actors being in residence and the creation of ongoing companies.[17]

*The Ford Foundation and San Francisco, 1967*

The talks between the Ford Foundation and the San Francisco Chamber of Commerce began on 9 September 1966. At that time, Magnin spoke with foundation officials about a possible $250,000 grant for the company's training program, while overtures were being made by the National Endowment for the Arts, a fledgling federal program. The actual announcement of the first Ford grant came on 30 January 1967, in the form of the foundation's standard matching grant. ACT's press release read, "William Ball, General Director of the American Conservatory Theatre of San Francisco . . . today announced A.C.T. has received a $245,000 Ford Foundation grant to help consolidate the theatre by supporting its training and production program for the 1967–1968 season.[18] Ball explained the nature of the matching grant: The $245,000, which must be more than matched by Bay Area contributors of $425,000, represents a major stimulus to the economic vitality of the area."[19]

The Ford Foundation quickly became the muscle behind the survival of ACT. With McNeil Lowry's support, the company seemed to be instantly recognized as a true resident company in San Francisco. The community feeling at this point was that San Francisco was a fertile theatrical ground and that ACT was fated for it. Mortimer Fleishhacker wrote about the community's need for ACT:

With its long tradition of support for the performing arts, the Bay Area is a natural home for A.C.T. And, as a capital of the West for educational, scientific, financial, shipping and corporate headquarters, the Bay Area needs A.C.T. If it is granted that theatre, with opera, symphony, visual arts such as painting and sculpture, dance, and more recently public television, supplementing each other in creating a cultural atmosphere, this area, with its background of sophistication, should strive for excellence in all of these fields. A.C.T. has demonstrated that it has the potential of excellence. The theatre has undergone many changes in the United States since World War II; it is now acknowledged that New York has lost its pre-eminent position in the world of theatre.[20]

With the understanding that San Francisco was a major cultural area of the United States the funds would come for the needed subsidy. The continuing hope of the directors was that ACT would receive this support privately. Said Fleishhacker, "If San Franciscans are to enjoy a lively, permanent resident theatrical company, they should begin to think of supporting it in the same measure as they support libraries, museums and concert halls. Hopefully, the major contributors—business, industry and foundations—will offer their full, traditional share of support while the base is broadened to include small donations from interested members of A.C.T.'s audience and the general public."

This statement was printed in the *San Francisco Chronicle* on 1 February 1967, under the title "A.C.T. Deserves Public Support." The urgent need to raise matching funds was recognized by the COC, and it rallied to help collect their pledge.

At the end of ACT's first season, the COC members who were active in the company formed the nonprofit California Theatre Foundation, or the CTF. (The name was changed in 1973 to the California Association for the American Conservatory Theatre—CAACT.) Melvin Swig was the first president; Mortimer Fleishhacker was chairman of the board. "By agreement, the sole function of this Foundation was to raise money in the Northern California area to subsidize A.C.T.'s annual visit to San Francisco."[21] There would be a yearly arrangement whereby the CTF would pledge its funds according to a "best-efforts" structure. The foundation would also attempt to meet the Ford Foundation's requirements of a matching grant.

### Federal Support: The N.E.A.

In addition to the local support pledged by the newly-created CTF, another source of support came from the federally funded National Endowment for the Arts, headed by Roger L. Stevens. One of the goals of the NEA was to "help create and sustain not only a climate encouraging freedom of thought, imagination, and inquiry, but also the material conditions facilitating the release of this creative talent."[22]

This philosophy had inspired Public Law 209–89, which created the National Endowment for the Arts and the Humanities in 1965. The act declared the need to encourage support of the arts by the federal government, while support would concurrently continue from private sources. Federal support hinged on the nonprofit status of the arts organizations. The belief of the federal government was that culture, in its essence, was a democratic entity. These federal funds added to the list of possible sources of subsidies to the arts. The addition could, therefore, enhance the regional theatre movement afoot at the time.

ACT was appropriated $160,000, the largest grant made by the NEA in the fiscal year of 1966. Moreover, the grant was made while the company was still itinerant. The fifteen other grants to resident theatres totaled $660,000. The indication was clear: if ACT could find a home, the NEA would continue to subsidize the operation. Once again the goal of the NEA was for ACT to permanently settle into a community.

The NEA was working in coordination with the Rockefeller Foundation in a matching-grant appropriation during ACT's itinerant period of 1966. The $160,000 appropriation was $10,000 more than the previous maximum grant given by the NEA. The NEA saw great potential in ACT, as Ruth Mayleas, former official of the NEA, stated: "In the case of the A.C.T. (and that was exceptional) we were very much involved with a joint project. In the one case actually to get the organization started—and in the other (which was, I think, two years after that first grant) in seeing that it got a firm hold, and got a very high level grant to enable it to match that with far more money from the community."[23]

### The Hotel Tax Fund and the City of San Francisco

ACT's highly successful twenty-two-week season of 1967 in San Francisco brought added local support. The city of San Francisco had instituted a fund called the Hotel Tax Fund. This fund was a 3 percent tax added to all hotel rooms. The accrued revenues were distributed to areas that would advertise San Francisco: "The California Government Code, Section 26100, allows local governments to levy a special tax 'for the purpose of inducing immigration to, and increasing the trade and commerce of the county.' Under that provision, in 1961, the City and County of San Francisco established the Hotel Tax."[24]

To be eligible to receive hotel tax revenues, a program had to enhance San Francisco's reputation outside the city and also had to have a positive economic impact on the city itself. By 1967 ACT had fulfilled these requirements and appropriated $30,000 from the tax fund that year. The amount clearly indicated that the city government was a serious contributor to the ACT concept in San Francisco.

The Ford Foundation pledged $300,000 to ACT, to be matched by the CTF for ACT's first full San Francisco season from 1967 to 1968. But most surprising of all the grants was the NEA's matching grant of $350,000. Bushnell explained why ACT needed and deserved such a subsidy:

A repertory company which is also a full-scale theatre training institute can no more be expected to be self-sustaining than the nation's opera companies, museums, or symphonies.

A center of advanced education and research whose methods and techniques are being widely adapted by major universities may justifiably claim—as many universities and research institutes do—the need of subsidy.

There is a myth, that theatres should be self-supporting. However, the alarming decline of Broadway productions over the past few seasons indicates clearly that quality theatre cannot survive today in a purely commercial market.

Subsidy funds should be available only as a supplement to a healthy box office. If the theatre is consistently performing to a house which is two-thirds empty, then it can hardly justify asking for funds from foundations, corporations or private contributors. The work on stage is obviously not satisfying the artistic, entertainment and educational needs of the community, and subsidy becomes purely "relief."

But a growing theatre whose business is good must be subsidized so that quality and creativity may advance and thrive and in order to keep its ticket prices at a moderate level so that it can attract a broad-based audience and be of maximum service to the community.[25]

The NEA's grant to ACT in 1967 was a major step by the federal funding program toward the support of the regional theatre movement. The generous grant was made partially through the influence of the Ford Foundation as Ruth Mayleas explained:

An organization, now called the American Conservatory Theatre, was getting started. That was a case where we did come in at the beginning. Something we rarely do. However, the circumstances were special. I mean that nucleus of people and that director had an exceptional track record and a certain amount of organizational chaos in those early years. The artistic plan and all that was basically very sound. I think that's been proven.

At any rate, we made two very large (for us certainly in those years) major grants in cooperation with private foundations. In one case it was Rockefeller and in one case it was Ford. But they were for us (at that time) massive grants to A.C.T. . . . we did play a very important part in their beginning.[26]

### Financial Crisis: 1968

In spite of the pledged support, the cost of ACT's second season, combined with the costs of the conservatory, increased the already critical need for that support. ACT's ambitious projected budget created a crisis, and raising the funds was essential as the 1968 season came to a close. The CTF was short of the $400,000 subsidy that was to be used for the matching grants; $104,000 more was needed by 31 July 1968 if the matching grants were to become a reality. This was the second of the perennial financial crises that were to plague ACT's fundraising arm, the CTF. On 19 July 1968, the *San Francisco Examiner* read,

The present crisis resulted from the failure of this year's fund drive to reach its goal of $400,000. A total of $296,000 has been raised, leaving a gap of $104,000.

The seriousness of the situation brought an appeal yesterday from Mayor Alioto, whose statement was read by Fleishhacker.

"A.C.T. has assumed a major role in our cultural life," said the mayor. "It has taken its place beside our opera, our symphony and our ballet, and has made our city more than ever a center for the performing arts. A.C.T.'s impact on the city—both cultural and economic—is a vital force. At this time, I urge all leaders of San Francisco's business and corporate community to take the initiative in raising the funds necessary to insure A.C.T.'s permanent residency here."[27]

The amount of behind-the-scenes pressure being applied by the Ford Foundation was hard to determine, but the fact remained that the Ford Foundation was very interested in seeing professional theatre succeed in San Francisco. To help speed up the collection of money for ACT, KQED, the local educational television station, presented a three-hour fund-raising program entitled, "A.C.T. Now." By the day of the telecast, 29 July 1968, the CTF was still $83,500 short of its goal. The television program featured scenes from several ACT productions along with special guest appearances by members of the APA (Ellis Rabb's theatre group). At the time Bushnell expressed his hope for the success of the program. "I hope 'A.C.T. Now' will put us over the top. It's a magnificent gesture on the part of K.Q.E.D. Our only worry is that the show will be so exciting people will be unwilling to leave it to call the theatre and make their pledge."[28]

The seriousness of the need for funds was recognized by California government officials. Ronald Reagan, then governor of California, sent ACT a telegram that read: "Wish you every success with your fund raising. I am sure the Bay Area's citizens will support this worthy cause."[29] (The state of California did not contribute.) The telethon raised $40,841.50 from more than 2,000 callers. Among the donations came a $10,000 pledge from the Crown Zellerbach Foundation of the paper industry and an additional $5,000 from the Zellerbach Family Fund. The total still needed for the completion of the pledged CTF support was $25,158.50.

The full amount of the $83,000 was raised at the eleventh hour, mostly through the accumulation of small contributions. The amount of $400,000 did not seem like too much to Mortimer Fleishhacker, who felt that the Bay Area could afford this price. But raising that amount for the theatre was unexpectedly difficult. When the first crisis year ended the sigh of relief did not last long.

### 1969: A Year of Crisis and Change

The CTF announced another goal of $400,000 in 1969 for the continuing support of ACT in San Francisco. The amount was to go toward a matching grant of $350,000 from the Ford Foundation. The feeling at this point was that ACT was a vital part of the San Francisco economic scene. As Fleishhacker wrote,

Business and corporate leaders have come to realize the economic soundness of supporting cultural activities. They know that these sources produce an expanded economy and that, equally important, the most imaginative and productive employees are invariably attracted to a community offering a rich and varied cultural and entertainment life.

A.C.T. is a major commercial venture, too, operating on a year-round schedule with an annual budget of $2,500,000 and a full-time staff of 150 professional directors, actors, trainers, designers, craftsmen, technicians and administrators. In terms of dollars alone, the yearly economic activity generated by A.C.T. is estimated at more than $3,000,000. That figure will undoubtedly grow if the Bay Area continues—and increases—its support of A.C.T.[30]

Mayor Alioto urged the business community to support ACT to enable it to reach its local subsidy goal. The deficit that ACT was to face by the end of the 1968–1969 season was staggering. The CTF, though well-intentioned, was not able to raise the necessary funds quickly or efficiently.

During the first three seasons ACT grew rapidly. Large sums of money went into creating the repertory and conservatory programs. The double repertory company of close to fifty members required tremendous planning and huge financial resources. The upheavals that occurred by the end of the 1968–1969 season were a natural outgrowth of dealing with a new and daring theatre program, but the resulting instability caused ACT to rely heavily on the additional financial support as well as on community acceptance of its productions. However, the community was a fickle base of local support: only when the plays were popular would the fund raising become easier.

The general incentive to raise the funds came from the dedicated members of the CTF—Fleishhacker in particular—and the strong-armed support of McNeil Lowry and the Ford Foundation. Fleishhacker and Lowry were not only backing the company and its founding principles, but they were ultimately backing Bill Ball.

When Jim McKenzie came to San Francisco in early 1969, he saw a growing distrust by the CTF directors of the ACT administration. McKenzie explained:

By the end of the season of '68–'69, they [the ACT administrators] were in the position of being one-half million dollars in debt. There was a poor accounting being done, terrible . . . through a local firm hired through politics . . . the staff were all hiding bills because they were afraid of the sponsors. They were afraid of having a reconciliation. I put it together and realized it was a disastrous situation.

They had a big company meeting at the Geary after a succession of Saturdays coming around with no payroll. The actors weren't insulated, they didn't get paid. We called a special meeting on a Saturday. Mortimer Fleishhacker showed up and assured them that by Monday they'd get their checks and pay their rent and eat. So we all kept working. This went on, on two or three different occasions within a period of a month.[31]

There was little doubt that the presence of Mortimer Fleishhacker reassured the company. How much actual money in "forgiven" loans or outright gifts to ACT was given by Fleishhacker is hard to determine, but Fleishhacker was devoted to ACT's survival. As Goldsby said, "It was Mort Fleishhacker, more than anybody, that provided operating capital for the theatre through the first three years."[32] Bill Bushnell reiterated that there could be no doubt that Mort Fleishhacker had "bailed out" the company on several occasions.[33] Yet the fact remained that in return Fleishhacker had very little say in the workings of ACT. McKenzie explained: "In effect we never allowed the two (boards) to meld. Mortimer Fleishhacker had been invited to be on the ACT board, but he declined. After that we never allowed a single person from the community to be on the ACT Board, whether Ball loved them or not, because of that principle (the need for separate boards). So the two boards ran parallel for years."[34]

When ACT was faced with the internal turmoil and the need for more fiscal responsibility in 1969, an important meeting took place between Fleishhacker and Lowry at Fleishhacker's home. The CTF fund drive had fallen significantly short of the $400,000 goal. ACT was spending this expected amount creating a deficit. McKenzie saw two solutions to the salvaging of ACT and its financial dilemma:

One, Mac Lowry came out and made some very strong negotiations with Morty Fleishhacker, who at the time was head of the CTF . . . . In fact, he went down to Morty's house in Palo Alto. He had such a difficult negotiation with Morty that Mac ended up taking a bus back to San Francisco—W. McNeil Lowry, vice president of the Ford Foundation. But he got what he went for—a $200,000 guarantee against matching [funds] from Ford. So $400,000 was there immediately to solve our half-million-dollar problem, or help to solve it.

At the same time, or roughly the same time, I arranged for us to coproduce *Hair*, and to postpone the season and gamble everything on the success of that to get us the rest of the money we needed. That's what we did.[35]

At the meeting with Lowry, Fleishhacker was asked to keep a closer eye on the management of ACT's finances. He "agreed, at that time, to move into more active management of the theatre," said Goldsby.[36]

A press release, issued on 26 March 1969, announced the newly created executive committee composed of Fleishhacker, Swig, and William Porter of the CTF, along with Ball and McKenzie. This committee was to help guide ACT's overall policy making. Ball explained the need for the committee at the time:

We find ourselves confronted by two major needs, first, a need to increase our box office income while maintaining expense control, and second the need to participate more effectively in C.T.F.'s fund raising campaign.

The new committee provides us with a greater confidence and a sense of permanence with the community, closing the gap between our productions and the sponsors of A.C.T. This cooperation will lead to more effective fund raising and operating methods and it certainly will be of great value to us to be in close touch with spokesmen of the community regarding the plans and the programs of our company.[37]

Though this statement appeared to give the CTF policy-making powers, in reality it did not. What it did was to bring the CTF into the discussions of budgeting:

In December of 1969, a new agreement was negotiated between A.C.T. and C.T.F. It was determined that in the best interest of both organizations, separate legal entities would be maintained, but complete and timely exchange of all operating information would occur on a continuing basis. This exchange included a detailed budget of A.C.T.'s income and expenses for each season, calendars, all plans for subscription and fund-raising, organizational charts, monthly operating statements compared to budgets, emergency stand-by plans in the event of unfulfilled projections and the formation of a joint committee of representatives from each organization to meet regularly for consultation and exchange of information and advice.[38]

The essence of this agreement was to facilitate a more open exchange of information between the two groups. It had become increasingly difficult for the CTF to create the necessary support for ACT as the two organizations stood. The most difficult problem facing the CTF was working for the company despite its lack of a permanent commitment to San Francisco. ACT's image as an itinerant company was confirmed in several official statements that expressed the company's fierce independence from any locale. In a formalized fashion, the new agreement put to rest, in part, CTF's fear that ACT would leave the city, while ensuring that control of policy making for the company remained with Ball.

Because Ball had great hopes and "thought big," he was not considered to be a fiscal conservative. Thus, the CTF asked for some safeguards to help create the subsidy, and to keep it from escalating. McKenzie explained the new arrangement:

Each year we'd go over budgets, agree on an annual budget, and agree on a fund-raising total. It was always a difficult thing. We'd postpone the season if they didn't give us more money the next season. Or they'd say, "We won't give you any more money unless you do this or that." Many times there were hard feelings from our early local support boards because we would never let them select our plays or really make policy decisions that were important to us. They kept thinking, "Well, you're artists—you should have control of the art; we should have control of the money, because it's San Francisco money." We learned, long ago, that you can't separate art and money. Money is art. So we never went for that ploy, never gave an inch of control of our operation. It was very bitter. . . . Businessmen don't normally join boards of directors just to raise money to support something they have no control over. It's against all their training.[39]

Through McKenzie's belief in the separation of the boards and his sensitive bargaining, he convinced the CTF to continue its support. Mortimer Fleishhacker gave a substantial gift to help match the Ford Foundation grant that kept the company going during the 1969 planning stages. The speculated amount of the gift was fifty thousand dollars, given anonymously through the guise of the San Francisco Foundation. The last one hundred thousand dollars of the needed five hundred thousand dollars was generated while ACT went to the ANTA festival in New York during the fall of 1969. Meanwhile, *Hair* played in the Geary Theatre while ACT was in New York, and the latter shared in the box-office profits. In a press release issued 3 February 1970, McKenzie praised this arrangement, saying, "It was most helpful in picking up the financial slack and in paying off a good share of our accumulated deficit from past seasons."[40]

During the 1968–1969 financial crisis, ACT realized that it had to lower some of its goals. It became evident that the theatre would continue to increase its deficit if some reorganization did not take place. One solution was to do away with the double repertory in the two theatres, and thus ACT settled for performing only in the Geary. The double repertory was dropped for the 1970–1971 season, never to be renewed. Ball gave an additional reason for the change:

It became too difficult. We had people running from one theatre to another. We had another where we opened *Tiny Alice* at 8:30 and the other one up the hill at 8:40, because we didn't have enough actors to do those two shows together unless the people that played the two monks in the first scene of *Tiny Alice* could get up the hill. We had to have two separate opening times, so the monks could make their appearances in *Tiny Alice* and get off stage and run up the hill. You'd see these two monks holding their dresses running up the hill to change and to get on in time for the curtain. Also, we started producing plays that I didn't like in order to keep the two theatres functioning. We started doing plays for the wrong reasons because it didn't have any set, or because it had parts for a fat actor or something like that. We weren't doing organic plays. I was beginning to miss opening nights. I did consider that as a serious reason for giving up the double rep. If you can't keep in personal touch, that was one of the reasons we are as small as we are; we are large but also small. We're constantly lopping off what we call ancillary activity. We have many opportunities to expand. The American disease is expansion. If you're doing well, why don't you expand? Many people say, "Well, now you're doing that, what else are you going to do?" What we are doing is quite enough. We found that if I—it is true of any leading director—if you can't reach out and touch, personally, all the actors you are responsible for, then your company is too big.[41]

By corporate standards, ACT, with its 157 members in 1970 and 1971, was a small organization. But by American theatrical standards ACT was a large theatre company. The maximum size of the company was reached in the 1969 season when the members numbered 250.

ACT also set its sights on a smaller season subscription total. The second season produced 18,000 subscribers, and the third saw only 10,000. This was owing, in part, to the large number of revivals that were being done to fill the schedule of the two theatres, as was discussed earlier. *Tiny Alice, Tartuffe,* and *Under Milkwood* had all been revived at least twice. Since this created fewer subscribers, ACT dropped the Marines' booking. Instead, touring shows were booked at the Marines', with ACT profiting in a share of the proceeds generated. Being dependent upon public acceptance of the shows, this plan met with mixed results, nevertheless it reduced the overall financial risk. The new company structure and scheduling plan was accomplished mainly through McKenzie's urgings. Said Ball, "Jim McKenzie is one of the most knowledgeable, dedicated, clear-minded theatre businessmen I know. It's thanks to him that we have confidence as a company and that we are on a much more sound fiscal footing with sponsorship. He has brought sober structure, a good budget and respectability with the foundations upon which we rely."[42] McKenzie also subsequently developed dependable bookkeeping and accounting systems for ACT. The accounting firm of Lutz and Carr was commissioned to do ACT's yearly audit.

## 1971–1972: New Financial Security

Matching grants continued to be awarded to ACT for the 1970–1971 and 1971–1972 seasons from the Ford Foundation, ensuring ACT's survival. The funds totaled more than seven hundred thousand dollars. The CTF pledged amounts to be raised as matches during those two seasons, and did their best under their new, more active role to raise their pledged subsidy. ACT boasted of a more financially stable situation by the end of the 1972 season. Ball explained ACT's financial plights in retrospect: "Our early years—my pink period—were survival years, years in which we had to spend all sorts of energies and pull all sorts of rabbits out of our hats in order to stay alive as a company. We were very demonstrative about it, doing some pretty survivally, wacky things to stay together, constantly shouting, 'Somebody give us a home! Give us security, some place where we can work!'"[43]

By the time it began its 1972–1973 season, ACT had its home as well as strong local support. The support was hard-won, and mainly emerged owing to the urging of ACT's major patron, the Ford Foundation. There can be little doubt that the Ford Foundation made possible ACT's continued existence. Ball explained:

McNeil Lowry was a great champion of the performing arts. He . . . was personally committed to our company . . . he and Mortimer Fleishhacker, are the two men most responsible for our existence. He supported us through all sorts of unreasonable times. The thing is, it is easy to support a successful artist. What takes guts is to support an idea which has not been demonstrated, a principle which hasn't been proven. That's what Mac Lowry could do. He supported the principle and a commitment and he lent his power to that commitment. Essentially, he caused our company to come into existence.[44]

### The Ensemble and the Lack of An American Aristocracy: Conclusions

It has always been essential for companies to gain some form of financial security away from the pressures of box-office solvency. Historically, many European ensembles owed their success to subsidy by the aristocracy. The United States has never had a philanthropic aristocracy that could subsidize the theatre. Grants from foundations set up as tax shelters form the closest analogy to such philanthropic gestures. The original great captains of industry, with their large earnings, learned to make use of these shelters, and their second- and third-generation descendants used them as well. The family names are familiar to most Americans: Ford, Rockefeller, Mellon, and Carnegie.

The support of the arts by these foundations at different times during the second half of the twentieth century has been remarkable, but their support fluctuated with the degree of their interest in certain projects. Thus, the Rockefeller Foundation aided ACT for a three-year period and then ended its support. The Ford Foundation, mainly because of McNeil Lowry, created a fertile base for many regional theatres with the belief that eventually local support would take over, cancelling out the need for additional foundation money.

The original CTF had the altruistic philanthropist, Mortimer Fleishhacker, without whom ACT may not have survived its first three expensive years. By 1971, Cyril Magnin had taken the leading role in the active local support. These men and the Rockefeller and Ford foundations can be seen, in some respects, as the aristocratic support enjoyed by so many historical ensembles. Shakespeare's King's Men, Molière and the *Comédie Française*, the duke of Saxe-Meiningen, and Goethe all enjoyed this type of support. (Later, the Moscow Art Theatre would have had difficulty surviving without its governmental patronage.)

ACT emerged during a period in which decentralization of the theatre away from New York City was the trend. Because of this, more Americans could enjoy what was available to only a few until the 1950s. The "cultural boom" of the 1960s was based on the belief that more well-educated citizens should have access to as many varied cultural activities as possible. Theatre thus came to be categorized with museums, opera, and symphony orchestras.

As ACT shouldered increased fiscal responsibility, it had to adapt to its limitations. First, it dropped its double repertory; second, it sponsored touring shows to increase its earned income; and finally, it created a more open communication with its local fund-raising board, the California Theatre Foundation, while still maintaining policy-making control. While it implemented these changes, ACT's core remained the same. It still existed primarily to provide continued employment for its actors and to maintain, concurrently and inseparably, its training and repertory programs.

# 6

# The ACT Style of Acting

## The Concept of Professionalism

"When I began ACT," said Bill Ball, "I wanted to create a company with a dual purpose: resident repertory performance, and concurrent and inseparable training, for all members of the company."[1] The concept of providing training concurrently and inseparably with repertory performance was new in the history of the American theatre. ACT's program aimed to unify the theatrical styles of the older and younger actors in a professional setting and to continue the training of the professional actors already in the ACT company:

Many companies in the United States offer classes and apprentices in fundamentals of voice, fencing, or acting, for example, but A.C.T. is the first theatre to be founded on the conservatory concept, recognizing that a professional actor (just as any serious artist) must study continuously if he is to grow in his art. At the same time an educational theatre program must be administered under professional standards and in conjunction with professional performance. In order to provide himself with the opportunity to study his craft, to discover new techniques, to research and experiment in training methods and new production possibilities, the theatre artist must earn a living through performance. By performing in a year-round theatre, he acquires the necessary sense of continuity allowing him to give serious attention to training himself at an advanced level which enables him to reach new high levels of excellence in performance.[2]

Ball thought that American actors were not getting the necessary training actors needed either at the university level or at the professional level. He declared that "university training is notoriously bad."[3] One of the points Ball made in his theatre manifesto (ACT's statement of purpose) was that "such training as exists in universities and professional schools often suffers from inadequate standards and is often limited by highly individualistic stamps of one teacher or method."[4] Consequently, ACT was created to raise the level of professional acting in America. "Ball bluntly places the load upon the 'profession' of acting as it exists today to bring itself up to the levels of the other professions. An actor should be complete, capable of eliciting any emotion imaginable upon the stage."[5]

Ball's strongest criticism was aimed at the style of acting that prevailed in America in the 1950s and 1960s. He thought that actors needed to find the proper technical skills for the art and then to exercise those skills, much as a ballet dancer would exercise to remain in performance shape. Ball explained:

I thought [actors of that time] had no right to call themselves professionals any more than you would have a butcher enter into an operating room and perform an operation on your brother. No more would I call these mushy unknowledgeable actors that were working for me professionals. They had no professional standards. So our effort was initially to establish certain techniques which constitute definition: professionalism—the standards by which professionalism was made. The things that a professional actor has to know and have at his command are not only the "Method"—in other words, only one-half of the acting technique, only one book of Stanislavsky.[6]

Ball's attempt to standardize the profession was initially a reaction against the American "Method" acting prevalent at the time of ACT's inception—a style that had developed through the work of Lee Strasberg at the Actors' Studio in New York. Until the emergence of the Group Theatre there was no American school of acting, per se, to train acting students in an indigenously American style. The hope was that ACT would become the flagship, or model, of a new American standard for acting:

The student's close association in class and on stage with the professional serves to fulfill a larger, though less tangible standard of American acting. A.C.T. and Conservatory staff and faculty agree that actors in this country are often inhibited in their development by the lack of an indigenous training upon which they can draw (we still look to London and Moscow, for example, for models). A.C.T., therefore, emphasizes the responsibility of mature American artists to pass on what they have learned over the years to younger members of the profession—"to conserve" in the literal sense of the word.[7]

Thus, part of ACT's self-definition reads: "The training program of the *Conservatory* will be concurrent with the program of presentations. Training will be woven into the rehearsal pattern by stage managers specifically engaged for the purpose of preparing the daily schedule and assignments of personnel (*Estudientenlieder*). Our goal is to awaken in the theatre artist his maximum versatility and expression."[8]

American actors had too often been forced to develop on a hit-or-miss basis in the professional arena. Either they relied solely on the development of their stock type or on their personality. Except through the efforts toward naturalistic acting spearheaded by the Group Theatre, no actor was able to find concentrated training. As Harold Clurman noted, "There are enormous resources of talent in our country, but little coordinating discipline or formative enterprise. We are eager for the fruit, but we do not care about the tree."[9]

### The Model: Michel Saint-Denis

Ball chose as his model for ACT the work of the French director and teacher Michel Saint-Denis. Ball explained:

This theatre (ACT) is based on a concept that Michel Saint-Denis had but was never able to make effective. He tried it with the Young Vic School, then he tried it with the Strasbourg Theatre in France. Then he was about to try it at the Julliard School, but he was too old then and too ill to develop it further.

He believed that a school, a training academy, and a professional company worked together, hand in hand. This theatre, here, is a tribute to his design. We saw that he had spent his life trying to get that theatre into existence. In a sense I said, "It sounds like the best idea in the whole world; let me have a go at it."[10]

Michel Saint-Denis (1897–1971) was Jacques Copeau's nephew and formed his own theatre in the 1930s called the

*Compagnie des Quinze* (company of fifteen) composed of former Copeau students. The company performed in the remodeled Vieux Colombier Theatre and was known for its ensemble playing. When it toured London in 1934, one person impressed by its playing was Tyrone Guthrie, who subsequently invited Saint-Denis to operate the London Theatre School from 1935 to 1939 and to direct at the Old Vic. Around Saint-Denis and Guthrie was created a new school of acting in England attended by the likes of Edith Evans, Flora Robson, Peggy Ashcroft, Laurence Olivier, Maurice Evans, Michael Redgrave, Alec Guiness, Ralph Richardson, Anthony Quayle, and others.

After World War II, Michael Saint-Denis, with the assistance of George Devine and Glen Byam Shaw, established a theatre school in coordination with the Old Vic. It was called the Young Vic School, and its members performed for children in the newly patched Old Vic Theatre, which had suffered bomb damage.

Saint-Denis had great respect for the ensemble company of the Group Theatre. He saw their attempt to create an ensemble company in America as vital to the art of the actor, as was illustrated when he said, "look at the American Group Theatre. Did they not bring something new to realism itself? Will not their names go down in theatrical history because they were based on an attempt at permanence and continuity?"[11]

Saint-Denis' understanding of the need for continuity enabled him to bring to England Copeau's ideals of acting technique. He formed the connection between the continental and English styles of acting. Saint-Denis described the connection in his book *Theatre: The Rediscovery of Style*:

Unity of style can be obtained only by working together and getting used to each other's physical and emotional reactions. Occasionally one may succeed without it and directors and actors of genius delight in winning against the odds: it's so much more exciting! But a theatre cannot establish an artistic policy unless it gathers together a well composed group of collaborators around a permanent company of actors, with partial renewal every year.

Even a variety of interesting plays and the talent of a director is not enough to give expression to a policy without the continuity of the actor's presence. For it is the company that gives the place its spirit. The public is attached to men and women they can see in the flesh.[12]

Saint-Denis believed that continuity of style is created by a permanent company and that the education of young actors is the essence of creating a tradition, two ideas that parallel Ball's philosophy. Saint-Denis saw his role as an *ensemblier*: "An *ensemblier*, according to the dictionary, is 'an artist who aims at unity of general effect.' We were '*ensembliers*.' We set out to develop initiative, freedom, and a sense of responsibility in the individual, as long as he or she was ready and able to merge his personal qualities into the ensemble."[13]

Like Copeau, Saint-Denis saw the theatrical artist as a servant to the playwright. The primary artist was the writer, all other work on plays was interpretation of the script. However, he realized that the only way an actor could interpret well was through strong and precise technical skill: "We applied certain other basic principles in order that techniques should never be allowed to dominate and supersede invention and interfere with what is called truth. But we impressed on everybody that there was no possibility of expressing truth, especially truth to a theatrical style, without a strongly developed technique."[14]

Developing technique demanded classwork before performance. The actor needed to learn his craft (a philosophy that also mirrored Ball's). Saint-Denis explained some of the rigor of his school: "For the student's interpretative work we like to use whole plays or acts rather than isolated scenes, so that they would learn to consider their relationship with the other actors and to relative values of the different parts of the play. For detailed work on language and textual style, we used scenes from plays only in exceptional circumstances."[15]

The actual length of the learning process was two years in England (the first year at the Young Vic and the second at the Drama School) and three years at Strasbourg. According to Saint-Denis, three years was the ideal length of time to spend in the classroom, and he was quick to point out that in Russia the length of the acting course was four years.[16] Three years was the minimum length of teaching that a training actor needed, "mainly because of the lengthy nature of the work that has to be done on the voice and on the practice of language in various styles."[17] According to Saint-Denis, the purpose of his schools was "to bring reality to the interpretation of all theatrical styles, particularly the classical, and to achieve the greatest possible freedom in their practice," and "to enlarge the actor's field of expression and to equip him in such a way that he could mime, sing, dance, perform acrobatic tricks, without specializing beyond the normal requirements of an actor."[18]

In order to meet acting demands, the school first trained the actor's body ("which is the first technical need of the actor") and then began vocal training, which was never-ending during the actor-education process.[19] Criticism by all instructors was encouraged, and the first opportunity to criticize students' work came after the first-year student's initial performance of a Shakespeare play in England following a three-week rehearsal period. All instructors kept in constant touch with each other in order to provide students with a continuity of criticism.

The training was broken into sections—"cultural, technical and a central section that was concerned with improvisation and interpretation"—but there was never an attempt to isolate one section from the others.[20] "Each section was approached from a dramatic point of view. Academic attitudes were avoided. Behind all scholarly knowledge or intellectual considerations there had to be the requirements of dramatic necessity."[21] While movement and language training were essentially the responsibilities of the directors of those particular divisions at Saint-Denis' schools, students always had contact with the directors of interpretation and improvisation.

It was Saint-Denis' belief that an actor must begin his training with the classical plays that are full of verse and poetic images. That material would lead the actor toward the realization of character by means of the playwright's words. To Saint-Denis, realism was a style that left much unsaid and, as such, a beginning actor would not have the facility to discover a character or a truth. Realistic acting on a Chekhov text, for example, could be done only after classical training.

Saint-Denis' schools never completely bridged the gap between a training institute and a professional theatre. The Young Vic students performed for children while the Strasbourg students performed for young audiences and toured often. However, Saint-Denis' intention was not to deprive the students of professional experience: "A school of this kind should not exist in isolation. It should be *related to an actual theatre*, the actors from which might find it profitable, from time to time, to return to school, to improve or develop one aspect or another of their talent."[22]

### Eclectic Training, Not "Method"

The unfulfilled dream of simultaneous performance and training is the basis of Ball's conservatory-theatre concept. However, Ball also felt the need to root his theatre in a particularly American style of acting. His theatre was intentionally called the American Conservatory Theatre to reflect the fact that the enterprise was indigenously American.

In addition to the Group Theatre and the Actor's Studio, an actor-training institute that had an impact on postwar American theatre was the Yale Drama School. During the 1940s and 1950s the acting department of Yale was said to have been dominated by Constance Welch,* a former voice teacher whose eclectic approach to actor training was reputed to have run counter to internal method acting, and whose influence on American acting has never been fully understood. Welch developed exercises that added to the inner motivational structure. "She never denied that as a foundation," said Goldsby.

Both the original conservatory director, Goldsby, and his successor, Allen Fletcher, had been students of Welch. While she had a strong interest in speech, Constance Welch seems to have had a deep understanding of the problems of acting as well, be

---

* Very little has been written about Constance Welch. The opinions expressed in this chapter were compiled through interviews with four of her former students: Thomas Tyrell, professor of acting at San Francisco State University (interviewed on 23 April 1982); Christopher Hampton, Ph.D., professor of theatre at San Francisco State University (interviewed on 26 April 1982); Allen Fletcher, former conservatory director of ACT (interviewed on 23 November 1981), and Robert Goldsby, professor of theatre at the University of California at Berkeley (interviewed on 27 October 1981).

they physical, vocal, or motivational. Because she seems to have been able to determine just what device or language was necessary to correct the acting flaws of her students, she was never stamped as having created just one method of acting; rather, she was known as a master of eclectic training. This style of training was precisely the style that Ball chose to use in building the technical skill of his actors, though he too never fully discarded the Method tradition. "'Do the act and the feeling will follow' is Ball's byword," wrote Eric Atkins in the *Saint Petersburg Times* in 1969. "His belief is that the very muscular contractions will help to release the feeling in the actor. 'Within the four basics—dynamics, pitch, rate and volume—lies the perfect architecture of a sentence.' Ball tells us . . . through all the other technique that is taught at A.C.T., it is obvious that Ball considers the voice as the actor's most important instrument." [23]

One of the greatest criticisms of Method acting was its concentration on emotional truth at the cost of vocal or physical expression. By concentrating on the external first, Ball chose sides in an old acting argument: internal versus external presentation. Denis Diderot (1713–1784), who had been fascinated by David Garrick's ability to transmit emotion through the manipulation of the expressions of his face, wrote an argument for the external-first style of acting in his *Paradox of Acting*.

If the actor were full, really full of feeling, how could he play the same part twice running with the same spirit and success? Full of fire at the first performance he would be worn out and cold as marble at the third. But take it that he is an attentive mimic and thoughtful disciple of nature, then the first time he comes on stage . . . faithful copying of himself and the effects he has arrived at, and constantly observing human nature, will so prevail that his acting, far from losing in force, will gather strength with the new observations he will make from time to time. He will increase or moderate his effects, and you will be more and more pleased with him . . . the actor who plays from imitation of some ideal type, from imagination, from memory, will be one and the same at all performances, will be always at his best mark; he has considered, combined, learnt, and arranged the whole thing in his head; his diction is neither monotonous nor dissonant. His passion has a definite course—it has bursts, and it has reactions; it has a beginning, a middle and an end. The accents are the same, the positions are the same, the movements are the same; if there is any difference between two performances, the latter is generally better.[24]

This argument between the outside-in and the inside-out philosophy of acting has never been resolved. The realization that a company like ACT would choose to "do the act first" as a starting point for its training helps to clarify what was used as the curriculum of the conservatory.[25] Still, Ball did not wish to eliminate Method acting from the education of his actors or students. Said Ball:

No. . . . We are not anti-Method as we understand that term. We want our actors to have as many methods as they need to fulfill themselves and make them feel freer. We want our actors to perfect techniques and not rely solely on feeling.

In our company the younger people learn from the experienced artists. What a wonderful thing it would have been, for instance, to have had a Bert Lahr in a permanent company who could pass on his knowledge to young people. The heritage could have been preserved.[26]

Instead of narrowing to externals the possible experiences of the actors during training, ACT trainers undertook to synthesize internal style and external technique: "The Method relies upon the use of his emotional and sense memory, the human relationship between himself and the character he is portraying. Ball considers it basic to any actor's training. However, he adds, it is inadequate when it becomes the only tool a performer brings to every assignment. A.C.T. combines Method principles with constant and rigorous exploration of every actor's vocal, physical, emotional, and intellectual resources."[27]

The conservatory itself was meant to educate not only students, but also the practicing professional actors in the company. Allen Fletcher explained: "people that worked here, actors, were expected also to be teachers and students at the same time. That was the basic philosophy which was behind it. That has evolved into the fact that we now have what is formally called a school, a professional school which takes students and trains them to a point to where we feel they can be useful actors in the best repertory company in this country, our own."[28]

## *The Beginning of a Structure of Training*

The evolution of the conservatory into a school took place over the first six years of ACT's existence, beginning in Pittsburgh in 1965. There was a twofold program of education in progress during ACT's initial Pittsburgh season, one for the students of Carnegie and the other the aborted company training called exploratories.

During A.C.T.'s first season in Pittsburgh, Pennsylvania, in 1965, the student program consisted of a curriculum of study offered to students of Carnegie Institute of Technology (now Carnegie-Mellon University). Students received a minimum of 20 hours of class study per week and were directed in one studio production per semester giving no less than two performances. In addition, trainees received three hours per week of study in stage and costume design. Trainers in almost every case were members of the A.C.T. company. Emphasis was on innovation—experimental techniques brought to A.C.T. by the trainers from other schools and companies.[29]

Ball instituted for his actors less structured classes, the exploratories, which consisted of informal voluntary seminars. The topics of the seminars ranged from comedy to melodrama to outrageous imitation. Ball explained the rationale for the exploratories:

At that time my idea was, I would watch the actors after the performance and they would sit around the bar for an hour and a half or two and unwind after performances. They'd be so vigorous and so splashy and imaginative in the bar, I thought what a waste of all that creative energy—if we could give them as much beer as they wanted, or booze and hamburgers or whatever they wanted to eat, but we would use the creative energy ... [in] what we called exploratories. Actors' Equity got down on us and they ultimately wrote rule number sixty-three, which was written specifically for my benefit, to prohibit any form of party or classes. First of all we had classes and they said, "You must not have any classes." So we said, "Well, we'll have parties." Then they rewrote the "law" so you couldn't have classes or parties or anything resembling company meetings required or voluntary.[30]

The Actors' Equity ruling was later renumbered as rule sixty-four. It reads "All members of the company are prohibited from attending so-called voluntary classes, and the theatre agrees not to request members to attend such classes."[31]

Subsequently, ACT was able to negotiate a "rider" for the actors' standard contracts whereby the actors would mutually agree to train as required, or to teach along with their normal acting duties of rehearsals and performances. Equity permitted a work week of up to fifty-two hours. The time not used in rehearsal or performance could be devoted to taking classes. With the new agreement, ACT was given more freedom to institutionalize an actual training program in its San Francisco seasons.

Mark Zeller, a voice teacher with ACT's first San Francisco company, was made nominal head of the conservatory in early 1967. Some classes were held then for the company members, and six students were accepted and used as apprentices in small and walk-on roles of the repertory.

### The Initial Summer Training Program

Applications were taken for a summer training program in 1967. Two hundred applicants were processed and auditioned, and more than forty students were accepted. Most of the ACT acting company was on tour to Stanford and Ravinia, which left only a few members in San Francisco to teach. It was during this ten-week, three-hundred-hour program period that Robert Goldsby was named director of the conservatory. Goldsby recalled being asked to devise the summer program: "Bushnell started talking to me about it (the summer program) because I was, after all, a professional teacher for years. There was a lot of jockeying around about what the program was going to be. Of course, there were classes at ACT the first year, but they were for the company."[32]

The training program proved to be a successful pilot for what eventually was called the Summer Training Congress. The following season's classes were taught to the company again and a small number of students were taken on as fellows. The fellows performed in class projects and in minor roles during the 1967–1968 season. Up to this point in ACT's history the conservatory had not developed past courses for the company members and peripheral, apprentice-like students. It was in the summer of 1968 that the conservatory arm of ACT began to mature and take shape as a school. Ball decided to have a ten-week intensive program for two hundred students during the summer: "The aim of the Congress was to introduce the student/actor to the theatre techniques which must be studied and developed over a much longer period if the student wants to pursue an acting career."[33]

Goldsby thought the task one of gigantic proportions:

Bill was insistent that we do this very large training program for a number of reasons. One, he believed in thinking big like that. He thought it was a way of getting national attention. Two, it would be a real big source of income. Three, he thought there was no reason why we couldn't use existing facilities and people on the staff to teach. Four, he had already sent out this huge colored poster, that I didn't even know about. . . . I was told that it was my responsibility to do this thing. . . . I, naturally, kind of fell into this position. They gave me an assistant and said, go to it. Four months later we had the first training congress and we had two hundred students and we did this program and it was very successful.[34]

The Summer Training Congress of 1968 was ambitious, as were all of ACT's activities in the 1967–1968 period. In an attempt to accomplish the original goals that Ball had set for the company, the congress was formed quickly, but with a sound philosophical ideal behind it. The congress was also a precursor to the actual Conservatory Advanced Training Program which was being plotted for the fall of 1969. While some of those teaching were specialists (Mark Zeller in speech, Frank Ottiwell in the Alexander technique), most were actors in the repertory company. The use of actors as teachers gave fruit to Ball's theory that young actors should learn from practicing professionals. Goldsby explained: "Most of the students came from colleges around the country. . . . [Here at ACT] they were working with actors in a professional theatre. So they had the authority . . . these actors would say, 'I don't know how to teach.' We'd sit down and talk about it and they'd start. But they knew something about acting and they would have a different tone. . . .

they just started working on scenes and told the students about how they went about rehearsing.[35]

The opportunity for students to study with the professional actors was a revolution in theatre training. Deborah Sussel, an original actor-teacher during the first Summer Training Congress explained the effect of the ACT training ideal: "A lot of the reason why ACT is so exciting, professional, and stimulating is there really is an opportunity for these people not to be in a kind of unreal world of the drama school, but to be in a real theatre world."[36]

Another aim of the Summer Training Congress was to give as many actors as was possible full-year employment, an aim that was in keeping with one of the cornerstones of the ensemble philosophy of ACT of providing continuity of employment for the actors. The actors could stay in residence during the summer by teaching, thereby ensuring employment. By the 1968–1969 season, year-round employment was almost a reality for many ACT actors.

## The Advanced Training Program

Problems became evident as the conservatory program embarked on a larger scale in the fall of 1968. The biggest problem was scheduling classes so that they did not interfere with rehearsals. The 1968–1969 season had a sixteen-play schedule in repertory, and since many teachers were used in productions, time conflicts were inevitable. Goldsby stated, "When we started the '68–69 season there was a full-time training program scheduled while the company was rehearsing all these plays. It became even more manic. This time the training ran into more substantial problems . . . the basically simple reason was that in the summer everybody was there for every class and there were just ten weeks of teaching; nobody had outside commitments. However, in the fall and winter all the teachers were actors, directors. . . . It created an extremely difficult teaching situation."[37]

The breakneck pace of acting, rehearsing, training, and teaching kept ACT members on the verge of hysteria. Goldsby described this high state of energy:

It was part of ACT that you were doing fifty different things at the same time. That was just part of the excitement of the place. So one adapted to teaching that way and the students adapted to learning that way. They got a lot of different sort of things out of it . . . it was wide and varied and exciting and flamboyant. Their days were filled with doing things, meeting all kinds of people, watching different directors work. I defended it many times because it was not like a university situation. It was not like the Actor's Studio. It was another kind of learning, and a kind of learning that had a meaning and a rationale and a kind of pragmatic excitement about it.[38]

The 1969–1970 season, which saw much internal dissension and many changes, was the first year of the conservatory's Advanced Training Program, also known as the ATP. It was produced by Allen Fletcher, who became the conservatory director. The ATP with its structured one-year program of class work, was a step toward institutionalizing the training program. The small number of students accepted were used as walk-ons and bit players in the new modified repertory. Fletcher explained: "Under Bob [Goldsby], who sort of ran what at that time we called a training program, [the students] were really more like apprentices in a stock company. They did walk-ons and they had classes: occasionally they did sort of projects. When Bob quit and I began running the program, I tried to make it a little more scheduled. I tried to make it a little more officially . . . school.[39]

With the shorter repertory and only the Geary Theatre in use, Fletcher was able to keep more students in class. He also was able to create a more serious atmosphere of training. Recalled Fletcher,

We got rid of some people who simply weren't interested in being students, who just wanted to be on the fringe of the company and come in and do walk-ons, and maybe become an actor by osmosis. [The ATP] got formalized amazingly fast, within two maybe three years we had a system that is basically the same system that we are using now. That is a two-year school, a two-year program. For the first couple of years it was sort of one year, as far as classes went. If you hung around and you came back, you were sort of a junior member of the company.

The more serious attention placed on the school atmosphere and the lessening demand for stage time on these young actors helped the conservatory to organize itself in a short time. By 1972, only four years after the first Summer Training Congress, ACT stabilized its conservatory and kept the same basic structure for the next decade. The number of students that entered into the first year was approximately forty-five. The second year approximately one-half of those students were invited back for more advanced training. With this structure in place, ACT easily rivalled any American theatrical training institute. ACT also paralleled the size and type of actor education envisioned by Michel Saint-Denis when he created his school in England.

## The Mechanics of Training

The first requirement of the students in training was that they possess a certain attitude, one of positation, that would influence their entire experience. (From 1972 onward Ball had personal meetings with these students during the first or second week of their training.) The philosophy of positation demanded that each student find something good or positive to say about anything that was attempted during his or her classwork. Ball transmitted the idea that each student had the right to fail, and that learning only proceeded from this base. The idea of being positive also helped to create the ultimate goal of ACT, that being the unity of the company's work or the ensemble playing of all actors in the company. Fletcher explained the effects of positive thinking: "This is a philosophy which comes essentially from Bill's positation. . . . The philosophy behind this is what one feels in the productions, a spirit in the rep company and in the school, itself, an unusual amount of energy which goes into the productions."

The training was structured around the idea that students could try any acting technique without fear of failure, thus permitting the training at ACT to be eclectic rather than bound to one school of acting. Eclecticism shaped what might be termed ACT's style of acting. Fletcher explained the choices he and his staff made when creating the classes that were available to the conservatory students:

[The training] places a great deal of emphasis on what I call mechanical skills, skills which have to do with the training of the body, the flexibility in the use of the voice, equipping an actor to do anything in the repertory. In terms of the approach to acting, it is Stanislavsky-based, as almost everything is. My own taste in acting is not original. It is shaped by teachers like Constance Welch at Yale, Lee Strasberg at the Actor's Studio. It is shaped a lot by that and by whatever contributions I can make to this acting theory and techniques out of my experience and everything that I have tried over the last thirty years. It has to do with the truth of basic communication on the stage just as strongly as it has to do with a necessity for those bodily skills, verbal and vocal skills, but also a great truth of mainly communications and vitality that comes from commitment to your imaginative given circumstances and your objectives.

In order to create a synthesis of skill and communication, the teaching staff at the ATP worked closely together, never segregating one aspect of training from any other. In essence, this aspect of ACT mirrored the structure of Michel Saint-Denis' schools, whereby the different divisions were in constant communication with each other: "What is admirable about us is that we all work together. The voice teachers recognize the necessity for truthful communication and motivation, just as much as the acting teachers are the first ones to tell the students that they need to work vocally and acquire those skills."

The atmosphere of open communication among trainers and the positive attitude encouraged among the students resulted in a healthy learning situation. The students were encouraged to take risks and were shown a number of acting techniques and theories. The training as a whole was bent toward creating what Ball saw as the essential qualities of a professional actor: "a powerful stage presence, a vigorous and agile body, intelligence, endurance, kindness and an ensemble spirit." [40]

The courses offered to the students during their two-year residence were required courses. The classes were given in the ACT classrooms, all of which were on the premises (the two adjacent buildings that ACT's conservatory and administration occupied were at 450 and 466 Geary Street respectively, across from the Geary Theatre, which was ACT's performance space). The rehearsing of the repertory plays also took place at the same address. Therefore, during the course of a day there was a constant intermingling between the repertory actors and the students of the ATP.

### The First-Year Students

With the division made by 1972 between the first-year and second-year students, a curriculum was devised for each portion. The first-year students were scheduled to train for forty hours a week, five days, Monday through Friday. The training took place over thirty-one weeks, roughly parallel with the repertory season. The first-year students' work was strictly classroom work; the students did no performing with the ACT repertory company. The training focused on the fundamental acting skills necessary for repertory acting, meaning the "development of the physical instrument and the actor's technical skills," and the "development of the actor's work process."[41]

The class was broken into three sections of not more than fifteen each to ensure that students received individual attention. A daily schedule of classes was maintained for the proper balance of classes. The following is a list of the classes offered to the first-year student:

| | |
|---|---|
| Voice | 3 hrs/wk |
| Phonetics and Ear Training | 3 hrs/wk for the first 6 wks |
| Scansion | 1½ hrs/wk every 2 wks |
| Dance | 2 hrs/wk |
| Ballet | 2 hrs/wk |
| Tap | 2 hrs/wk |
| Awareness in Movement (Alexander and Feldenkrais) | 1½ hrs/wk |

| | |
|---|---|
| Fencing and Combat | 1½ hrs/wk |
| Singing | 1 hr/wk |
| Working Theatre Technique (gymnastics, mime, voice) | 2 hrs/wk for 10 wks |
| History and Period Style | 1½ hrs/wk |
| Music Theory | 1 hr/wk |
| Acting | (Remainder of the time per wk[42] as scheduled) |

These classes were shifted to accommodate scene work or other special gatherings requiring student attendance for a large block of time. Among these assemblages were the performances of scenes by the first-year students in each week of the first ten weeks of training. Every student was expected to prepare a scene for presentation every three weeks during that period of time. The scenes were viewed as works-in-progress, so that students did not feel an unnatural performance anxiety. The course work up to the time of these performances was integrated into the rehearsal and preparation of scenes. The actual performances were not open to a general audience, but were used specifically as a learning process for the students. The performances were critiqued by the staff on "the basis of acting process and technique rather than interpretation."[43]

When the first ten weeks were over, the student actors began work on their first projects. The projects consisted of rehearsing the plays of an American playwright; for example, William Inge, N. Richard Nash, Clifford Odets, Arthur Miller, or Eugene O'Neill. In this way the students were able to draw upon their knowledge of American literature as well as on their own indigenous understanding of their country and environment: "The projects are directed by acting teachers, who function primarily as tutors or coaches, guiding the students in the application of their process and lightly coordinating the individual actor's work into an interpretation of the play."[44]

The time allotted to "acting" sections was used for rehearsal during this period. The technical classes continued on a revised schedule to accommodate the needs of rehearsals and performances. These projects warranted the same attention for criticism as did the scenes. Performances were open to interested company members in addition to all the students and trainers.

After the first projects were completed, a period of seven to eight weeks was spent on scene work and classwork until a second set of projects was introduced. The second project was to pose an atmospheric problem; for instance, one of difficult language, or unfamiliar locale. The difficulties faced in the second project were meant to challenge the newly acquired skills of the students in their technical and acting classes. Under conditions identical to those of the first projects, rehearsals began on plays written by some of the following playwrights: Pinero, Terrance Rattigan, James Barrie, Jean Anouilh, and Ferenc Molnar. Criticism followed the performances of the projects.

Trainers wrote reports twice yearly on both first-year and second-year students that evaluated their progress on the following disciplines: physical skills, speech, voice, and acting. At the end of the school year approximately half the entering class would be invited to return for a second year of training.

The selection process created an inevitable atmosphere of competition among the actors. This competitive atmosphere was considered important by the staff, reflecting the fact that the world of theatre outside of the ATP was harsh. This realization brought into focus the insular nature of the conservatory; since the size of the ACT company could not expand infinitely, there was a pervasive hope that what was learned by the rejected students would be transmitted to other theatres through out the country. In this way, ACT could have a nationwide impact on acting standards and on theatre life in general in the United States.

## The Second-Year Students

The students who were chosen for the second year of training were expected to perform with the repertory company. This meant that they attended rehearsals with the company members and began to exercise the skills they had been taught while they still were continuing their training.

After an initial individual review was made of each second-year student they began work in more technical classes. Initially scene work centered on the works of Shakespeare, and speech and articulation practice became more focused and intensive. The class work was also bent more toward the performance of material, as opposed to the more sheltered work in the first-year class.

By the third month of the season the students began rehearsing "genre" plays, naturalistic plays that involved the understanding of a particular period and style in history. Chekhov was most frequently employed in these projects, although Gorky and Yeats were used as substitutes. Twelve weeks of rehearsal for these projects were scheduled. The emphasis was on discovery rather than on mere performance. Students, teachers, company members, and invited guests viewed the project, and criticism was offered at the end. All classroom work was geared toward a full understanding of the period and style of the chosen project.

A second project, begun immediately following the end of the genre plays, made greater demands on the actors. Plays chosen for this project were normally either Shakespearean, Restoration, or eighteenth-century in period. Essential costumes, props, and scenic elements were employed as was required by the script. The performance of this more difficult range of material culminated the two years of training and onstage experiences.

## An ACT Style

The two-year training put into effect by Allen Fletcher by 1972 differed markedly from that of Michel Saint-Denis. In fact, training was the converse of Saint-Denis' curriculum. ACT stressed the naturalistic and familiar first, whereas Saint-Denis emphasized the lyric and unfamiliar first, leaving the naturalistic for last. ACT had developed an indigenous style, in which American playwrights were initially performed while continuing training of the voice and body enabled students to tackle difficult material requiring technical proficiency by the culmination of the work. The ultimate impact of the Group Theatre's ensemble style had taken shape in naturalistic training, which served as the base for other training in acting technique. Specific objectives and imaginative exercises were the foundation of the acting school of the ATP. After the students understood these basics, they could apply them to all unfamiliar material.

ACT training, like Saint-Denis' training, strongly emphasized technical skill. For both first-year and second-year students, classes in voice, phonetics, singing, dance, and movement were held throughout the course. In an effort to round out this technical training, ACT introduced several classes that were an attempt to stretch the students' capabilities. Most notable of these subjects were yoga, Alexander (a technique of body alignment), and classes created by Ball including Yat (described later), laughter, and connotations. The addition of these subjects contributed heavily to the distinctive ACT style of acting. As Mike Steele of the *Minneapolis Tribune* pointed out, "For all the variety of plays, there is an A.C.T. style, a very theatrical style devised by Ball based on technical skills. It's a physical, commedia del'arte style, the opposite of the Method, which begins with physical activity and works inward toward inner emotions."[45]

For the most part, the actors Ball employed during ACT's first years had the energetic quality of acting that has been the company's hallmark. (Two of Ball's standout comedic actors during the first five seasons were René Auberjonois and the late Michael O'Sullivan.) The ensemble playing of these actors created the ACT style, an achievement that can, in part, be credited to the "in-training" attitude that Ball instilled. Julius Novick of the *New York Times* observed,

Perhaps because of the Conservatory, perhaps because the actors have been cannily chosen, perhaps because of the way they are directed, this company is developing a style distinctively its own.

His actors address themselves to the spectators first of all; they and their directors seem always conscious of the need to be interesting, picturesque, vivid, "theatrical." Their work is designed, shaped, elaborated, figuratively and often literally; these actors like to wear capes, and to swirl them—not at random, but in different ways at different times, to express different things.[46]

The physical acting and energetic staging that typified ACT's presentations lent verve to the comic plays that were performed. The playing of comedy was considered to be ACT's forte. (ACT's comic bill during the first San Francisco season included *Beyond the Fringe, Charley's Aunt, Man and Superman, Arsenic and Old Lace, Dear Liar, Tartuffe,* and *Torch Bearers.*) Part of Ball's philosophy was that American actors were not taught comic techniques in the Method school, and he sought to rectify that training flaw. Novick praised ACT's comic abilities: "[Ball] mentioned the lack of opportunity most young American actors have to learn its sparkling techniques. The double-take, the timing and the style that comedy demands. But he did not stress what he had in mind, in 1967. Indeed perhaps he did not know. Now, however, there can be no question that A.C.T. is the outstanding company in the United States as far as the Comic-Muse is concerned."[47]

Though its strength lay in comic performances, one of the most notable aspects of ACT during the first five San Francisco seasons was its ability to handle an eclectic schedule. While Ball's stamp on his company's style was indelible, he employed several other directors and, as noted elsewhere, allowed each to practice their art free of any interference. (Some of the directors of the first five seasons were: René Auberjonois, Richard A. Dysart, Allen Fletcher, Edward Hastings, Jerome Kilty, Edward Payson Call, Robert Goldsby, Nagle Jackson, Gower Champion, Edward Sherin, Francis Ford Coppola, Jack O'Brien, and Ellis Rabb). No matter which director was working, the actors had a common language among themselves that they developed from working closely together and taking ACT training.

The actors attained their common language through a series of artistic choices made by Ball in his training philosophy. Ball explained what an actor needed to know and what he needed to be capable of doing on stage at any time:

He had to know the phonetic alphabet and be able to have complete command of every sound that came out of his mouth. He had to have a powerful and interesting voice, to know how many inflections there are in the English language and to know how to use them. An actor had to know how to laugh on cue, to know how to structure Shakespeare or any language that was written before the twentieth century. . . . . He must know how to fence, to fall, to fight without being hurt, to dance, tap-dance, to play musical instruments, to play guitars, banjos and pianos. An actor has to know how to sing, to sight read. An actor should know how to put himself into what is known as presence or thereness, he has to know how to place himself. An actor has to know how to listen carefully. He has to know how to rehearse, how to break down a script. . . . An actor should be skilled, in my opinion, in meditation and yoga, things that are not in formal education.[48]

Because Ball felt that the time had arrived to create a school that addressed these actors' needs, he sought teachers capable of giving proper instruction. It was with this intention that he popularized several areas of actor training, including the teaching of scansion, phonetics, yoga, Yat, Alexander, and comic technique.

Ball himself taught the initial classes in comic technique, which included classes in laughter, double-take, and timing. He also taught a class in suspense, which centered on the actor's ability to keep an audience from knowing an important fact in a story. Ball's class in connotations analyzed nonverbal gestures used to elucidate the story as well as feeling and position of dominance during scenes of a play. Ball gave examples:

Do you remember when the Miser gives away a gold piece? When he parts with the money, the money won't leave his hand. The coin won't leave his hand no matter how hard he tries to give away the money. . . . Very simple things like when people die they usually lie down in some manner of speaking. It's funny, in the last act of *Tiny Alice*, the man is dying but he talks for two pages and it's hard to connote to the audience that he is dying because he is so energetic. This consideration is from Shakespeare's advice to the players: "suit the action to the word and the word to the action."[49]

The method of teaching speech that ACT used was influenced by the late Edith Skinner, a master teacher at Carnegie and later at Julliard, and also at ACT's ATP. Her techniques included the teaching of Shakespearean scansion and phonetics, an art neglected by many American acting schools during the 1950s. Skinner explained her philosophy of the importance of stage speech in her book, *Speak with Distinction*:

Since it is generally accepted that: through voice and speech, more than any other qualities, the actor lays bare before the audience the *soul* of the character impersonated . . . . since, the word expresses the meaning of what the actor says, and, his *tone of voice* reveals his feelings about what he says, the actor's vehicle for carrying words, the voice, must be flexible. . . . So that, he can reveal the inner feelings of the most hidden emotions he is portraying: in the most effective, convincing, revelatory and satisfactory way that is possible.

The speech of the character must *bring to life* the character itself.[50]

A catch-all heading for what seemed to be a mysterious subject at ACT was "Yat." The Yat system is a jargon phrase for the Yat Malmgren movement, a gesture discipline method for actors. (Yat Malmgren, presently working in London, is a Swedish movement teacher who expanded upon Rudolph Laban's exercises of gesture to aid an actor's communication on stage.) Yat Malmgren has used his teaching techniques in London since 1954 and taught several times in the ATP during the 1970s. In 1960, he explained his philosophy of movement in an article called "The Actor and his Actions":

That an actor shall be able to move well is not at all to say that he should move in a particular way, but simply to insist that no barrier may interpose itself between the emotion he entertains and the audience to which he addresses himself. This is a technical achievement that should lie within the range of any actor, given the will to improvement. In so doing he will also obtain certain important by-products: stamina, awareness, a common terminology through which he can make a direct approach to the problem of his work and avoid the wordy circumlocutions into which technical discussions usually disintegrate. He will also obtain a sense of communion within a group.[51]

Besides Yat Malmgren and Edith Skinner, several outstanding voice teachers, including the late opera singer Robert Weede, joined ACT's impressive staff over the years. All these teachers have helped to shape the company's highly technical acting style, thus fulfilling Ball's original goal of bringing together the finest teachers to train his actors. The training itself has also fulfilled the goal of setting standards for the art and practice of acting. Therefore, Ball can be seen as a builder of ensemble spirit within a company or, to use the better word employed by Michel Saint-Denis, an *ensemblier*.

# 7

# The Acting Company

## ACT: A Sense of Community

When actors were contracted by the American Conservatory Theatre they were expected to do more than merely rehearse one role and play one part. ACT, from its inception, was a repertory company. An actor could expect to play in several plays and have several roles, sometimes alternating major roles on the same day. Also, as chapter 6 made clear, an actor was expected to train. Another aspect of working at ACT for some actors was the teaching of either acting or a specialty. Finally, some actors also doubled as directors. All this activity made ACT a unique environment. The actors' duties were varied in order "to restore to the creative artist, himself, the right to leadership in shaping and fulfilling his own potential."[1]

Two very important accomplishments crucial to ACT's success must be credited to Ball. The first was his ability to attract many talented and willing actors to adhere to ACT's philosophy, and the second was his maintenance of a creative environment for the actors. Ball had a successful track record before ACT, beginning with his production of *Ivanov*. The environment he created with ACT was based on both cooperation and an almost monastic approach to performance, with actors spending their nights and days onstage.[2] Ball recalled his emphasis on a positive attitude when the actors first formed a company in 1965: "I asked them to work from an attitude which would form a uniting principle of governance to work which, essentially, was a positive attitude. I had been in a lot of theatre situations in my experience where the attitude was most destructive and difficult. The frequent characteristics were such that a lot of times individuals were running down each other's energies and making it absolutely oppressive and stressful. So we said we'd do it a different way, and we'd limit ourselves to positive thought."[3] [All quotes from William Ball throughout this chapter are drawn from the personal interview cited in note 3.]

The most important aspect of the creative environment for the acting company was performance in repertory. Under the conditions of repertory, an ACT actor could anticipate playing in many different types of plays and, during the height of a season, in several styles of plays during the space of a week. Thus, the repertory element was an added strength in ACT's ability to attract and interest good actors. Ball explained: "We have perpetuated the belief that repertory theatre can work, that it is healthful to the actors, and that rotating repertory is the best form of theatre. We have also illustrated or added this piece of information to the general theatre history: a theatre company that is dedicated to the health of the actors is likely to produce the best possible theatre."

When Ball formed ACT he sought actors who would agree with his basic premise, and who were not "dogged soloists." His overall purpose was to sustain the continuity he desired in his company. A man prone to metaphors, Ball explained how he envisioned the ACT ensemble: "I have this feeling that we're all going down a river in our tiny, tiny little boats and . . . I like the feeling of a lot of boats going more or less at the same rate and more or less in the same direction without too much incident. There is always incident, but the refinement of incident becomes the songs, the chants that are passed on forth, from boat to boat, the needs that are fulfilled, without being asked because what one boat wants to be rid of, another boat is in search of."

Thus, Ball looked for actors who displayed not only talent but also a "positive free spirit first. I look for enthusiasm and imagination." He considered these virtues necessary because of the intradependence of members of the ACT community.

The community of artists at ACT has been depicted from its earliest days as having the atmosphere of a family. Al Alu, an actor with the company both during its Pittsburgh and San Francisco years, was quoted as saying in a 1967 press release, "It may sound corny but there aren't any other words to describe A.C.T. except to say it's a family. We have the conflicts from time to time that you find in any large group, but we are all theatre people. We know each other as few people outside theatre ever get to know one another because we work together under constant tension."[4]

In fact, Alu even suggested that the itinerant period helped to solidify the feeling of community within the company. He pinpointed this feeling to June 1966, when ACT was in residence in East Haddam, Connecticut. Alu explained: "It was like a kibbutz. We worked together and we played together. We were only doing two shows so we had more free time than usual."[5]

An analogy to ACT's stay in Connecticut during the early part of its history can be seen in a similar stay in Connecticut by the famed Group Theatre of the 1930s, where they too had an early residence. The isolation from other distractions may have helped forge the community spirit, but it was mainly through Ball's leadership that ACT found its philosophy of ensemble.

DeAnn Mears,* a charter member of ACT, felt that an early sign of the company becoming something "special" was its reception during its hectic Pittsburgh season.[6] ACT performed the repertory to overwhelmingly positive acceptance in Pittsburgh.

With the philosophies of ACT in place, the sense of a community of actors was strong from its inception. Still, not until the first full season, 1967–1968, when the hint of security emerged along with the feeling that the company had a perma-

---

* De Ann Mears came to ACT after an appearance on Broadway in Shaw's *Too Good To Be True* and was seen Off-Broadway as Gwendolyn Fairfax in *Earnest in Love* and in *A Sound of Silence* and *The Decameron*. She began her acting career in the national company of William Inge's *The Dark at the Top of the Stairs*. Some of the ACT productions she appeared in were *Tartuffe*, *Tiny Alice*, *Man and Superman*, and *Under Milkwood*.

nent home in San Francisco, did ACT truly begin to be an ensemble. Ray Reinhardt* explained the change in the company that season: "The first year of anything—the President's administration or anything—is a shakedown. I think it became a company when it found its permanent home in San Francisco."[7]

Frank Ottiwell,† ACT Alexander teacher and a company actor, concurred with Reinhardt on this point. Said Ottiwell, "when we moved [San Francisco] we moved with a family of two hundred people. It was a fabulous way to come to San Francisco . . . . in the first couple of years people didn't know other people, hadn't established lives outside at all. We literally lived together. The Curtain Call (a local bar) was another office. When you wanted to discuss your contract you did it at the Curtain Call. They posted the schedule there every day."[8]

The cohesiveness of the company, owing to what Bushnell termed their "monastic" commitment, was made possible and livable through Ball's philosophy of positation. Also contributing to the sense of community were the heavy demands on the actors' time compared with the less demanding schedule of most other theatres.

These great demands made on ACT's members during the first years in San Francisco are graphically illustrated by two incidents. The first was Jay Doyle's playing roles in two ACT plays (as described here) that were performed on the same night in ACT's two theatres, the Geary and the Marines'. "Doyle makes his appearance as Madam Pace, the brothel keeper in the second act of Pirandello's classic *Six Characters in Search of an*

---

* Ray Reinhardt appeared in the original New York production of *Tiny Alice*. He was well known for his performances at the Phoenix Theatre, including *Hamlet*, *The Plough and the Stars*, and *Henry IV*, as Iago in *Othello* and Mack the Knife in *The Threepenny Opera* at the Arena Stage in Washington, D.C. His early ACT roles included Sir Toby Belch in *Twelfth Night*, Peterbonon in *Thieves' Carnival*, Mr. Webb in *Our Town*, the First Voice in *Under Milkwood*, Astrov in *Uncle Vanya*, Mangiacavallo in *The Rose Tattoo*, and Stanley Kowalski in *A Streetcar Named Desire*.

†Frank Ottiwell came to San Francisco from Montreal via New York. His theatrical experience was gained first with the Canadian Art Theatre in Montreal. He began training in teaching Alexander technique in 1955. He performed in ACT's production of *The Three Sisters*.

*Author* at the Marines' Memorial Theatre. When he finishes his role in *Six Characters* he's due for the third act of Moliere's *Tartuffe* at the Geary Theatre two blocks away. He has only twelve minutes between the time he's off stage at the Marines' and his scheduled appearance in *Tartuffe*."[9]

The second illustration of the almost superhuman stamina required occurred during the same time period, in 1967. ACT had just opened its *Man and Superman* by Shaw, which includes one of the largest roles ever written in the English language, that of Jack Tanner. The role was played by René Auberjonois.* At that point, Auberjonois was ACT's leading comic actor and had endeared himself to the San Francisco audiences.[10] During the first week of the run of the Shaw play, Auberjonois lost his voice: when he was not in *Man and Superman*, he was performing in *Endgame* and in *Beyond the Fringe* (which he had directed), in addition to playing the leading role in *Tartuffe*. At the same time that he played these five roles, he was also in rehearsals for *Charley's Aunt* and *Under Milkwood*.

The circumstances were more than Auberjonois, with all his energy, could handle. However he did regain his health, proclaiming, "The only time [actors] complain is when they don't have enough work to do."[11]

Peter Donat,* who joined the ACT company in the 1967–1968 season, described the experience of coming into this hectic atmosphere of time-consuming rehearsal and performance:

When I arrived at ACT mid-season, 1968, I was put immediately into rehearsal for a revival of Bill Ball's production of *Tartuffe* by Molière, with René Auberjonois in the title role. It was a wonderful production, fast moving, funny, two feet off the ground from the word "go", with a damn good cast. I was replacing somebody as Cleant, the *raison-*

---

* René Auberjonois was with ACT from its inception and held an incredible record at that time. He had created more than forty-five roles in four years, including twenty roles in productions with the Arena Stage in Washington, D.C. He graduated from Carnegie Institute of Technology.

* Before joining ACT, Peter Donat appeared in several Broadway plays including *The Chinese Prime Minister*, *The Entertainer*, *The Country Wife*, and *The First Gentleman* (for which he won the Theatre World Award as best featured actor). He was also with the Canadian Stratford Festival for six seasons and acted with the APA.

*neur*. It was like being in the middle of a hurricane. In the small, cramped elevator that took us to the street level and to the various ACT offices and rehearsal rooms I once asked René if it would be possible for me to try a few ideas and pieces of blocking of my own in the rehearsals instead of merely repeating exactly what was done before. He said, "Yes, it is possible but a little difficult. It is like trying to show a card trick to a passing freight train!" [12]

DeAnn Mears, who left the company in 1970 and later rejoined ACT in 1979, recalled her feelings about the first ACT seasons:

The company is better organized now, perhaps because the pace isn't so hectic. In our first season in San Francisco, from January to May, 1967, we did 17 plays. That was a short season. The following season (1967–68) we did 27 plays.

It was a frantic pace. We'd sometimes get mixed up running between the Geary and the Marines' Theatres, sometimes forgetting which theatre we were supposed to perform in. But it was a wonderful learning experience. After a time, however, I was exhausted and felt I needed a change of scenery, which is why I left the company. [13]

The business of the actors created a sense of excitement that helped mold a unity among them. Angela Paton,* a member of the first San Francisco company, and founder of the Berkeley Stage Company, recalled the feeling of excitement: "It was almost like being in paradise because you'd go up the elevator, you'd be talking about theatre, you'd go down the elevator, you'd be talking about theatre. You'd go to the coffee shop and you'd meet actors and it was a terrific sense of excitement—that something wonderful was happening. It was really exciting to be a part of it." [14]

### Casting for Repertory

As McKenzie saw it, in some ways ACT's repertory was constructed much like an old stock company. He explained:

---

* Actress Angela Paton graduated from Carnegie Institute of Technology and performed Off-Broadway in *The Trojan Women* and in *Autumn Garden* and in leading roles at the Arena Stage in Washington, D.C. She also performed at the Showcase Theatre in Evanston, Illinois and at the Hearst Greek Theatre in Berkeley, California. She

ACT's casting is much like an old-fashioned stock company. Actors used to receive contracts "as cast" in that system. Then casting might change according to the needs of a play.

At ACT an actor was to have a similar attitude, a company attitude, where casting might change and that an actor might play large and small roles in different plays during the course of a season. That is why Peter Donat has played cameos and alternating performances. We are able to give them the security of knowing they are loved while they are here and as long as they want to be here at ACT.

There is a definite acting company commitment. We seldom, if ever, use jobbers.[15]

What this statement by McKenzie meant was that when actors became part of the ACT company they knew how long their employment would last. With this security they would be assigned roles by Ball and, owing to circumstances, the assignment might be changed. Seldom would actors be brought in for a single show as "jobbers." In fact, this rule was broken after the first few years only to allow returning ACT actors to perform with the company again. (Sada Thompson in *The Cherry Orchard* in 1974, and René Auberjonois in *The Ruling Class* in 1975, are two examples.) ACT actors knew that they would be used in a variety of roles both large and small. The actors would surrender their time and services to the company and would be used at the discretion of the management, and ultimately, at the discretion of Ball.

Given the large number of plays during the 1967–1969 period, almost all the senior actors were cast in leading roles, doubling in smaller roles as the situation demanded. But Ball also used some actors in featured roles and gave them shows off, using journeymen or fellow actors in the smaller roles as both an expedient and as an educational device for the novices. Ball also double and triple cast some roles, making it usual in the same play to feature different ACT actors.

A grand total of fifty-five productions was mounted between 1967 and 1969. Thirty-three Equity actors and twenty-two acting fellows were employed during the 1967–1968 sea-

---

performed more than fifty leading roles as an Equity actress and became artistic director of the Berkeley Stage Company, which she founded.

son. The total number of actors was fifty-five. All actors were employed in performances and rehearsals by means of a challenging juggling act.

ACT's programs reflected the ideal of equality by listing the cast in order of appearance. No special attention in billing was paid to those who emerged as local favorites. Along with the order of appearance, all the roles that were rehearsed by different actors also were listed. The first actor whose name appeared would be the one performing that day. The example below is the cast list of the 1967–1968 season performance of Shakespeare's *Twelfth Night, or What You Will.*

CAST
*(Cast in order of appearance)*

| | |
|---|---|
| Orsino, Duke of Illyria | Paul Shenar |
| | Philip Kerr |
| | James Ragan |
| Curio | Mark Schell |
| | Larry Ferguson |
| | Don Watson |
| Valentine | James Ragan |
| | Kimo Perry |
| Viola, sister to Sebastian | DeAnn Mears |
| | Ellen Geer |
| | Dana Larson |
| A Sea Captain, friend to Viola | Patrick Tovatt |
| | Herman Poppe |
| | Larry Ferguson |
| Sir Toby Belch, uncle to Olivia | Ray Reinhardt |
| | Harry Frazier |
| | George Ede |
| Sir Andrew Aguecheek | Glen Mazen |
| | Peter Donat |
| | Herman Poppe |
| Clown, servant to Olivia | David Grimm |
| | Scott Hylands |
| | David Dukes |

| | |
|---|---|
| Olivia | Carol Mayo Jenkins |
| | Deborah Sussel |
| | Kate Hawley |
| Malvolio, steward to Olivia | Ken Ruta |
| | Barry Kraft |
| | Patrick Tovatt |
| Antonio | George Ede |
| | Glen Mazen |
| | John Schuck |
| Sebastian | Mark Bramhall |
| | Mark Schell |
| | Ray Laine |
| Fabian | Michael Lerner |
| | David Dukes |
| | Terry Mace |
| Priest | Barry Kraft |
| | Terry Mace |
| | Gil Turner |
| First Officer | Herman Poppe |
| | Robert Feero |
| Second Officer | Robert Feero |
| | Gil Turner |

Changes in the casting of a play would be brought on by the exigencies of repertory and not necessarily by the wishes or demands of the actors. As McKenzie explained, "If we have to change casting, because we change the play or what have you, we give [the actors] a mutual agreement on the change. At a place like ACT I'm afraid it's not really mutual because they realize that for the good of the company they have to change a role. If they don't change it they are probably not company people and probably shouldn't be here. The next year they probably wouldn't be here." [All quotes from James McKenzie throughout this chapter are drawn from the personal interview cited in note 15.]

The practice of casting from within the ACT company eventually provoked the objection that casting was either being done subjectively or in contrast to the normal typecasting, which was done in commercial theatre. The practice of casting from within the company was criticized by the local media on several occasions. One of the featured actors at ACT in the early seasons was Paul Shenar.* He was cast as Brother Julian in ACT's hallmark production of *Tiny Alice* (much controversy raged over Ball's adaptation of the Albee script, quite apart from the casting issue). He was also cast as Hamlet and Oedipus. Several of the local critics questioned Shenar's capacity to play Oedipus. Nevertheless, Ball stuck to his commitment to allow actors to grow by being stretched past the limits of their capabilities, and Shenar proved equal to the task.

Peter Donat's casting in several leading roles also raised some eyebrows, not to mention Donat's own feeling of not being "right for a role." [16] Donat, a nephew of Robert Donat of *Goodbye Mister Chips* fame, had worked as a character actor for several years at the Shakespeare Festival in Stratford, Ontario, and with Ellis Rabb's APA company. With ACT he was cast as Hadrian VII in the play by the same name in 1970. He was very surprised at the offer to do the role. He recalled: "By 'not being right' for a role I simply mean being cast against type. If you look at me in an ordinary conversation I don't think you would regard me as the obvious actor to play Hadrian VII or Shylock or Cyrano de Bergerac, and yet I made those different parts and many others work. This was largely due, of course, to Bill Ball's ability to say, 'Who says you're not right for a role?' and then casting me in it without hesitation or question." [All quotes from Peter Donat throughout this chapter are drawn from the personal interview in note 12.]

In the same vein, DeAnn Mears expressed her disdain for New York typecasting as opposed to repertory acting: "In New York you get very type-cast. You hear, 'Oh well, she does Noel Coward very well, she is very witty and that veneer.' That whole thing. They don't think you can do anything else. They just stamp you. That is rotten, because it isn't true about most of us. There is a problem with most actors, particularly in New York, they don't grow, they don't expand." [17]

Ball used actors in the company without regard for the

* Paul Shenar was a charter member of ACT. He made his New York debut at the Circle-in-the-Square and appeared with the Repertory Theatre of Lincoln Center.

critics' opinions in order to create a fertile base for the actors' growth. This supportive atmosphere paid great dividends to the individual actors. Said Donat,

I love the repertory idea—I feel that it is very good for actors to develop discipline and range. They prefer to do one show at a time, run in it, close it, then go into rehearsal for another show. That is the "stock company" approach. The difference between a stock company and a repertory company is immense, both philosophically and creatively. And I salute Bill Ball for holding out, not only for the impractical, difficult, expensive repertory idea, but also for the repertory-conservatory idea, turning a professional repertory into a beehive of creative activity with classes occurring continually that seasoned performers can take if they wish, along with students. It's a great idea, a great concept. And the experienced performers can also teach, passing their knowledge and skills.

I don't know how the atmosphere is established at ACT but it must be partly due to Ball's belief in "positation." From "no" nothing happens, from "yes" anything and everything can happen. In any case the company feeling is very supportive, non-bickery, non-jealous. The atmosphere and accomplishments are pretty great—not always, but often enough to be admirable and amazing.

Ken Ruta,* a member of ACT's acting company during its first six San Francisco seasons and also a member of the Guthrie Theatre of Minneapolis, explained his feelings about ACT's repertory:

We're close to being an opera company. Most repertory theatres in this country don't really alternate like we do. They play four or six different shows, but they play them one at a time. The Tyrone Guthrie Theatre plays four or five in rotating repertory, but that can't compare with thirty-one [sic] plays in forty weeks. And even though the Guthrie alternates plays, it doesn't alternate actors in roles. . . . I don't think we can touch the Guthrie with regard to physical production because the emphasis here is not on spectacle. With our schedule we

---

* Ken Ruta graduated from the Goodman School of Theatre and was with the Minnesota Theatre Company as a leading actor for four years before joining ACT. He appeared in the Broadway productions of *Inherit the Wind*, *Separate Tables*, *Duel of Angels*, and *Ross*, in addition to Off-Broadway productions at the Circle-in-the-Square and the Phoenix Theatre.

need a staff like the Metropolitan Opera ... at the Guthrie we had two weeks of solid dress rehearsal. A week before that we had all the props and the set was all done. But we only did four plays. Here the emphasis is on the actor. ... I don't know of any other company where the people have such consideration for one another. There's no caste system, which is incredible.[18]

Josephine Nichols,* a member of ACT's company from 1967 to 1969 and a veteran of Broadway, Off-Broadway, and television, explained her desire to be in a repertory theatre:

I really think I've been a repertory actress all my life. I think that is the appetite I've had for theatre. When I graduated from the University of Oklahoma, I was accepted as an apprentice in a repertory theatre that Beulah Bondi and Elmer Rice were beginning in New York. I was so excited because this was what I deeply wanted—a chance to play in repertory theatre. A month before the theatre was open, I got a letter saying that due to insufficient funds, they were not opening. So between then and now, I am the product of all the battle scars I have acquired in all aspects of theatre, television and film. But finally, now, I am right where I want to be when I started out. And as long as I can function in a creative atmosphere, I can continue to grow as a creative artist and, hopefully, reach some degree of artistry I know I could not reach if I spent most of my time either in one commercial production after another or looking for work. I think all of us are here because we feel within ourselves a deep need for this kind of theatre. The satisfaction comes when we feel that ACT and this kind of theatre needs us.[19]

Paul Shenar explained his experience of repertory at ACT:

There's something very strange about the way in which you grow from role to role—that is, going back and forth in the repertory from doing a comedy to doing a heavy play, to doing a farce or whatever. Even now, I had the experience of just completing the mounting of "Devil's Disciple" and I have been playing Hamlet now for about eight months ... and because of playing Dick Dudgeon, Hamlet has grown tremendously. He's gotten wider and stronger and bigger. It's really extraor-

* Josephine Nichols joined ACT after three years in daytime television serials, two Broadway productions, and six Off-Broadway plays, including a season's run as Cassandra in the prize-winning production of *The Prodigal*. For seven years she was an assistant professor at Adelphi University.

dinary to go out on the stage, and for some reason or other the old role changes completely because of the new one.[20]

Michael Learned,* who was married to Donat during her ACT years, was a company member from 1967 to 1972, after which she moved on to national fame as the mother in the television series of *The Waltons*. She described her experiences at ACT: "This [A.C.T. company] has a special quality. There's no back biting. People seem to be joyful for each other. We all have our bad days, and we all know how to comfort one another. There are no cliques—no running one another down. It's a difficult company to come into—you feel like you're breaking into a family—coming to people who've been together so long."[21]

Learned also expressed the feeling that "A.C.T. provided me with the most profoundly creative years of my life. Bill Ball has created a family for his actors and for the San Francisco Bay Area and A.C.T. is an integral part of the city."[22]

Bill Paterson,* who came to ACT in 1967 after twenty years with the Cleveland Playhouse and has been continuously employed at ACT ever since, explained his attitude about working with the company: "[A.C.T. is] the happiest company I've ever known. Not that there haven't been some unhappy times, but being an actor here is so satisfying that it just seems people are generally happy. In a company like A.C.T., it's hard not to speculate about rivalries for certain roles."[23]

Paterson compared the Playhouse to ACT:

The big difference is that ACT plays in repertory. Essentially, that difference and the difference of the school here—the conservatory. . . . When I was there [in Cleveland] it was very much a company of

* Michael Learned had appeared as a leading actress with the Canadian Stratford Festival resident and touring companies and with the Shakespeare Festival in Stratford, Connecticut. She played Irina in *The Three Sisters* at the Fourth Street Theatre in New York, and played in the Off-Broadway production of *A God Slept Here*. Her television credits include several leading roles for the Canadian Broadcasting Company, including Estella in *Great Expectations*.

* William Paterson acted with stock companies in the East and on television in New York until 1947, when he became a leading actor with the Cleveland Playhouse. He toured nationally with one-man shows of *A Profile of Benjamin Franklin* and *A Profile of Holmes*.

people who had been together a long time. They were a real ensemble
... in recent years they have tended to job more people in for particular shows which we don't do at ACT—at least, we do that very
rarely. I think it is an advantage to ACT that it uses its own company
for all the plays except in very rare circumstances. I think more and
more, regional theatres are tending, in the last four or five years, to
job people in—which probably results in better type casting at
times. . . . Whereas, in a company like ACT people are sometimes a
little miscast because every role has to be cast out of the company.
But, it's very good for the actors because they are therefore asked to
stretch themselves in ways that they might not in other places. So I am
very enthusiastic about the idea of using one group of actors for a
season—casting entirely out of the resident company.[24]

Ray Reinhardt, a continuous member of ACT since Pittsburgh in 1965, was asked to join the company after Ball saw
his Broadway performance in *Tiny Alice*. Reinhardt considered
the repertory environment a healthy one for actors to work in:
"As an actor I love the variety that you get in a repertory situation. You're asked to stretch constantly. That's a great plus for
me personally, because I think my needs are gargantuan—I have
to experience vicariously as much as I possibly can. If you're a
glutton for behavior, for different styles and ideas, a repertory
company is where you should be. It's a museum idea in part,
but it's not a bad idea."[25]
Reinhardt also explained his feelings about ACT as an ensemble company:

People work together, and when they are proficient and sure of themselves and a certain amount of good loss of ego—you have to have a
certain amount of ego to get on stage. I think ensemble acting happens
when the more successful you are, the more that you succeed, the
more generous you become in any aspect of life.
But what that means in terms of acting is that you are willing to
set up things for your fellow actors in the scene to make the play
work. You don't become petty. You don't try to shine at the expense
of the other actor, and/or play, and/or the costume—whatever it is.
There's a sense of—it's a good sense of superiority. In other words,
you're very confident because the actor isn't pushing too hard. And
imagine when eight or ten or fifteen actors are doing that in a com-

pany. . . . Part of what's called ensemble is that. It's everyone doing just the right amount of work—no more, no less.[26]

Deborah Sussel,* an actress with ACT since 1967, also explained the positive feelings an actor gets within the ACT company:

I did get a very good feeling right from the beginning, but I'm really shy and it takes me a while to feel at home. The first year I felt out of it, but that was just personal. When I came back for my second year, then it was very homey and I really felt connected to everybody. I felt that everybody felt the same way. Everyone was pulling for each other. That is one of the really special things about ACT. It was a great atmosphere. It is because of Bill. It starts with him. It is so important. The theatre is such a treacherous place sometimes, he can't stop gossip or peoples' feelings; some people are at different points of their careers. The leader of whatever organization sets the tone or the mood or the feeling for the whole company. He has really made what he calls positation a living reality, it works. It is so important because as an actor, even more than a teacher—you can learn to teach pretty much on your own—but as an actor you are so vulnerable. . . . To have that attitude of cooperation and support is so helpful.[27]

Marc Singer,† an ACT actor who began with the company in 1970 and gained his national fame with his portrayal of Petruchio in the 1973 PBS production of *Taming of the Shrew*, expressed his feelings toward ensemble playing:

We know we're shooting for the same thing—greater uniformity of style and purpose. This allows for vitality to increase within the company . . . for us to roll in the same direction.

---

*Deborah Sussel was the recipient of a Fulbright-Hays grant for study at the London Academy of Music and Dramatic Art. She worked with the Bucks County Playhouse in Pennsylvania, the Mineola Playhouse in Long Island, and at the Goodspeed Opera House in East Haddam, Connecticut. She joined ACT after a year with the Theatre of the Living Arts in Philadelphia and a critically acclaimed tour of *Room Service*.

†Mark Singer acted with the San Diego Shakespeare Festival in the roles of Demetrius in *A Midsummer Nights Dream*, Lucentio in *The Taming of the Shrew*, and Menas in *Antony and Cleopatra*. At the Seattle Repertory Theatre he played Camille in *A Flea in Her Ear*, Sandy in *Hay Fever*, and La Fleche in *The Miser*. He performed in summer stock companies and with Seattle's A Contemporary Theatre. He is a graduate of the University of Michigan.

A.C.T. is bringing newer and newer theatrical blood into San Francisco. It is a strengthening of a new-found American heritage—new-found to some—and confirms to American audiences that this company is in reality telling them about themselves. Overall, it is a reaffirmation of the lifeblood of American Theatre.[28]

Kitty Winn,* who acted as a fellow during ACT's 1967 season and eventually assumed major roles until the 1970 season, including Irina in ACT's production of *The Three Sisters*, gained her fame in the film *The Panic in Needle Park*, playing opposite Al Pacino. In 1971 she looked back on her ACT experience: "The time was a truly rare and incredible experience. First of all, there was a different play every night, and sometimes two different plays in a day, from Arthur Miller to Moliere. And there was also a training program that went along with it, in which we were offered lessons in tap dancing, ballet and guitar. So it was a total theatre experience. I'd like to do it again."[29]

## The Regional Actor

René Auberjonois, who left ACT after the 1967–1968 season, had an interesting perspective on regional acting. He was asked what problems most frequently beset the actor in the regional theatre.

I believe that there are roughly three species of regional acting: (1) the actor (like myself) who is a relatively pure product of the theatrical hinterland, and whose entire training and experience has been in regional theatre; (2) the actor who has tried the "commercial scene" and given it up; and (3) the actor who is considered and/or considers himself a visiting dignitary (doing a bit of soul-cleansing—slumming perhaps). For the time being I have left the "movement." I am not sure whether I am a graduate or a drop-out.

I am convinced that most actors involved in regional theatre are schizophrenic in the sense that they cannot reconcile the feeling that they should be fighting the fight of commercial theatre with the feeling

---

* Kitty Winn graduated from Boston University and worked with the Lebo Theatre, the Centenary Little Theatre, and the Tufts Arena Theatre, and appeared on tour in *Measure for Measure*, directed by Margaret Webster.

that they are chosen members of some great and holy theatrical crusade. This dilemma gives rise to a working climate which could be compared to a monastery filled with self-consciously zealous monks suppressing the desire to ravage the neighboring village.

There is undoubtedly, much to be said for the "womb of the rep" which affords the freedom to make mistakes which may lead to brilliance, but one must contend also with the nagging fear that one is copping out and losing perspective. There is the danger that the constant pressure to create leaves no time to stop and take stock of one's work—to learn from those mistakes. . . .

I don't mean to deny that the training and exposure afforded by regional theatre is the only practical way for a young actor to mold himself into a useful artist. I mean that most actors will admit that they are actors because of a driving desire to be loved. It follows that to be loved on the grandest scale by the greatest number of people is an important if not primary objective.[30]

Auberjonois touched upon one of Ball's basic beliefs: the avoidance of the commercial settings of New York or Los Angeles. By locating in San Francisco, ACT minimized distractions for its actors. Still, several of ACT's actors have gone on to fame in other mediums. Of the male actors these include Peter Donat, Dana Elcar, Marc Singer, Ramon Bieri, Paul Shenar, and Richard Dysart. Some of the actresses that have gained fame away from ACT have been Michael Learned, Marsha Mason, Sada Thompson, Kitty Winn, Carol Mayo Jenkins, Lee McCain, and Ann Weldon.

Many ACT actors felt that it was healthy to leave ACT and then return "refreshed" by other experiences. The most outspoken of all the actors on this point was Peter Donat. Donat had established himself nationally before joining ACT, and during his years with the company he has taken several "sabbaticals" to do film, television, and Broadway productions. Donat explains:

I remember my early days in New York, the struggle to get someone to notice me, to give me a job, and my determination to make my way as a full time actor, not part-time with jobs in other fields to keep me going. So I went wherever there was work, anywhere and everywhere.

Too many young performers refused to leave New York, thinking that attaining a Broadway show would open all doors and be a magic key to the future. Nonsense. In the meantime they were not working as performers, they were just "making the rounds." I did summer stock in Provincetown, Cape Cod, one show per week at a salary of thirty dollars; went to Mayo Jones Arena Theatre in Dallas for a winter season; did several national tours (the old railroad tours, which my children can't believe!); did summer stock all over the East; did live T.V. and radio in New York, as well as some plays off and on Broadway; was a member of the Shakespeare Festival company in Stratford, Canada, for six years; and finally came to Los Angeles in 1967 to look into another great and formidable medium, motion pictures. I had never done anything in feature films and thought it was time. God knows, anyone who has grown up in the theatre can always use more money and exposure to larger audiences which work in films provides. It also provides added disciplines and refinements and skills to the difficult art of acting. Well, I hadn't been long in Los Angeles when I heard from Bill Ball who was bringing ACT to San Francisco. We had met several times over the years, in Stratford, Canada and also with various APA projects, and had stated that we would like to work together. ACT in San Francisco was the perfect opportunity. And we have worked together most of those years since then. In the early years I was totally involved in the ACT repertory from September to June. But over the years I have been able to modify that so it is possible for me to do interesting T.V. and film projects if and when they come up. And this is good, both for me and ACT. It is good to circulate among other directors, actors, designers, writers, and return to ACT with what one has learned.[31]

One of the hopes of ACT's development, expressed by Bushnell and quoted earlier, was that it could become a "mother" company. It would be a home for great American actors to leave and come back to, much as the Royal Shakespeare and the National Theatre companies of England operate.

ACT has been able to accommodate actors who have left and then decided to return. Of course, the actors' returning depended upon their willingness to spend a large amount of time in San Francisco which takes them away from the mainstream of Los Angeles and commercial work.

John Schuck,* an actor with ACT from 1967 to 1970, was one of the first ACT actors to be featured in a major motion picture and then to return to the company. He, along with G. Wood and René Auberjonois were cast in *M.A.S.H.* At that time, Schuck expressed his desire to be able to perform with ACT and continue to develop as a film actor: "This is a problem for A.C.T. to accept, but I think now Bill Ball realizes that actors benefit from outside experience. Movies give us a chance to pick up quickly a comparatively large salary, to learn by the experience, and to return refreshed, and I hope movies, too, will be enriched by the proximity of A.C.T.'s talent."[32]

Bill Paterson conforms to what Auberjonois describes as a product of the regional theatre. Paterson has been content to live the life of a regional actor.

The reason that I've stayed in regional theatre all of my career is that it offers you a continuity of employment and I feel very fortunate to do what I want to do all the time. There are very few actors who can say that. It does result, at times, in playing roles that are not very significant, but that's part of the ensemble. And I'm very happy to do these roles in order to be part of such a company. . . . The acting profession in general is a very precarious one, and there are always so many more talented people than there are jobs . . . I feel enormously lucky to be here. I wouldn't dream of going anywhere else; of course I would if a play came up. But I wouldn't sever my connection here. It's like the old theatres in Europe where a company settled in for life—for their careers.[33]

Reinhardt was also attracted to ACT, even though he had thoughts of trying different theatre experiences: "What if there isn't anything better? The main reason for leaving would be to have a greater variety of roles, to work with new directors. Why leave if I have good roles and A.C.T. can bring directors in like Gower Champion and Tom Moore . . . so it's still the best place to be."[34] Reinhardt also supported the rationale for not siting ACT in Los Angeles or New York:

* John Shuck appeared in more than one hundred plays in the five years before his first ACT season and was featured in the Off-Broadway productions of *The Shrike* and *The Streets of New York*. He also acted on television in *Route 66*, *East Side*, *West Side*; and *The Cultural Arts of Washington*.

Why not New York? Because the pressure is unbearable. No repertory company has been able to make it in New York over a length of time. APA did have some wonderful seasons, but the pressure becomes too much. It's more and louder and faster and funnier and—I don't know. The temptation is always there for other things . . . . I'll tell you why not Los Angeles. Obviously, in Los Angeles every actor would be going to Bill and every director saying, "Oh, just one day out, just one day's shooting on a film, one day on a television program." It would be impossible. Up in San Francisco, it is a very good choice because you are away from the commercial pressure. You're in a cosmopolitan city. It still, as far as . . . social living is concerned . . . perhaps the best city in the United States to be.[35]

Deborah Sussel explained her relationship with her New York agent during her first years at ACT:

I was told by my agent, who I had in New York, that I could stay at ACT for a year or two at the most. After that you just couldn't be there. If you were a New York actor and you took it seriously in the profession you move on. I really felt, I knew, that she didn't want me to stay. After my second season I was still coming back here, she was getting more and more disgusted. She was writing me off after my third year, fourth year and it was like I kind of ceased to interest her in the New York professional way. There was a real conflict between, do I want more than just a career. That's the wonderful thing about ACT. You got an enormous amount of acting experience. That's what I wanted. . . . When you were at ACT you worked as an actress.[36]

Several of the ACT actors during the 1967–1972 period could be seen as products of the regional theatre, as was suggested by Auberjonois. Other actors who performed with ACT, often at Ball's urging, had considerable experience in both regional and New York theatre. Thus, the company was a mixture of mature and maturing actors. The aspect of ACT that made it stand out as special among other regional theatres was the conservatory training. As Donat suggested,

What people don't realize is that we are more than a stock company. We are a conservatory, a school for young actors and actresses. We have classes in dance, yoga, fencing, voice, all sorts of things they need. It's the life of the theatre, a tremendously dynamic thing. A stock company does one play, and then it does another. That is not a repertory company. And ACT is intimately connected to a school, its own conservatory, the "C" in ACT. In the conservatory, experienced performers can be both teachers and students, learning from both positions. We're basically like the *Comédie Française* in this—experienced performers helping those coming up.[37]

The effect of the training, according to Donat, is to set the actor free: "I don't know that there's any one way to label ACT's type of acting, but I'm glad there is an emphasis on technique, physical techniques like movement and vocal enrichment. Technique sets us free to perform, it gives us wings. There are emotional and intellectual techniques taught also, to allow the performer to create at a maximum, to get the gold out of the script. I think ACT is creating a group of well-trained American actors. I have a feeling that the well-trained American actor is the most versatile in the English speaking world."[38]

Michael Learned also thought highly of ACT's training program: "I don't know of any other theatre in North America where you can watch young actors starting as students and growing into experienced performers. At A.C.T., they expand their consciousness as well as their talent, and the Conservatory benefits actors and audiences alike. A.C.T.'s training program has a reputation. All over the country—kids call me in Los Angeles and ask if I can help them get into it."[39]

The general attitude toward ACT's conservatory was positive. Ball's initial plan of concurrent and inseparable training and repertory created an extremely active environment. It also created a common language for the company to use. Auberjonois stressed this: "The most one should hope or try for is a company in which actors have a common vocabulary allowing them to investigate and comprehend each other's methods of creating roles. I like to think this would create 'ensemble' which would in turn be what some might call 'style.' If 'style' means a generally accepted standard of good speech and physical control, then its necessity seems obvious."[40]

### Artist Advisory Council

One other structure of the acting company was the Artist Advisory Council, made up of ACT actors. In essence, the council served as a means of venting certain frustrations within the company while also creating solutions. As Frank Ottiwell, a long-standing member of the council explained, "The Artist Advisory Council . . . is not so much a place to complain, but a place to bring solutions rather than problems. There is the fact that there has to be a solution implied that a problem had developed."[41]

While all ACT actors were part of a national union, the Actors' Equity Association, the management of ACT (McKenzie, Ball, Fletcher, and Hastings) saw the need for an in-house organization to help solve immediate problems. McKenzie explained the management's solution of a committee of artists:

We have fifty-two people in the company and eighty-six students and about twenty more people who are in the artistic community of the company. So that's one hundred and sixty people who are very much involved with the artists' lives moment to moment. Rather than have it dealt through Equity, arbitrations, deputies to meet with committees, things like that, Ball initiated early on the Artist Advisory Council. The idea is that we don't recognize unions as being anything but a salary-protection device for the employees. We do post bond, it guarantees that they will get their salary if we close mid-week. Beyond that, we don't do anything.[42]

In other words, the council gave the actors an open forum outside union involvement to discuss problems that could be quickly solved:

We on the council anticipate union or personnel problems; we think of them as "people problems." We have one person selected from each area: one senior actor, one senior actress, one first-year student, two second-year students, and so forth. It ends up with about fifteen or twenty people representing one hundred and sixty people. They meet or try to about once a month; it is not on a regular basis. We do it when there is enough to talk about. The meetings are to solve any problems between the company, any part of the company, and the actors. If the actors say it's too cold backstage, we have a problem and we solve it before they go to a mediator and have a grievance committee.

The council was an attempt to get feedback and input from the actors so that the management of the company would not be isolated from the company's daily problems. The same philosophy of positation, or positive action, that Ball postulated for the entire operation—that is, to contribute, not to criticize—was the basis of the council. If a problem existed there was a solution. The company was thus invested with some power of internal self-rule, while Ball held the reigns as *regisseur* over the artistic endeavors of ACT.

# 8

# Conclusion

Bill Ball set out in 1965 to create a theatre that would ensure actors continuity of employment and the opportunity to train and play in a large and eclectic repertory. Thus, the acronym of ACT stood for a theatre that was specifically American, a theatre that was a conservatory, and a theatre that was professional. He patterned ACT after the great European ensembles, the *Comédie Française* and the Moscow Art Theatre. He was inspired by the Group Theatre's attempt to create a company that had a commitment to its actors. Finally, he was influenced by the move toward creating a healthy theatre for actors that Ellis Rabb initiated with his APA.

Ball himself designed a management structure that would ensure his own permanence with ACT. One aspect of this structure was the separation of the financial support organization from the artistic management of the company. ACT was colored by its time in history, during which performing arts organizations took on the corporate structure of organization. However, ACT was different from other arts organizations in that it was protected from the whims of power-conscious business people. ACT's policy board was made up of respected artists, not of business or community leaders. The American Conservatory Theatre Foundation was a producing entity unto itself. The overall effect of this structure was a continuity in the artistic leadership that Ball himself chose to maintain during the dynamic early part of the group's existence. With that continuity assured, a philosophical continuity was also intact.

Along with the ACT jargon of inseparable and concurrent training and repertory came the philosophical term—indeed, ACT's driving force—*positation*. Positation comprised Ball's ideal of the "right to fail" in the creative process of the actor. The associated effect of the philosophy was the willingness to take risks in production as well as in casting.

Ball's idea of a resident repertory acting company was the basis of the ensemble. The resident company ensured continuity of employment for the actors and a managerial commitment to securing their well-being. Thus, Ball searched for actors who would reciprocate with a commitment to his philosophies. Two of these philosophies were positation and the need for actors to grow through training and repertory performance. Ball was able to find actors who surrendered their services for a full season in return for the modest financial security ACT offered them. Some actors found ACT so amenable to their needs that they decided to stay with the company for the remainder of their acting careers. Other actors were either poorly suited to the company concept, or chose to seek more recognition and the financial cornucopia of the commercial acting world in film, television, and Broadway. Still others were able to manage both the commercial and the regional theatre worlds. In all cases, the actors who have been with ACT have recognized the need to commit themselves to Ball's philosophies in order to create the ensemble that Ball envisioned.

There were no stars in the ACT company, but top American talents worked with the company during its first five San Francisco years, and they have continued to work with ACT since. Stratification within the company became apparent through the use of the mature actors in many major roles of the repertory and the use of journeymen actors to fill out the minor roles of the repertory. Yet the senior members did perform in minor roles or cameos, and often alternated in other roles, while the younger performers acted in major roles as the plays of a season were demanded. When actors signed on with ACT, they were fully aware that their roles might change as the situation demanded, or that they might be asked to play roles that were not particularly significant.

Another aspect of the resident-repertory-company concept was Ball's casting of actors out of type. This kind of casting was meant to enrich the actor's experience in ways that would not occur in the commercial theatre, while it also showed ACT's great respect and commitment to the individual actors.

The argument that ACT should create a stable environment to become a "mother" company may not be economically or geographically possible. Although San Francisco is near Los Angeles, the film capital of the United States, accommodating those actors whose interest is solely film stardom and the economic advantages it brings is almost impossible. Owing to Ball's acclaimed loyalty to ACT actors (attested to by several actors interviewed here), he has been willing to use actors who have left the company but who have had the time to perform with ACT again. However, the goal of training actors for ACT has sometimes superseded the desire to re-hire former ACT actors. Ball's determination not to "job" new talent in, except under unusual circumstances, created an ensemble in which actors had a common vocabulary.

The training at ACT helped to standardize the profession; simultaneously it resulted in a style of acting that could rightly be called ACT's own. The structure of the conservatory changed and matured over the first five years in San Francisco, from a loosely run set of seminars to a two-year training academy. The introduction of the ten-week summer training program in 1968 set the pattern for the more refined scheduling and curriculum of the Advanced Training Program of 1972. Combining the school and the professional repertory broke new ground in the American theatre by giving professional actors a chance to hand down techniques, thereby "conserving" the art.

Historically, ACT evolved in the context of the regional theatre movement in America of the 1950s and 1960s, when public and private support for the arts was at a peak. As with many other resident professional theatres outside New York City, ACT gained the commitment of, first, the Rockefeller Foundation in Pittsburgh and second, the philanthropic Ford

Foundation initiated by McNeil Lowry. As was true for many ensembles throughout history, ACT gained patronage that reduced its need to rely on box-office income. American arts have never had the relative advantages that royalty provided or the financial support that the aristocracy often offered in other countries. The closest analogy to the Old World aristocrats has been the foundations, which essentially are tax shelters for the "captains of industry" and their descendants.

The support by the Ford Foundation was meant to help create matching funds at the local level for arts organizations. ACT had the good fortune to have had two Renaissance-like local patrons in San Francisco, but the company never surrendered policy-making powers to them. The first, Mortimer Fleishhacker, backed ACT and secured its existence, especially during its first three years in San Francisco, through the California Theatre Foundation. Later, Cyril Magnin led the way in raising the pledges that would help to eliminate ACT's annual deficit.

The deficit incurred by ACT was owing to the high costs associated with maintaining the repertory and to the large company of actors, plus the fact that ACT charged inexpensive ticket prices. ACT wished to make performances available to as many San Franciscans as possible. Audience response to ACT's first full season was surprisingly enthusiastic. When subscriptions dropped off for the 1968–1969 season and the costs of operating the double repertory escalated, ACT adjusted its schedule. Much credit was due to the professional producing abilities of James McKenzie in staving off possible closure. By the 1972 season a standard was set: approximately nine plays were produced in repertory exclusively at the Geary Theatre. A simplified subscription was put into place and fewer revivals were produced. These changes helped to create a more fiscally responsible atmosphere for the continuation of the ensemble.

Ball held reign as the *regisseur* of ACT in the classical mold. His "benevolent dictatorship" came at some cost, and almost resulted in the deterioration of the company's morale in 1969 when, owing to illness, he was unable to be active in the day-to-day management. Despite the factionalism that ensued, a new and revitalized ACT emerged in 1970. Three key members of the management departed during the period of upheaval: William Bushnell, Robert Goldsby, and John Seig. They were replaced by Allen Fletcher and James McKenzie, who were more consonant with Ball's philosophies than their predecessors.

As with the leadership in other ensembles in history the *regisseur's* leadership was balanced by another, less autocratic presence, in this case Edward Hastings, Jr. Hastings can be seen, in some respects, as playing the role of Chronegk in the Meiningen troupe or Schiller in the Goethe theatre. His communicative abilities and his practicality had in the day-to-day functioning of the company proved invaluable during times of crisis.

ACT operated along the lines of the great European companies of the *Comédie Française* and the Moscow Art Theatre, although on a smaller scale. It was committed to its actors and their careers. Ball, as *regisseur*, has seen to its managerial continuity and to the continuity of its philosophic base, which has remained intact throughout ACT's existence. Ball's aim of creating a ballet-company atmosphere was accomplished quickly and with a sustained force throughout the first years of its existence. The company's success in those years was a testimony to Ball's insight and sense of the organizational philosophy of ensemble playing. ACT, in essence, fulfilled a need in modern American theatre.

Thus, ACT is consistent with the definition of a true historical ensemble acting company, the elements of which, for convenience, are listed once more below:

1. A permanent company of actors.
2. A consistency in acting style.
3. A commitment of the actors to the ideal.
4. Equality in and cooperation among all members of the acting company.
5. Unified productions created either by a particular playwright or by the company's *regisseur*.
6. Financial security to allow for growth and experimentation toward furthering of the art.

7. Often, but not always, a no-star system of acting, whereby small and large roles alike are shared by all in the acting company.

8. An overriding ideal often based on the societal factors of the company's environment and engendered by the company's management.

Appendixes
Notes
Bibliography
Index

# Appendix A

## Statement of Purpose
## of the American Conservatory
## Theatre Foundation

1. WHEREAS, The United States is the only country in the civilized world without a national conservatory of theatre art, and there is no immediate likelihood of one being created within our existing theatrical structures;

2. The commercial theatre is so heavily burdened with the pressures of immediate projects, that it cannot be expected to provide development and training for theater artists;

3. Such training as exists in universities and professional schools often suffers from inadequate standards and is often limited by the highly individualistic stamp of one teacher or method;

4. There is no consistently available link for young professionals of these schools and the competitive commercial theater;

5. The creative artists in many professional theatre structures often find their work limited or dominated by institutionalism, financial or pedagogic interference or the personal whim of a proprietary interest;

6. The theatrical trade unions generally refuse or are unable to use their power to initiate constructive programs toward revitalizing the theatre;

7. The metropolitan theatre audience consists mainly of hit-followers; the minority of thoughtful theatre lovers is offered little in the way of a sustained meaningful repertoire;

8. A handful of drama critics find themselves in a position to shape the canons of theatre art and the tastes of the entire nation; that their

mere opinion may make or break the self-esteem, progress, and longevity of an artist or company;

9. The exaggerated values of "fame and fortune" and the panicky competitiveness accompanying them have intimidated most theatrical artists to the point of paralysis; these myths have misled others in the conviction that their work has achieved an incontestable excellence, that their venerated talents are no longer in need of training and extension;

10. Everyday, innovators announce new theatre projects, each determined in his own way to solve the problems of today's theatre; but lacking valid experience and research they are frequently unaware that their formulas for tomorrow's theatre have already proven yesterday's mistakes;

### Therefore We Resolve to Found:
### The American Conservatory Theatre

1. As a non-profit tax exempt educational institution resembling the European concept of Conservatory—adapted so that development and performances are integral and inseparable parts of the professional's creative life. Training and production shall be indigenous, the one to the other, not working as separate programs with separated personnel. All participants in the Conservatory—as in a ballet company—will always be in training;

2. To bring together the finest directors, authors, playwrights, actors, and educators in the theatre arts to provide comprehensive advanced training to a large professional company and to make this aggregate training available to representatives of regional theatres and educators in university and professional schools of drama;

3. To restore to the creative artist himself the right to leadership in shaping and fulfilling his own potential;

4. To determine the qualifications for membership and welcome as participants in the Conservatory any union person who demonstrates creative ability and who agrees to participate in the triple role of student, instructor, and production artist. It shall not, however, demonstrate prejudice against gifted young talent merely because they are not union members;

5. To engage artists on long contracts so that within an explorative atmosphere, with reasonable security, the adventuresome artist may test his potential;

6. To structure the Conservatory-Theatre to insure the maximum freedom from proprietary interference, and to vest in the artistic directors of the Conservatory the authority to determine continuity and policies of the Foundation;

7. To build and rely completely upon a subscribed membership audience offering a meaningful repertoire at a popular, accessible ($4.95 top) price scale;

8. To enlist the cooperation of national leaders, publishers, editors and theatre critics themselves in an experiment by which television and journalistic reviewing will be limited to exclude both praise and disparagement of the repertory performances for a period of three years; in return, the Conservatory-Theatre will agree to limit advertising to exclude "quotes" from any source;

9. To found the AMERICAN CONSERVATORY THEATRE upon the observed and reported experience of all related theatre projects; principles derived from research and experience collated from former theatre projects with the aim to avert the misjudgements that have caused so many projects to founder; to leave provision for expansion and adjustment within the Charter and By-Laws; to encourage, through future programs (already drafted) the growth of playwrighting, criticism, design, architecture, opera, mime, and theatre literature; to provide a receptacle for the focus of isolated theatre projects and to aid all efforts towards unity and economy in the national theatre.

### *Definition*

THE AMERICAN CONSERVATORY THEATRE combines the concept of resident repertory theatre with the classic concept of continuous training, study and practice as an integral and inseparable part of the performer's life.

THE AMERICAN CONSERVATORY THEATRE is simultaneously an educational and performing organization. The purpose in the first three years is to provide actors, craftsmen, directors, and designers with a triple-pronged program. Each participant in the program will:

1. Develop his own artistic potential through study
2. Teach the younger professionals
3. Perform wide repertoire

As the project is aimed at broadening the expressive ability of the actor and director, all available techniques for acting and directing will be used as sources. An eclectic program will be explored with a wide range of theory and experiment, while performance will serve to apply and test techniques.

The training program of the CONSERVATORY will be concurrent with the program of presentations. Training will be woven into the rehearsal pattern by stage managers specifically engaged for the purpose of preparing the daily schedule and assignments of personnel (*Estudientenlieder*).

Our goal is to awaken in the theatre artist his maximum versatility and expressiveness.

# Appendix B

## The 1967 Acting Company Roster

### Associate and Journeymen Actors

Lynne Arden
René Auberjonois
Ramon Bieri
Dion Chesse
Barbara Colby
Peter Donat
Jay Doyle
George Ede
Patricia Falkenhain
Harry Frazier
Ellen Geer
Will Geer
Robert Gerringer
David Grimm
Scott Hylands
Phillip Kerr
Ruth Kobart

Michael Learned
Barry MacGregor
DeAnn Mears
Judith Mihalyi
Josephine Nichols
William Paterson
Angela Paton
Charlene Polite
Marguerite Ray
Ray Reinhardt
Ken Ruta
John Schuck
Paul Shenar
Deborah Sussel
Patrick Tovatt
Ann Weldon

### Acting Fellows

Mark Bramhall
David Dukes
Robert Feero
Larry Ferguson

Terry Mace
Glenn Mazen
Kimo Perry
Herman Poppe

Kate Hawley
Karen Ingenthron
Carol Mayo Jenkins
Enid Kent
Barry Kraft
Dana Larson
Michael Lerner

James Ragan
Mary Ellen Ray
Mark Schell
Izetta Smith
Gil Turner
Don Watson
Kitty Winn

# Appendix C

## ACT Play Schedule 1965–1973

### *1965–1966—Pittsburgh*

| PLAY | AUTHOR | DIRECTOR |
|------|--------|----------|
| *Tartuffe* | Molière | William Ball |
| *Six Characters in Search of an Author* | Luigi Pirandello | William Ball |
| *Tiny Alice* | Edward Albee | William Ball |
| *The Rose Tattoo* | Tennessee Williams | William Francisco |
| *King Lear* | William Shakespeare | William Ball |
| *Death of a Salesman* | Arthur Miller | Allen Fletcher |
| *The Apollo of Bellac* | Jean Giraudoux | René Auberjonois |
| *Antigone* | Jean Anouilh | Jay Harnick |
| *Noah* | Andre Obey | William Young |
| *The Servant of Two Masters* | Carlo Goldoni | William Francisco |
| *The Devil's Disciple* | George Bernard Shaw | Harold Stone |
| *In White America* | Martin Duberman | Harold Stone |
| *Under Milkwood* | Dylan Thomas | William Ball |

| | | |
|---|---|---|
| *Beyond the Fringe* | Alan Bennet, Peter Cook, Jonathan Miller, Dudley Moore | René Auberjonois |

1967—San Francisco, Six-Month Season

| PLAY | AUTHOR | DIRECTOR |
|---|---|---|
| *Beyond the Fringe* | Alan Bennet, Peter Cook, Jonathan Miller, Dudley Moore | René Auberjonois |
| *Endgame* | Samuel Beckett | Edward Payson Call |
| *Charley's Aunt* | Brandon Thomas | Edward Hastings |
| *Man and Superman* | George Bernard Shaw | Jerome Kilty |
| *Arsenic and Old Lace* | Joseph Kesselring | Allen Fletcher |
| *Our Town* | Thornton Wilder | Edward Hastings |
| *Dear Liar* | Jerome Kilty | Jerome Kilty |
| *The Torch-Bearers* | George Kelly | Edward Payson Call |
| *Long Day's Journey into Night* | Eugene O'Neill | Byron Ringland |
| *The Seagull* | Anton Chekhov | Edward Payson Call |
| *A.C.T. One-Acts: The Zoo Story* | Edward Albee | Richard A. Dysart |
| *Krapp's Last Tape* | Samuel Beckett | Scott Hylands |
| *Tartuffe* | Molière | William Ball |
| *Tiny Alice* | Edward Albee | William Ball |
| *Six Characters in Search of an Author* | Luigi Pirandello | William Ball |
| *Death of a Salesman* | Arthur Miller | Allen Fletcher |
| *Under Milkwood* | Dylan Thomas | William Ball |

# ACT Play Schedule 1965–1973

## *1967–1968—First Full Season*

| PLAY | AUTHOR | DIRECTOR |
|---|---|---|
| *Two for the Seesaw* | William Gibson | Byron Ringland |
| *The Crucible* | Arthur Miller | Allen Fletcher |
| *Thieves' Carnival* | Jean Anouilh | Jerome Kilty |
| *Twelfth Night* | William Shakespeare | William Ball |
| *An Evening's Frost* | Donald Hall | Marcella Cisney |
| *The Misanthrope* | Molière | David William |
| *A Delicate Balance* | Edward Albee | Edward Hastings |
| *A Streetcar Named Desire* | Tennessee Williams | William Ball |
| *Don't Shoot Mable, It's Your Husband* | Jerome Kilty | Jerome Kilty |
| *Deedle, Deedle, Dumpling, My Son God* | Brian McKinney | Patrick Tovatt |
| *Long Live Life* | Jerome Kilty | Jerome Kilty |
| *In White America* | Martin Duberman | Nagle Jackson |
| *Caught in the Act* | Nagle Jackson | Nagle Jackson |
| *Albee Acts* | Edward Albee | Richard Dysart |
| *The American Dream* | Edward Albee | William Ball |
| *Dear Liar* | Jerome Kilty | Jerome Kilty |
| *Under Milkwood* | Dylan Thomas | William Ball |
| *Tartuffe* | Molière | William Ball |
| *Tiny Alice* | Edward Albee | William Ball |
| *Our Town* | Thornton Wilder | Edward Hastings |
| *Long Day's Journey into Night* | Eugene O'Neill | Robert Goldsby |

| | | |
|---|---|---|
| *Charley's Aunt* | Brandon Thomas | Edward Hastings |
| *Endgame* | Samuel Beckett | Edward Payson Call |

### 1968–1969

| PLAY | AUTHOR | DIRECTOR |
|---|---|---|
| *A Flea in Her Ear* | Georges Feydeau | Gower Champion |
| *The Devil's Disciple* | George Bernard Shaw | Edward Hastings |
| *Little Murders* | Jules Feiffer | Nagle Jackson |
| *Staircase* | Charles Dyer | Robert Goldsby |
| *Three Sisters* | Anton Chekhov | William Ball |
| *The Promise* | Aleksei Arbuzov | Edward Hastings |
| *Rosencrantz and Guildenstern are Dead* | Tom Stoppard | William Ball |
| *The Architect and the Emperor of Assyria* | Fernando Arrabal | Robert Goldsby |
| *Room Service* | Allen Boretz and John Murray | Nagle Jackson |
| *Glory! Hallelujah!* | Anna Marie Barlow | Edwin Sherin |
| *The Hostage* | Brendan Behan | Allen Fletcher |
| *Oh Dad, Poor Dad, Mamma's Hung You in the Closet and I'm Feeling So Sad* | Arthur L. Kopit | Edward Hastings |
| *A Delicate Balance* | Edward Albee | Edward Hastings |
| *In White America* | Martin Duberman | Nagle Jackson |

### 1970—Short Season (twenty-two weeks)

| PLAY | AUTHOR | DIRECTOR |
|---|---|---|
| *The Importance of Being Earnest* | Oscar Wilde | Jack O'Brien |

# ACT Play Schedule 1965–1973

| | | |
|---|---|---|
| *Oedipus Rex* | Sophocles | William Ball |
| *Saint Joan* | George Bernard Shaw | Edward Gilbert |
| *The Blood Knot* | Athol Fugard | Gilbert Moses |
| *Little Malcolm and His Struggle Against the Eunuchs* | David Halliwell | Nagle Jackson |
| *Hadrian VII* | Peter Luke | Allen Fletcher |
| *The Rose Tattoo* | Tennessee Williams | Louis Criss |
| *The Tempest* | William Shakespeare | William Ball |
| *The Tavern* | George M. Cohan | Ellis Rabb |
| *Rosencrantz and Guildenstern are Dead* | Tom Stoppard | William Ball |
| *Six Characters in Search of an Author* | Luigi Pirandello | Mark Healy |

## 1970–1971 *(no double repertory)*

| | | |
|---|---|---|
| *The Merchant of Venice* | William Shakespeare | Ellis Rabb |
| *The Relapse* | John Vanbrugh | Edward Hastings |
| *The Latent Heterosexual* | Paddy Chayefsky | Allen Fletcher |
| *The Time of Your Life* | William Saroyan | Edward Hastings |
| *An Enemy of the People* | Henrik Ibsen | Allen Fletcher |
| *The Selling of the President* | Hample, James, O'Brien | Ellis Rabb |
| *The Tempest* | William Shakespeare | William Ball |
| *Hadrian VII* | Peter Luke | Allen Fletcher |

Appendix C

*1971–1972*

| Play | Author | Director |
| --- | --- | --- |
| *Caesar and Cleopatra* | George Bernard Shaw | William Ball |
| *Antony and Cleopatra* | William Shakespeare | Allen Fletcher |
| *Dandy Dick* | Arthur Wing Pinero | Edward Hastings |
| *Paradise Lost* | Clifford Odets | Allen Fletcher |
| *The Contractor* | David Storey | William Ball |
| *Sleuth* | Anthony Shaffer | Ellis Rabb |
| *Rosencrantz and Guildenstern are Dead* | Tom Stoppard | William Ball |
| *The Tavern* | George M. Cohan | Peter Donat |

*1972–1973*

| Play | Author | Director |
| --- | --- | --- |
| *Cyrano de Bergerac* | Edmond Rostand | William Ball |
| *The House of Blue Leaves* | John Guare | Edward Hastings |
| *The Mystery Cycle* | Nagle Jackson | Nagle Jackson |
| *A Doll's House* | Henrik Ibsen | Allen Fletcher |
| *You Can't Take it with You* | Kaufman and Hart | Jack O'Brien |
| *That Championship Season* | Jason Miller | Allen Fletcher |
| *The Merchant of Venice* | William Shakespeare | Robert Bonaventura |
| *The Crucible* | Arthur Miller | William Ball |

# Notes

*1. Ensemble Theatre Companies*

1. Gerald Eades Bently, *The Jacobean and Caroline Stages: Dramatic Companies and Players*, 2 vols. (Oxford: Clarendon Press, 1941) vol. 1, pp. 3–4.

2. Ibid., pp. 68–69.

3. Toby Cole and Helen Kirch Chinoy, eds., *Actors on Acting* (New York: Crown Publishers, 1949), p. 147.

4. Peter D. Arnott, *An Introduction to the French Theatre* (Totowa, N.J.: Rowan and Littlefield, 1977), p. 310.

5. Pierre Louis Ducharte, *The Italian Comedy*, trans. Randolph T. Weaver (New York: Dover Publications, 1966), p. 6. Cole and Chinoy, *Actors on Acting*, p. 147.

7. Arnott, p. 147.

8. Cole and Chinoy, *Actors on Acting*, p. 147.

9. John H. Terfloth, "The Pre-Meiningen Rise of the Director in Germany and Austria," *Theatre Quarterly*, vol. 6 (1976), p. 66.

10. Ibid.

11. Ibid., p. 67.

12. Ibid., p. 68.

13. Ibid., p. 69.

14. Ibid.

15. Cole and Chinoy, *Actors on Acting*, p. 257.

16. Terfloth, pp. 78–79.

17. Ibid., p. 79.

18. Ibid., p. 84.

19. Marvin Carlson, *The German Stage in the Nineteenth Century* (Metuchen, N.J.: The Scarecrow Press, 1972), p. 13.

20. Ibid., p. 15.

21. Ibid., p. 20.

22. Max Grube, *The Story of the Meininger*, trans. Ann Marie Koller (Coral Gables, Fla.: University of Miami Press, 1963), p. 33.

23. Ibid., p. 39.

24. Ibid., p. 37.

25. Ibid., p. 28.

26. Ibid., p. xi.

27. John A. Henderson, *The First Avant-Garde, 1887–1894* (London: George Harrap, 1971), p. 48.

28. Cole and Chinoy, *Actors on Acting*, p. 223.

29. Oscar Brockett and Robert Findlay, *Century of Innovation* (Englewood Cliffs, N.J.: Prentice-Hall, 1973), p. 101.

30. Maxim Newmark, *Otto Brahm, the Man and the Critic* (London: G. E. Strechert, 1938), p. 141.

31. Ibid., p. 146.

32. Cole and Chinoy, *Actors on Acting*, p. 268

33. Ibid., p. 30.

34. Marc Slonim, *Russian Theatre* (New York: The World Publishing Company, 1961), p. 101.

35. Vladimir Nemirovitch-Dantchenko, *My Life in the Russian Theatre*, trans. John Cournos (New York: Theatre Art Books, 1968), p. 101.

36. Slonim, p. 133.

37. Nemirovitch-Dantchenko, p. 156.

38. Ibid., p. 144.

39. Ibid., p. 146.

40. Ibid., p. 156–57.

41. Slonim, p. 110.

42. Norris Houghton, *Moscow Rehearsals* (New York: Grove Press, 1962), p. 76.

43. Bernard Hewitt, *Theatre U.S.A., 1668–1957* (New York: McGraw-Hill, 1959), p. 161.

44. Ibid., p. 161.

45. Ibid., p. 219.

46. Ibid.

47. David Belasco, *Theatre Through Its Stage Door* (New York: Harper & Row, 1919) pp. 90–91.

48. Hewitt, pp. 365.

49. Oscar Brockett and Robert Findlay, *Century of Innovation*, p. 494.

50. Harold Clurman, *The Fervent Years: The Story of the Group Theatre and the 30's* (New York: Harcourt Brace Jovanovich, 1975), p. 23.

51. Ibid., p. 33.

52. Ibid., p. 36.

53. Ibid., p. 57.

54. Ibid., p. 281.

55. Ibid., p. 287.

56. Alïce J. Kellman, "Joseph Chaikin the Actor," *The Drama Review*, 20 (3 September 1976), p. 18.

57. James Godfrey, "William Ball: the Cornerstone of a Great Company," *San Francisco Theatre Magazine*, 1 (Summer 1978), p. 52.

2. *The American Conservatory Theatre*

1. Julius Novick, *Beyond Broadway* (New York: Hill and Wang, 1969), p. 223.

2. William Ball, interview with Bill Hillman, *Voice of America*, (15 May 1971).

3. Novick, p. 223.

4. Ellaine Hershberger, "The Pittsburgh Playhouse," *Player's Magazine* no. 48, vol. 4 (1973), p. 99.

5. Steven Winn, "The Enigmatic Man Behind A.C.T.," *San Francisco Chronicle* (4 October 1981), p. 21.

6. Ellis Rabb, interview with Bill Hillman, *Voice of America*, (15 May 1970).

7. Ball, *Voice of America*, (15 May 1971).

8. Unpublished paper, Archives of the American Conservatory Theatre, p. 3.

9. Joseph Zeigler, *Regional Theatre: The Revolutionary Stage* (Minneapolis: University of Minnesota Press, 1973), p. 137.

10. American Conservatory Theatre Statement of Purpose, 1965, p. 1.

11. Ibid., p. 3.

12. Unpublished paper, ACT Archives, p. 3.

13. American Conservatory Theatre Statement of Purpose, 1965, p. 5.

14. Dennis Powers, "The Story of A.C.T., a New Concept in the American Theatre," press release 1969, p. 3.

15. Carl Maves, "A.C.T. at Eight," *Big Times* (19 October 1974), p. 6.

16. Leigh Weimers, "That Live Feeling," *San Jose Mercury News*, 14 October 1973.

17. William Ball, interview with Joan Sadler, Archives of the American Conservatory Theatre, 1979.

18. Ibid.

19. Ibid.

20. Ibid.

21. Ibid.

22. American Conservatory Theatre Institutional Self Study (typewritten, 1977), pp. 4–5.

23. Ibid., p. 5.

24. Ball, interview with Joan Sadler, 1979.

25. Ibid.

26. Powers, "The Story of A.C.T.," p. 3.

27. Julius Novick, "Hinterlands II: Cleveland, Pittsburgh and Points South," *Nation* (6 June 1966) p. 691.

28. Dayle Hilbourn, "William Ball and the American Conservatory Theatre," (typewritten, 30 July 1975), p. 4.

29. Powers, "The Story of A.C.T.," p. 4.

30. Zeigler, *Regional Theatre: The Revolutionary Stage*, p. 138.

*3. A Theatre in Search of a City*

1. James B. McKenzie, interview with author, San Francisco, 17 November 1981.

2. Walter Kerr, "Why this grass? Rosemary asked." *New York Times* (29 January 1967), sec. 2, p. 1, col. 1.

3. William Ball, interview with author, San Francisco, 2 February 1982.

4. American Conservatory Theatre Statement of Purpose, 1965, p. 1.

5. Charles A. Church to the American Conservatory Theatre Foundation, 17 May 1965, Internal Revenue Service, Washington, D.C.

6. James B. McKenzie, interview with author, San Francisco, 17 November 1981.

7. American Conservatory Theatre Institutional Self-Study (typewritten), p. 105.

8. James B. McKenzie, interview with author, San Francisco, 17 November 1981.

9. Edward Hastings, Jr., interview with author, San Francisco, 11 January 1982.

10. American Conservatory Theatre Institutional Self-Study (typewritten), pp. 106–7.

11. Cyril Magnin, interview with Joan Sadler, Archives of the American Conservatory Theatre, 1979.

12. James B. McKenzie, interview with author, 17 November 1981.

13. Frederick H. Gardner, "The Actor's Workshop is Dead," *The Nation* (19 September 1966) p. 256.

14. Ibid., p. 257.

15. Cyril Magnin and Cynthia Robins, *Call Me Cyril* (San Francisco: McGraw-Hill Book Company, 1981), p. 282.

16. Ibid.

17. William Ball, interview with the author, 2 February 1982.

18. American Conservatory Theatre Institutional Self-Study History of C.A.A.C.T. (typewritten), p. 1.

19. Magnin and Robins, p. 285.

20. *New York Times* (23 January 1967), p. 29, col. 1.

21. John Wasserman, "A.C.T. Opening: A Rousing Success," *San Francisco Chronicle* (23 January 1967), p. 37.

22. Powers, "The Story of A.C.T.," p. 8.

23. *Performing Arts*, vol. 1, no. 1 (November 1967) p. 22.

24. *New York Times* (23 January 1967), p. 29, col. 1.

25. *New York Times* (6 July 1967), p. 40, col. 1.

26. William Bushnell, interview with author, 12 December 1981.

27. Edward Hastings, Jr., interview with author, 11 January 1982.

28. William Bushnell, interview with author, 12 December 1981.

29. Mortimer Fleishhacker, "A.C.T. makes permanent home in San Francisco," press release (6 September 1967).

30. Lawrence E. Davies, "S.F. Keeps Repertory Unit," *New York Times*, 8 September 1967, p. 33, col. 4.

31. Ibid.

32. Julius Novick, *Beyond Broadway: The Quest for Permanent Theatre* (New York: Hill and Wang, 1969), p. 230.

33. William Ball, interview with author, 9 February 1982.

34. Stanley Eichelbaum, interview with author, San Francisco, 21 December 1981.

35. Magnin and Robins, p. 260.

36. Welton Jones, "Invigorating Place for Theatre," *San Diego Union*, 11 August 1974.

37. Gerald Nachman, interview with author, San Francisco, 2 November 1981.

38. Jones, "Invigorating Place for Theatre."

39. Mike Steele, "Theatre Wins Heart of San Francisco," *Minneapolis Tribune*, 5 May 1975.

40. Stanley Eichelbaum, interview with author, 21 December 1981.

41. Judy Stone, "The Right to Fail—and to Succeed," *New York Times* (7 May 1967), sec. 2, p. 5, col. 1.

42. Grover Sales, "A.C.T.—Can It Survive the Local Boosters?", *San Francisco Magazine* (January 1972), pp. 9–10.

43. Stanley Eichelbaum, interview with author, 21 December 1981.

44. Robert Goldsby, interview with author, 3 November 1981.

45. "Flower of the West," *Newsweek* (22 January 1968), vol. 71, p. 24.

46. R. Lyons, "San Francisco's Cultural Donnybrook," *Harper's* (March 1966), vol. 232, pp. 31, 32.

47. Rockefeller Panel Report, *The Performing Arts: Problems and Prospects* (New York: McGraw-Hill, 1965), p. 110.

48. American Conservatory Theatre Statement of Purpose, 1965, p. 3.

49. Novick, p. 231.

50. Douglas Johnson, "Appreciation of A.C.T.," *San Francisco Theatre Magazine*, vol. 1 (1978), p. 51.

51. Robert Goldsby, interview with author, 21 December 1981.

52. Ibid.

53. Stanley Eichelbaum, interview with author, 21 December 1981.

54. American Conservatory Theatre Institutional Self-Study, 1977, p. 8.

55. James B. McKenzie, interview with author, 17 November 1981.

56. Brian McKinney, press release, 27 December 1966, p. 1.

57. Joseph Zeigler, *Regional Theatre: The Revolutionary Stage* (Minneapolis, Minn.: University Press, 1973), p. 139.

58. Stanley Eichelbaum, "All in All, Good Season," San Francisco Examiner, *May 1970*.

59. Chris Curci, "1971—Bright, Encouraging Year," *The Daily Revue* (11 January 1972), p. 12.

60. Stanley Eichelbaum, "A.C.T.—The Outlook Has Never Been Rosier," *San Francisco Examiner*, 25 April 1972.

61. Sales, p. 9.

62. Tyrone Guthrie, "Repertory Theatre: Ideal or Deception," *New York Times* (26 April 1959), vol. 6, p. 40.

63. William Ball, interview with author, 9 February 1982.

64. Carl Maves, "A.C.T. at Eight," *Big Times* (October–November 1973), p. 8.

65. Bill Hillman, "Critic's Choice," *Voice of America* (15 May 1971), p. 4.

66. Charles R. Lyons, "Theatre in Review," *Educational Theatre Journal* (December 1971), p. 479.

67. Johnson, "Appreciation of A.C.T.," p. 51.

4. *The* Regisseur *and His Staff*

1. George Oppenheimer, "The Gentleman From San Francisco," *Newsday*, 25 October 1969.

2. Steven E. Markham, "A Summary Report to A.C.T.," (typewritten, 11 January 1979), p. 2.

3. Robert Taylor, "Margaret Webster," *Oakland Tribune*, 16 November 1972.

4. Margaret Webster, unpublished paper 1965, Archives of the American Conservatory Theatre, pp. 3–4.

5. Taylor, "Margaret Webster."

6. Oppenheimer, "The Gentleman from San Francisco."

7. John Adams, "The Thought Behind Conservatory Theatre," *Independent*, 7 October 1967.

8. Walter Blum, "The Man Who Shook Up Geary Street," *California Living* (23 April 1967), p. 7.

9. Fran Fanshel, "It's All Bill Ball," *California Living* (22 February 1976), p. 26.

10. Steven Winn, "The Enigmatic Man Behind A.C.T.," *San Francisco Chronicle Datebook* (4 October 1981), p. 16.

11. Ibid.

12. Fanshel, p. 25.

13. Robert Goldsby, interview with author, Berkeley, 3 November 1981.

14. James B. McKenzie, interview with author, San Francisco, 17 November 1981.

15. William Bushnell, interview with author, Los Angeles, 12 December 1981.

16. Robert Goldsby, interview with author, 3 November 1981.

17. Allen Fletcher, interview with author, San Francisco, 23 November 1981.

18. Edward Hastings, interview with author, San Francisco, 11 January 1982.

19. Robert Goldsby, interview with author, Berkeley, 27 October 1981.

20. Stanley Eichelbaum, "A Dazzling, Diamond-Hard Portia," *San Francisco Examiner*, 30 November 1970.

21. William Bushnell, "Letter to the Pinkie," *San Francisco Chronicle Datebook* (15 November 1981), p. 58.

5. *Means of Survival*

1. Dennis Powers, "Setting the Artist Free," *Performing Arts*, vol. 6, no. 3 (March 1972), p. 6.

2. Ibid.

3. Ibid., p. 7.

4. William Ball, interview with author, 2 February 1982.

5. Richard Hofstadter, *Anti-intellectualism in American Life* (New York: Vintage, 1973), p. 235.

6. Ibid., p. 236.

7. Powers, p. 7.

8. Alvin Toffler, *The Culture Consumers* (New York: Vintage, 1973), p. 230.

9. *New York Times* (30 September 1966), p. 7, col. 2.

10. Rockefeller Panel Report, *The Performing Arts: Problems and Prospects* (New York: McGraw-Hill, 1965), p. 113.

11. Ibid., p. 19.

12. Ibid. p. 107.

13. William Ball, interview with author, 2 February 1982.

14. Ibid.

15. Edward Hastings, interview with author, 11 January 1982.

16. Ibid.

17. William Bushnell, interview with author, 12 December 1981.

18. Jim Jones, "A.C.T. Ford Foundation Grant," press release, 30 January 1967, p. 1.

19. Ibid., p. 2.

20. Mortimer Fleishhacker, "Why the Bay Area needs the American Conservatory Theatre," *Performing Arts* (February 1968), p. 9.

21. American Conservatory Theatre Institutional Self-Study, History of the C.A.A.C.T. (typewritten), p. 2.

22. *United States Code Annotated, Title 20, Education*, (St. Paul, Minn.: West Publishing Company, 1974), p. 499.

23. Monty Neely, "The National Endowment for the Arts Theatre Program: An Historical Analysis," (Ph.D. dissertation, Wayne State University, 1976), p. 275.

24. Roger Boas to John R. Wilk, personal letter, September 1980.

25. Dennis Powers, press release, 7 November 1967, p. 2.

26. Neely, pp. 175–76.

27. Stanley Eichelbaum, "A.C.T.'s Ultimatum—$104,000 or Else," *San Francisco Examiner*, 19 July 1968.

28. Brian McKinney, "A.C.T. Near July 31, Deadline, is $84,000 Short of Goal," press release, 26 July 1968, p. 3.

29. Brian McKinney, "'A.C.T. Now' Telethon Raises More Than $40,000 in Pledges," press release, 30 July 1968, p. 3.

30. Mortimer Fleishhacker, "California Theatre Foundation Opens 1969 Fund Drive for A.C.T.," press release, 28 January 1969, p. 3.

31. James B. McKenzie, interview with author, 17 November 1981.

32. Robert Goldsby, interview with author, 27 October 1981.

33. William Bushnell, interview with author, 12 December 1981.

34. James B. McKenzie, interview with author, 17 November 1981.

35. Ibid.

36. Robert Goldsby, interview with author, 27 October 1981.

37. Dennis Powers, press release, 26 March 1969, p. 1.

38. American Conservatory Theatre Institutional Self-Study, History of C.A.A.C.T. (typewritten), p. 2.

39. James B. McKenzie, interview with author, 17 November 1981.

40. Ibid.

41. William Ball, interview with author, 2 February 1982.

42. John C. Mahoney, "A.C.T. Dancing Not Begging in the Streets," *Los Angeles Times* (7 March 1971), p. 30.

43. Ibid., p. 28.

44. William Ball, interview with author, 2 February 1982.

*6. The ACT Style of Acting*

1. William Ball, interview with author, 2 February 1982.

2. Dennis Powers, "The American Conservatory Theatre, a Concept," (typewritten), p. 1.

3. William Ball, interview with author, 2 February 1982.

4. American Conservatory Theatre Statement of Purpose, 1965, p. 1.

5. John Adams, "The Thought Behind Conservatory Theatre," Richmond, California *Independent*, 7 October 1967.

6. William Ball, interview with author, 2 February 1982.

7. American Conservatory Theatre Institutional Self-Study, p. 8.

8. American Conservatory Theatre Statement of Purpose, p. 3.

9. Stanley Eichelbaum, "S.F.'s Chance to Star on the Stage," *San Francisco Examiner*, 4 April 1967.

10. William Ball, interview with author, 2 February 1982.

11. Michel Saint-Denis, *Theatre: The Rediscovery of Style* (New York: Theatre Arts Books, 1960), p. 84.

12. Ibid., p. 91.

13. Ibid., p. 92.

14. Ibid., p. 93.

15. Ibid., p. 92.

16. Ibid., p. 94.

17. Ibid.

18. Ibid., p. 97.

19. Ibid.

20. Ibid., p. 98.

21. Ibid., p. 99.

22. Ibid., p. 108.

23. Eric Atkins, "The Power of Acting Comes Forth in A.C.T.," *Saint Petersburg Times*, 28 October 1969.

24. Cole and Chinoy, *Actors on Acting*, p. 182.

25. Atkins, "The Power of Acting Comes Forth in A.C.T."

26. Lewis Funke, "West Coast 'Tiny Alice' passes Albee's Scrutiny Here," *New York Times* (29 September 1969), p. 52, col. 1.

27. Dennis Powers, "The Story of A.C.T.," (typewritten 1969), p. 2.

28. Allen Fletcher, interview with author, 23 November 1981.

29. American Conservatory Theatre Institutional Self-Study, p. 9.

30. William Ball, interview with author, 2 February 1982.

31. "Agreement and Rules Governing Employment in Resident Theatres," *Actor's Equity Association Handbook*, 3 July 1978, p. 55.

32. Robert Goldsby, interview with author, 3 November 1981.

33. American Conservatory Theatre Institutional Self-Study, pp. 10–11.

34. Robert Goldsby, interview with author, 3 November 1981.

35. Ibid.

36. Deborah Sussel, interview with author, San Francisco, 24 May 1982.

37. Robert Goldsby, interview with author, 3 November 1981.

38. Ibid.

39. Allen Fletcher, interview with author, 23 November 1981.

40. American Conservatory Theatre Institutional Self-Study, p. 19.

41. Ibid., p. 21.

42. Ibid.

43. Ibid., p. 22.

44. Ibid., p. 23.

45. Mike Steele, "Theatre Wins Heart of San Francisco," *Minneapolis Tribune*, 5 May 1975.

46. Julius Novick, "Is Good Good Enough," *New York Times*, 27 July 1969, p. 1.

47. Ibid.

48. William Ball, interview with author, 2 February 1982.

49. William Ball, class lecture, San Francisco, 10 April 1982.

50. Edith W. Skinner, *Speak with Distinction*, (typewritten, New Jersey, 1965) p. i.

51. R. B. Marriott, "An Actor and his Action," *The Stage and Television Today*, 12 May 1960.

### 7. The Acting Company

1. American Conservatory Theatre Statement of Purpose, p. 2.

2. William Ball, interview with author, 2 February 1982.

3. Ibid.

4. Press release, 1966, p. 2.

5. Ibid.

6. DeAnn Mears, interview with author, San Francisco, 19 November 1981.

7. Ray Reinhardt, interview with author, San Francisco, 27 July 1982.

8. Frank Ottiwell, interview with author, San Francisco, 27 July 1982.

9. Press release, 12 March 1967.

10. Paul Emerson, "A.C.T.'s Auberjonois Sets Frantic Pace," *Palo Alto Times*, 31 March 1967.

11. Ibid.

12. Peter Donat, interview with author, San Francisco, 17 November 1981.

13. Jeane Miller, "An A.C.T. Alum Comes Back," *San Francisco Examiner*, 4 May 1979.

14. Angela Paton, interview with author, Berkeley, 6 February 1982.

15. James B. McKenzie, interview with author, 17 November 1981.

16. Peter Donat, interview with author, 17 November 1981.

17. DeAnn Mears, interview with author, 19 November 1981.

18. "Repertory Theatre: 'Home Base' for an Actor," *Performing Arts*, vol. 2, no. 1 (January 1968), pp. 6–7.

19. Ibid., p. 8.

20. Paul Shenar, interview with Bill Hillman, "Voice of America" (18 January 1969).

21. L. Pierce Carson, "Anxiety Rides Back Seat with Leading Lady," *Napa Register*, 25 March 1972.

22. Jeane Miller, "A Role Far from Her Walton Image," *San Francisco Examiner*, 25 March 1977.

23. John McClintock, "A.C.T. Patrons Will Never Forget His Face," *Palo Alto Times*, (22 February 1979).

24. William Paterson, interview with author, San Francisco, 28 October 1981.

25. Gwyneth Richards, "The World a Stage," *Theatre Magazine* (Winter 1977), p. 52.

26. Ray Reinhardt, interview with author, 27 July 1982.

27. Deborah Sussel, interview with author, San Francisco, 21 July 1982.

28. L. Pierce Carson, "New Directions in Acting Needed," *Napa Register* 24 November 1973.

29. Judy Klemesrud, "Her Name is Kitty Winn, as in Winner," *New York Times*, 11 July 1971.

30. Richard Schechner, ed., "The Regional Theatre: Four Views," *The Drama Review* (Fall 1968), p. 21.

31. Peter Donat, interview with author, 17 November 1981.

32. Paine Knickerbocker, "A.C.T. Actor Goes to Hollywood," *San Francisco Chronicle*, 1 July 1969.

33. William Paterson, interview with author, San Francisco, 28 October 1981.

34. "Reinhardt: A.C.T. is for Actors," *Oakland Tribune,* 19 January 1969.

35. Ray Reinhardt, interview with author, 27 July 1981.

36. Deborah Sussel, interview with author, 21 July 1982.

37. Lois Taylor, "The Face is Familiar, but . . . ," *Honolulu Star Bulletin,* 13 June 1979, p. 2.

38. Peter Donat, interview with author, 17 November 1981.

39. "Popular T.V. Star Back at A.C.T. to Raise Funds," *San Mateo Times,* 17 March 1977.

40. Schechner, p. 22.

41. Frank Ottiwell, interview with author, 27 July 1982.

42. James B. McKenzie, interview with author, 17 November 1981.

# Bibliography

*Books*

ARNOTT, PETER D. *An Introduction to the French Theatre*. Totowa, N.J.: Rowan and Littlefield, 1977.

BAUMOL, WILLIAM, AND BOWEN, WILLIAM. *Performing Arts: The Economic Dilemma*. New York: The Twentieth Century Fund, 1966.

BELASCO, DAVID. *The Theatre Through Its Stage Door*. New York: Harper & Brothers, 1919.

BENTLEY, GERALD EADES. *The Jacobean and Caroline Stages: Dramatic Companies and Players*, vol. 1. Oxford: Clarendon Press, 1941.

BLAU, HERBERT. *The Impossible Theatre*. New York: Macmillan, 1964.

BOAS, FREDERICK. *An Introduction to Eighteenth Century Drama 1700–1780*. Oxford: Clarendon Press, 1953.

BROCKETT, OSCAR G., AND FINDLAY, ROBERT R. *Century of Innovation: A History of European and American Drama Since 1870*. Englewood Cliffs, N.J.: Prentice-Hall, Inc., 1973.

CARLSON, MARVIN. *The German Stage in the Nineteenth Century*. Metuchen, N.J.: The Scarecrow Press, 1972.

CLURMAN, HAROLD. *The Fervent Years: The Story of the Group Theatre and the '30s*. New York: Harcourt Brace Jovanovich, 1975.

COLE, TOBY, AND CHINOY, HELEN KIRCH, EDS. *Actors on Acting*. New York: Crown Publishers, 1959.

———. *Directors on Directing*. New York: Bobbs-Merril Company, Inc., 1963.

DALY, JOSEPH F. *Life of Augustin Daly*. New York: The Macmillan Company, 1971.

DAVIS, R.G. *The San Francisco Mime Troupe, the First 10 Years*. Palo Alto, Calif.: Rampart Press, 1975.

DUCHARTE, PIERRE LOUIS. *The Italian Comedy*. New York: Dover Publications, 1966.

FELHEIM, MARVIN. *Theatre of Augustine Daly*. Cambridge, Mass.: Harvard University Press, 1956.

FORD FOUNDATION REPORT. *The Finances of the Performing Arts*, New York: Ford Foundation, 1974.

GREEN, F.C., ED. *Diderot's Writings on the Theatre*. Cambridge: The University Press, 1936.

GRUBE, MAX. *The Story of the Meininger*. Coral Gables, Fla.: University of Miami Press, 1963.

GUTHRIE, TYRONE. *A Life in the Theatre*. New York: McGraw-Hill, 1959.

HENDERSON, JOHN A. *The First Avant-Garde, 1887–1894*. London: George Harrap, 1971.

HEWITT, BERNARD. *Theatre U.S.A., 1668–1957*. New York: McGraw-Hill, 1959.

HOUGHTON, NORRIS. *Moscow Rehearsals*. New York: Grove Press, 1962.

LANGLEY, STEPHEN, ED. *Producers on Producing*. New York: Drama Book Specialists, 1976.

LANGNER, LAWRENCE. *The Magic Curtain*. New York: E. P. Dutton, 1951.

MAGNIN, CYRIL, AND ROBINS, CYNTHIA. *Call Me Cyril*. San Francisco: McGraw-Hill, 1981.

MAMMEN, EDWARD W. *The Old Stock Company School of Acting*. Boston: Trustees of the Public Library, 1945.

MORISON, BRADLEY G., AND FLIEHR, KAY. *In Search of an Audience*. New York: Pitman Publishing, Inc., 1968.

NEMIROVITCH-DANTCHENKO, VLADIMIR. *My Life in the Russian Theatre*. New York: Theatre Arts Books, 1968.

NEWMARK, MAXIM. *Otto Brahm: The Man and The Critic*. London: G. R. Strechert, 1938.

NICOLL, ALLARDYCE. *A History of English Drama 1660–1900*, 6 vols. Cambridge: The University Press, 1967.

NOVICK, JULIUS. *Beyond Broadway: The Quest for Permanent Theatres*. New York: Hill and Wang, 1969.

ROBERTS, PETER. *The Old Vic Story*. London: W. H. Allen, A. Howard & Wyndham, 1976.

ROCKEFELLER BROTHERS FUND. *The Performing Arts: Problems and Prospects*. New York: McGraw-Hill, 1965.

RYAN, KATE. *Old Boston Museum Days*. Boston: Little, Brown, and Co., 1915.

SAINT-DENIS, MICHEL. *Theatre: The Rediscovery of Style*. New York: Theatre Arts Books, 1960.

SKINNER, EDITH. *Speak with Distinction*. New Jersey: 1965 (typewritten).

SLONIM, MARC. *Russian Theatre*. New York: The World Publishing Company, 1961.

STANISLAVSKY, KONSTANTIN. *Building a Character*. Trans. by Elizabeth Reynolds Hapgood. New York: Theatre Arts Books, 1949.

———. *My Life In Art*. Translated by J. J. Robbins. New York: Theatre Arts Books, 1948.

STRASBERG, LEE. *Strasberg at the Actor's Studio: A Tape Recorded Session*. New York: Viking Press, 1965.

THROSBY, C. D., AND WITHERS, G. A. *The Economics of the Performing Arts.* New York: St. Martin's Press, 1979.

TOFFLER, ALVIN. *The Culture Consumers.* New York: St. Martin's Press, 1964.

WELCH, CONSTANCE. *Yale Radio Plays.* Boston: Expression Company, 1940.

ZEIGLER, JOSEPH. *Regional Theatre: The Revolutionary Stage.* Minneapolis: University of Minnesota Press, 1973.


*Articles*

"A.C.T. Cancels 20-week Chicago Season." *New York Times,* 6 July 1967, p. 40, col. 1.

ADAMS, JOHN. "The Thought Behind Conservatory Theatre." *Independent,* 7 October 1967.

"American Conservatory Theatre Withdrawal." *New York Times,* 21 December 1965, p. 49, col. 1.

ATKINS, ERIC. "The Power of Acting Comes Forth In A.C.T." *Saint Petersburgh Times,* 28 October 1969.

BALL, WILLIAM. "A.C.T. Finds a Home Port." *Performing Arts* vol. 1, no. 1 (November 1967): 8–9.

BART PETER. "A.N.T.A. Spokesman Scolds Film Stars." *New York Times,* 28 June 1966, p. 49, col. 1.

———. "Cronyn Says Acting Companies Not Edifices, Need Financial Aid." *New York Times,* 25 June 1966, p. 19, col. 6.

"Bathos by the Bay: Candidate for Mayor." *Time* (3 November 1967): 20.

"Bay City Boom, High Rise Buildings." *Newsweek* 71 (13 May 1968): 12–13.

BLAKESLEE, DAVID. "Did the Stork Bring you or Did you Buy a Ticket?" *Performing Arts* vol. 2, no. 4 (April 1968): 12–13.

BLAU, HERBERT. "Decentralization: New Frontiers and Old Dead Ends." *TDR* vol. 7 (Summer 1963): 55–58.

BLUM, WALTER. "The Man Who Shook Up Geary Street." *California Living,* 23 April 1967, p. 7.

BUSHNELL, JR., WILLIAM. "The Business of Show Business—and of A.C.T." *Performing Arts* vol. 2, no. 5 (May 1968): 15–16.

CARSON, L. PIERCE. "Anxiety Rides Back Seat with Leading Lady." *Napa Register,* 25 March 1972.

———. "New Directions in Acting Needed." *Napa Register,* 24 November 1973.

CHAIKIN, JOSEPH. "Notes on Character ... And The Setup." *Performance* vol. 1, no. 1 (December 1971): 76–81.

CURCI, CHRIS. "1971—Bright, Encouraging Year." *The Daily Revue,* 11 January 1972.

*Current Biography* vol. 35, no. 5 (May 1974): 3–6.

Bibliography

DAVIES, LAWRENCE. "American Conservatory Theatre Seeks Funds for Home Coast." *New York Times*, 20 July 1967, p. 31, col. 2.

DEAN, DOUGLAS. "In the A.C.T." *In Touch* (April/May 1975): 40–44.

DUKORE, BERNARD F. "West Coast Theatre: The Pleasure of Companies." *TDR*, vol. 9 (Spring 1965): 198–207.

EICHELBAUM, STANLEY. "A.C.T.—The Outlook Has Never Been Rosier." *San Francisco Examiner*, 25 April 1971.

———. "A.C.T.'s Ultimatum $104,000 or Else." *San Francisco Examiner*, 19 July 1968.

———. "All in All, Good Season." *San Francisco Examiner*, May 1970.

———. "A Dazzling Diamond-Hard Portia." *San Francisco Examiner*, 30 November 1970.

———. "S.F.'s Chance to Star on the Stage." *San Francisco Examiner*, 4 April 1967.

EIMERL, S. "Some Uncharitable Thoughts on Thespian Matters, American Conservatory Theatre." *Reporter* 38 (18 April 1968): 41–44.

EMERSON, PAUL. "A.C.T.'s Auberjonois Sets Frantic Pace." *Palo Alto Times*, 31 March 1967.

ERLANDSON, JAMES. "Likes Reviews." *The Argonaut*, 4 January 1969: 7.

FANSHEL, FRAN. "It's All Bill Ball." *San Francisco Chronicle*, 22 February 1967: 24–29.

"Flowers of the West? New Mayor." *Newsweek* 71 (22 January 1968): 24.

FLEISHHACKER, MORTIMER. "Why the Bay Area Needs the American Conservatory Theatre." *Performing Arts* vol. 2, no. 2 (February 1968): 9–11.

"Ford Grant to A.C.T. $800,000." *New York Times*, 12 September 1969: p. 85, col. 5.

FUNKE, LEWIS. "West Coast 'Tiny Alice' Passes Albee's Scrutiny Here." *New York Times*, 29 September 1969, p. 52, col. 1.

GARDNER, F. H. "Actor's Workshop is Dead." *Nation* (September 1966): 203, 256–57.

GODFREY, JAMES. "William Ball: The Cornerstone of a Great Company." *San Francisco Theatre Magazine* 1 (Summer 1978): 52–53.

GOLDMAN, ED. "Backstage with William Ball of the A.C.T." *Air California Magazine* vol. 9, no. 6 (October 1976): 28–32.

GUTHRIE, TYRONE. "Repertory Theatre: Ideal or Deception." *New York Times*, 26 April 1959, vol. 6, p. 40.

HASTINGS, EDWARD. "How Can You Believe Me When I Say I Love You When You Know I've Been A Liar All My Life?" *Performing Arts* vol. 2, no. 7 (July 1968): 13–15.

HERSHBERGER, ELLAINE. "The Pittsburgh Players." *Player's Magazine* vol. 48, no. 4 (February-March 1973): 97–103, 136–39.

HEWES, HENRY. "American Conservatory Theatre—A Floating Permanent Company." *Saturday Review* 50 (22 April 1967): 76.

"Interview with Josephine Nichols, Ray Reinhardt, Ken Ruta, Paul Shenar." *Performing Arts* vol. 2, no. 1 (January 1968): 5–9.

# Bibliography

JOHNSON, DOUGLAS. "The American Conservatory Theatre: An Appreciation of A.C.T." *San Francisco Theatre Magazine* 1 (Summer 1978): 50–51.

KERR, WALTER. "Repertory was the Improbable Dream." *New York Times Magazine*, 25 February 1973, pp. 36–44.

———. "San Francisco/'Hamlet,'" *New York Times*, 9 June 1967, II, p. 1, col. 3.

———. "Why This Grass? Rosemary Asked?" *New York Times*, 29 January 1967, II, p. 1, col. 1.

KELLMAN, ALICE J. "Joseph Chaikin the Actor." *TDR*, vol. 20 (September 1976): 18–26.

KELB, WILLIAM. "Dramaturgy at A.C.T.: An Interview with Dennis Powers and William Ball of the American Conservatory Theatre." *San Francisco Theatre Magazine* 1 (Summer 1978): 31–36.

KILTY, JEROME. "In Whom the Bell Tinkles." *Performing Arts*, vol. 1, no. 2 (December 1967): 9–11.

KLEMESRUD, JUDY. "Her Name is Kitty Winn as in Winner." *New York Times*, 11 July 1971.

KNICKERBOCKER, PAINE. "A.C.T. Catches the Spirit of a Restoration Comedy." *San Francisco Chronicle*, 7 December 1970, p. 61.

———. "A.C.T.'s Pledge For Survival." *San Francisco Chronicle*, 19 July 1968, p. 42.

———. "A Cheerful Schedule of A.C.T. Comedies Skillfully Staged." *San Francisco Chronicle*, 6 February 1972.

———. "A Mainstay of the A.C.T.—The Comic Parson." *San Francisco Chronicle*, 14 March 1970, p. 33.

———. "Arch an Eyebrow, Mr. Kerr, As We Level Accusations." *San Francisco Chronicle*, 21 September 1969, pp. 6–7.

———. "Ball's Cheerful Look at A.C.T.'s Finances, Future." *San Francisco Chronicle*, 19 May 1969, p. 46.

———. "Ellis Rabb—Still Thinking of A.P.A., but Happy to be Here." *San Francisco Chronicle*, 22 February 1970, p. 3.

———. "Humor May Be Better Than Honor, but Where to Learn It?" *San Francisco Chronicle*, 15 June 1969, p. 3.

———. Life and Behan's Hostage." *San Francisco Chronicle*, 23 July 1969, p. 47.

———. "'Oh Dad, Poor Dad' Stars Like the Repertory Way." *San Francisco Chronicle*, 18 June 1969, p. 48.

———. "The Dragon Yet to Be Conquered." *San Francisco Chronicle*, 29 March 1970, p. 3.

———. "The Responsibility for A.C.T.'s Crisis." *San Francisco Chronicle*, 24 July 1968, p. 45.

———. "The Return of O'Sullivan—An Actor's Big Decision." *San Francisco Chronicle*, 29 July 1969, p. 42.

———. "Tony Winner Set for A.C.T. Play." *San Francisco Chronicle*, 16 February 1974, p. 33.

————. "The Three Young Performers of A.C.T.'s 'The Promise.'" *San Francisco Chronicle*, 10 February 1969, p. 42.

KROLL, JACK. "On The Ball." *Newsweek* 70 (November 1967): 118.

LONEY, GLEN. "Getting into the A.C.T." *After Dark*, June 1969, pp. 32–40.

LOWRY, MCNEILL. "Speech to the Association of Graduate Schools." *ETJ*, vol. 14 (May 1962): 99–112.

LYNES, R. "San Francisco's Cultural Donnybrook." *Harper's* (March 1966): 31–32.

LYONS, CHARLES R. "American Conservatory Theatre, 1970–1." *ETJ*, vol. 23 (December 1971): 477–479.

MAGNIN, CYRIL. "A.C.T. Then and Now." *Performing Arts* vol. 5, no. 12. (December 1971): 29.

MAHONEY, JOHN C. "A.C.T. Dancing, Not Begging in the Streets." *Los Angeles Times*, 7 March 1971, pp. 27–28, 30–31.

MARRIOT, R. B. "An Actor and His Action." *The Stage and Television Today*. (12 May 1960).

MAVES, CARL. "A.C.T. At Eight." *Big Times* (19 October 1974): 6–9.

MCCLINTOCK, JOHN. "A.C.T. Patrons Will Never Forget His Face." *Palo Alto Times*, 22 February 1979, pp. 18–19.

MELROSE, FRANCES. "BALL BOOSTS COWARD'S 'PRIVATE LIVES.'" *R M N*, 11 July 1972, p. 48.

MILLER, JEANNE. "A Role Far From the Walton Image." *San Francisco Examiner*. 25 March 1977.

————. "Two of A.C.T.'s Venturesome Plays." *San Francisco Examiner*, 6 December 1978, p. 32.

"N.E.A. and A.C.T." *New York Times*, 3 June 1966, p. 28.

*New York Times*, 30 September 1966, p. 7, col. 2.

————. 23 January 1967, p. 29, col. 1.

————. 6 July 1967, p. 40, col. 1.

NOVICK, JULIUS. "Hinterlands II: Cleveland, Pittsburgh and Points South." *Nation* (6 June 1966): 691.

————. "Is Good Good Enough." *New York Times*, 27 July 1969, pp. 1 and 5.

————. "It's More Fun Than a Circus." *New York Times*, 19 April 1970, II, p. 12, col. 1.

————. "Theatre." *Nation* (19 August 1968): 125–26.

OPPENHEIMER, GEORGE. "The Gentleman From San Francisco." *Newsday*, 25 October 1969.

"Pittsburgh Begins Repertory Theatre." *New York Times*, 16 January 1965, p. 14.

"Popular T.V. Star Back at A.C.T." *San Mateo Times*, 17 March 1977.

POWERS, DENNIS. "Setting the Artist Free." *Performing Arts Magazine* (14 May 1967): 22.

REXROTH, K. "Renaissance by the Bay." *Saturday Review* 50 (23 September 1967): 35–36.

# Bibliography

RICH, ALAN. "Ball Bounces Back." *The World Journal Tribune Magazine* (14 May 1967): 22.

RICHARDS, GWYNETH. "The World's A Stage—A Conversation with Ray Reinhardt." *San Francisco Theatre Magazine* (Winter 1977): 52–57.

SALES, GROVER. "A.C.T.—Can It Survive the Local Boosters?" *San Francisco Magazine* (January 1972): 9–10.

SCHECHNER, RICHARD. "Ford, Rockefeller and Theatre." *TDR*, vol. 10, (Fall 1965): 194–98.

———. "The Regional Theatre: Four Views." *TDR*, vol. 10 (Fall (1968): 21–28.

STEELE, MIKE. "Theatre Wins Heart of San Francisco." *Minneapolis Tribune*, 5 May 1975.

STONE, JUDY. "The Right to Fail and to Succeed." *New York Times*, 7 May 1967: 5.

TALMER, JERRY. "Across the Footlights." *New York Post*, 27 September 1968. p. 48.

TAYLOR, LOIS. "The Face is Familiar, But . . ." *Honolulu Star Bulletin*, 13 June 1979, p. 2.

TAYLOR, ROBERT. "Margaret Webster." *Oakland Tribune*, 16 October 1972.

TERFLOTH, JOHN H. "The Pre-Meiningin Rise of the Director in Germany and Austria." *Theatre Quarterly*, vol. 6 (Spring, 1976): 65–68.

"$3000,000 Ford Grant to A.C.T." *New York Times*, 25 October 1967, p. 42, col. 1.

"Troupe to Settle in San Francisco." *New York Times*, 8 September 1966, p. 43, col. 4.

"Twelfth Night." *New York Times*, 2 November 1967, p. 62, col. 2.

"Two More Schools—Raise Acting Standards." *New York Times*, 16 March 1966, p. 49, col. 2.

WEIMER, LEIGH. "That Live Feeling." *San Jose Mercury News*, 14 October 1973.

WINN, STEVEN. "Bill Ball: The A.C.T. Years." *San Francisco Chronicle*, 11 October 1981, pp. 39–43.

———. "The Enigmatic Man Behind A.C.T." *San Francisco Chronicle*, 4 October 1981, pp. 16–21.

ZOLOTOW, SAM. "Foundation Aids Three Stage Projects." *New York Timmes*, 4 June 1965, p. 40, col. 5.

———. "Lincoln Center Theatre Sells Fewer Season Subscriptions." *New York Times*, 25 November 1966, p. 51, col. 1.


*Interviews*

BALL, WILLIAM. "Voice of America," with Bill Hillman. 15 May 1971.

———. San Francisco, with Joan Sadler, 1979.

———. Interview with author. ACT, San Francisco, 1 February 1982.

———. Interview with author. ACT, San Francisco, 9 February 1982.

BUSHNELL, WILLIAM. Interview with author. Los Angeles, 12 December 1981.

DEMENT, PAT. Interview with author. City Hall, San Francisco. 10 November 1981.

DONAT, PETER. Interview with author. ACT, San Francisco. 17 November 1981.

EICHELBAUM, STANLEY. Interview with author. San Francisco, 21 December 1981.

FLETCHER, ALLEN. Interview with author. ACT, San Francisco. 23 November 1981.

GOLDSBY, ROBERT. Interview with author. University of California at Berkeley, 27 October 1981.

———. Interview with author. University of California at Berkeley, 3 November 1981.

HAMPTON, CHRISTOPHER. Interview with author. San Francisco State University, 21 April 1982.

HASTINGS, EDWARD. Interview with author. ACT, San Francisco. 11 January 1982.

MAGNIN, CYRIL. San Francisco, with Joan Sadler. 19 July 1979.

McKENZIE, JAMES B. Interview with author. ACT, San Francisco. 17 November 1981.

MEARS, DeANN. Interview with author. ACT, San Francisco. 19 November 1981.

NACHMAN, GERALD. Interview with author. *San Francisco Chronicle* Building, San Francisco. 2 November 1981.

OTTIWELL, FRANK. Interview with author. ACT, San Francisco. 27 July 1982.

PATERSON, WILLIAM. Interview with author. ACT, San Francisco. 28 October 1982.

PATON, ANGELA. Interview with author. Berkeley, California. 6 February 1982.

RABB, ELLIS. *Voice of America*, with Bill Hillman. 18 January 1969.

REINHARDT, RAY. Interview with author. ACT, San Francisco. 27 July 1982.

SHENAR, PAUL. *Voice of America*, with Bill Hillman, 18 January 1969.

SUSSEL, DEBORAH. Interview with author. ACT, San Francisco. 24 May 1982.

———. Interview with author. ACT, San Francisco. 21 July 1982.

TYRELL, THOMAS. Interview with author. San Francisco State University, San Francisco. 23 May 1982.

*Unpublished and Miscellaneous works*

Audience Development Associates, Inc., "Agreement and Rules Governing Employment in Resident Theatres." *Actors Equity Association Handbook*, 165 West 46th Street, New York. 3 July 1978.

"A Study of Audience for the American Conservatory Theatre 1975–77." Minneapolis, 1978 (typewritten).

BALL, WILLIAM. Class Lecture, ACT, San Francisco. 10 April 1982.

# Bibliography

BOAS, ROGER, TO WILK, JOHN R. 21 September 1980.

CARNEY, SARALEIGH. "The Repertory Theatre of Lincoln Center: Aesthetics and Economics." Ph.D. dissertation, New York University, 1976.

"Certificate of Incorporation of the American Conservatory Theatre." New York, 1965 (typewritten).

CHURCH, CHARLES A., to the American Conservatory Theatre, 22 May 1965. Internal Revenue Service, Washington, D.C.

GELTNER, FRANK J. "A Letter on William Ball." 9 June 1975 (typewritten).

HILBORN, DAYLE. "William Ball and the American Conservatory Theatre." 30 July 1975 (typewritten).

"Institutional Self-Study." *American Conservatory Theatre*, San Francisco. December 1977 (typewritten).

MARKHAM, STEVEN E. "A Summary Report to A.C.T." 11 January 1979 (typewritten).

NEELY, MONTY. "The National Endowment for the Arts Theatre Program: An Historical Analysis." Ph.D. dissertation, Wayne State University, 1976.

*United States Code Annotated, Title 20, Education*. Saint Paul, Minn.: West Publishing Company, 1974.

WEBSTER, MARGARET. Unpublished paper 1965. On file with the ACT Archives, San Francisco (typewritten).

# Index

# Index